Upper Room Worshipbook

UPPER ROOM
WORSHIPBOOK

MUSIC AND LITURGIES FOR
SPIRITUAL FORMATION

Compiled and Edited by

Elise S. Eslinger

UPPER
ROOM BOOKS®
NASHVILLE

Upper Room Worshipbook

Music and Liturgies for Spiritual Formation

The Upper Room® Web site: www.upperroom.org

Cover art: Betty Jackson, courtesy of Sumatanga Camp and Conference Center, Gallant, Alabama
Cover design: Gore Studio / www.GoreStudio.com
Third printing: 2008

ISBN 13: 978-0-8358-9874-4
ISBN 10: 0-8358-9874-1

Manufactured in the United States of America

Contents

Foreword

Worship as delighting in the love of God is a rare thing today. Perhaps in our haste to create new worship resources, we have neglected the spiritual life of the worshiper!

Such is not the intent—nor the effect, in my opinion—of this new *Worshipbook*. The subtitle conveys the desire for spiritual formation—for individuals and communities—as they join in the songs and liturgies of angels and saints. Every prayer, every hymn, every page is for your formation and growth in Christ, so that you may grow in your delight of God.

Scripture knows this delight as mutual joy, shared by God and believer. The prophet sings, "I will greatly rejoice in the Lord, my whole being shall exult in my God (Isaiah 61:10). A few verses later God responds, "You shall no more be termed Forsaken . . . but you shall be called My Delight is in Her . . . for the Lord delights in you . . . (Isaiah 62:4). This mutual delight marks the faithful sabbath (Isaiah 58:13-14), fruit of a relationship of faithfulness and trust.

In this spirit of delight we offer the second edition of the Upper Room's *Worshipbook* to you. Building upon the liturgical life of The Academy for Spiritual Formation, which for more than twenty years has practiced an intimacy of communal life, shaped by the liturgy, the *Worshipbook* is a gift to the whole church. Individuals, small groups, retreat leaders, Sunday school classes may find here a resource that can sustain them through times of joy and sorrow.

While many hands helped shape the *Worshipbook*, we were and are indeed fortunate that Elise Eslinger, editor of the first edition, was again available for this new resource. There is no one better suited for the task. Her love for and involvement in The Academy for Spiritual Formation have continued all of these years. As a former General Board of Discipleship staff member and now a staff member at United Theological Seminary in Dayton, she knows the church well. She lives and breathes spiritual formation in all of its various genres: from Mississippi gospel roots (where she grew up) to St. Meinrad's Archabbey and Seminary in Indiana, where she received a master's degree in Theology and Liturgy during her sabbatical study. My deepest appreciation extends to Elise, as well as to the twenty or so contributors to this resource. May it be gift to you!

Jerry P. Haas
Director of The Academy for Spiritual Formation and Emerging Ministries
Upper Room Ministries

Editor's Introduction

L ike the original "blue book" over twenty years ago, this new edition of the *Upper Room Worshipbook* has been compiled to serve those who gather for worship not only on Sundays but also throughout the week. The new *Worshipbook*, while offered ecumenically, is grounded in that hospitable Wesleyan spirit that holds together what some might separate—personal and social holiness, sacramental and evangelical practices, warmth of heart and strength of mind.

The liturgies and music support the patterns, rhythms, and content of worship for The Academy for Spiritual Formation and other programs of Upper Room Ministries. However, these richly varied resources may enhance the worship of those gathered on retreats, in special conferences or learning events, and all who may seek *sabbath* refreshment and renewal. We pray that this new edition will serve a useful purpose for groups on the Christ-journey in many congregational settings and in missional contexts—gathered in the name of Jesus in a host of contemporary "upper rooms."

The new *Upper Room Worshipbook* expresses some primary theological and pastoral commitments through timeless liturgical patterns for daily prayer and the Eucharist and through a myriad of hymns, psalm settings, and prayer songs:

- Praise to God-in-three-persons, a Trinitarian spirituality
- Biblical vision and liturgical continuity providing roots *and* wings for the emerging church of the 21st century
- Prayer reflecting the full, honest emotive range of the Psalms
- Image-rich, Gospel-soaked texts—foundational, evocative, and formative
- Music, delightfully varied in origin and style yet broadly accessible
- Prayers for aching creation and peoples that embody hopeful expectancy of healing, restoration, and peace in God's *shalom*
- Eucharistic joy expressed in inclusive and hospitable ways
- Liturgical resources to enliven and support the movement toward recovery of the daily office and services of healing prayer
- Alternative eucharistic prayers and musical settings for Holy Communion

Denominational hymnals make readily available most beloved, traditional hymns, and many contemporary worship songs may be easily learned by rote. The new *Worshipbook* contains many newer or previously unpublished selections considered particularly worthy of inclusion. However, a unique, frequent feature is provision of several alternate texts for one single, worthy tune. Herein, along with the inclusion of a greatly expanded body of music from global sources such as the communities of Taizé and Iona, are contributions from many recognized, gifted authors and composers, as well as some previously unpublished in this particular format.

May this new *Upper Room Worshipbook* bless your community and assist you and your spiritual and ministry companions in offering grateful praise as living Alleluias!

Elise S. Eslinger, Compiler and Editor
Day of Epiphany, 2006

Liturgies for Daily Prayer

Praying the Daily Liturgies Together

It is winter in Wisconsin. The pale light of early morning gradually spreads itself out over the chapel pews where we are quietly gathered, most of us fresh from sleep. The silence is palpable: deep and rich and full.

"Psalm 63," the prayer leader gently prompts, and we turn the pages of our worshipbooks to find the familiar words laid out before us. We open our lips and our breaths are swept up together into one common melody:

"In the morning I will sing glad songs of praise to you."

What are we doing when we begin the day this way? When we also end the day together with the ancient and familiar words: "Lord, you let your servant go in peace . . . "? How is it that we are thus being shaped by this shared prayer into the persons God created us to be?

What we are doing is not an innovation. It was what the earliest Christians did before there were church buildings or even a common day off to observe Sunday, the Lord's Day. They gathered in the morning and the evening to pray. In so doing they made, and we make, God and the things of God the first and last thoughts of the day. In a sense we sanctify time, make it holy. We honor the human rhythms of waking and sleeping and the earth's rhythms of sunrise and sunset. We surround our day with the parentheses of prayer, setting it apart for God.

The early Christians did this in common, using shared and ancient words. There is a particular grace to sharing a common prayer. Whenever or wherever we pray, we are not alone. Prayer allows us access to the eternity of God's own time. In that time we are present not only to the divine but to each other. We are present to all those who pray, all over the earth, in diverse gestures and languages. We are also present to those who have prayed and who will pray: in the early church, in the intervening centuries, and in the centuries to come.

When we enter into prayer using shared and ancient words, we are using many of the same words that those early Christians did. We are ushered into a vast, infinitely rich reservoir of longing and hoping that is larger than ourselves. For millennia certain psalms and canticles have been associated with specific times of prayer. Psalm 63 and the Canticle of Zachary (Luke 1:68-79, which prophesies the coming of the light to illuminate the darkness) have long been associated with morning prayer. Evening prayer is traditionally observed with the Magnificat, the Canticle of Mary (Luke 1:46-55) and with Psalm 141, the "incense psalm" ("My prayers rise like incense, my hands like the evening offering").[1] Similarly, the day ends with night prayer, which includes the Canticle of Simeon (Luke 2:29-32) with its sentiments of peaceful reception: "Now I can go in peace, my eyes have seen the salvation meant for the nations."

We are shaped by the words we pray. When we pray The Lord's Prayer deeply, our lips and hearts give articulation to the core of our faith. So it is with the psalms and canticles that form the backbone of the daily liturgies. We are expanded by the praise ("My soul proclaims the greatness of the Lord"), summoned by the hope ("Blessed be the God of Israel who comes to set us free"), met in our lament ("Out of the depths I cry to you"), and consoled by the words into which we enter ("In the shadow of your wings I sing for joy; I cling to you, your hand keeps me safe").

When we sing we heighten our praying. We gather up breath and body; we give form and flight to the keenest longings of our hearts. Our whole selves engage in what we pray. "My whole being desires you like a dry, worn, waterless land," we sing, and the notes take the shape of our desire; they trace our thirst and ache with our longing for God.

All this happens when we sing these daily liturgies alone. But when we pray together, we come to know that we are small streams that run into wider, deeper channels that in turn flow into the vast ocean of prayer. We are made aware of the depth of our connection with one another. We become mindful of our common hope, our shared longing. We are also made conscious that we live that common hope in diverse and individual ways. Our commonality is not a rigid uniformity but a convergence at the level of our common humanity and our communion in Christ.

When our prayer is guided by the simple form of the liturgies of daily prayer (invocation, psalmody, scripture, canticle, the Lord's Prayer, benediction), we are praying with the ecumenical Christian community. For these daily liturgies, in simplified or more elaborated form, are practiced by Methodists, Lutherans, Presbyterians, Anglicans (Episcopalians), Roman Catholics, Eastern Orthodox, and other Christians.

"Come let us sing to the Lord," the psalmist exhorts us. Yes, let us pray this way together and be formed into the people God intends us to be.

Wendy M. Wright
Professor of Theology
Creighton University

---

1. Excerpt from *The Jerusalem Bible* © 1966 Darton, Longman & Todd, Ltd. and Doubleday, a division of Random House, Inc. Reprinted by permission.

8   A Liturgy for Morning Prayer

Stand or sit as indicated by the worship leader.

GREETING

O God, o-pen our lips, and we shall de-clare your praise.

WORDS: Ps. 51:15
MUSIC: Elise S. Eslinger
Music © 1985 The Upper Room

and/or

God said: Let there be light; and there was light.
And God saw that the light was good.
This very day our God has acted! Let us rejoice!
Alleluia! God's name be praised!

MORNING HYMN (or Psalm 95)

PRAYER

Let us pray together.
**New every morning is your love, great God of light, and all day long you are
working for good in the world. Stir up in us desire to serve you, to live
peacefully with our neighbors and all your creation, and to devote each day
to your Son, our Savior Jesus Christ. Amen.**[1]

PSALM

*May be recited or sung. Suggested morning psalms include Pss. 63 or 95; and, alternatively,
Pss. 5; 51; 100; 146–50.*

Silence

Psalm Prayer

SCRIPTURE

After the reading:
The Word of Life.
Thanks be to God.

Silence for prayer and reflection

1. *The Worshipbook: Services and Hymns* (Philadelphia, Penn.: The Westminster Press, 1970,
   1972), 57, adapt.

CANTICLE OF ZACHARY ("Benedictus," Luke 1:68-79) *See Nos. 10–12.*

or

SONG OF PRAISE

PRAYERS OF THE PEOPLE (*standing or sitting, as invited*)

In peace let us pray.

Here may follow prayers of thanksgiving and prayers for the world, for the church, for family and friends, and for the community.

After thanksgivings:

Loving God . . .
We give you thanks.

After petitions and intercessions:

Merciful God . . .
Hear our prayer.

A sung response to the prayers may also be chosen.

THE LORD'S PRAYER *or* PRAYER OF JESUS
(*Sung or spoken. See Nos. 453–58 for musical and paraphrased alternatives.*)

Our Father in heaven,
   hallowed be your name,
   your kingdom come,
   your will be done on earth,
   as in heaven.
Give us today our daily bread.
Forgive us our sins
   as we forgive those who sin against us.
Save us from the time of trial
   and deliver us from evil.
For the kingdom, the power, and the glory are yours
   now and forever. Amen.[2]

SONG OF PRAISE OR BLESSING

BENEDICTION
The grace of our Lord Jesus Christ be with you. **Amen.**

Signs of Christ's peace may be shared.

2. English translation of The Lord's Prayer © 1988 English Language Liturgical Consultation (ELLC).

10 Blessed Be the God of Israel

1. Blessed be the God of Is - ra - el who comes to set us
2. With prom-ised mer - cy will God still the cov - e - nant re -
3. My child, as proph-et of the Lord you will pre - pare the

free and rais - es up new hope for us: a
call, the oath once sworn to A - bra - ham, from
way, to tell God's peo - ple they are saved from

Branch from Da - vid's tree. So have the proph - ets
foes to save us all; that we might wor - ship
sin's e - ter - nal sway. Then shall God's mer - cy

long de - clared that with a might - y arm God
with - out fear and of - fer lives of praise, in
from on high shine forth and nev - er cease to

WORDS: Carl P. Daw, Jr.
MUSIC: Trad. English melody; arr. by Ralph Vaughan Williams
FOREST GREEN
CMD

would turn back our en - e - mies and all who wish us harm.
ho - li - ness and righ - teous-ness to serve God all our days.
drive a - way the gloom of death and lead us in - to peace.

In the Tender Compassion of Our God 11

In the ten - der com-pas-sion of our God the morn - ing sun from

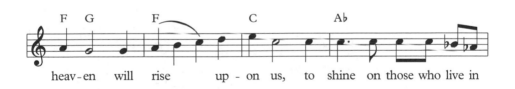

heav-en will rise up - on us, to shine on those who live in

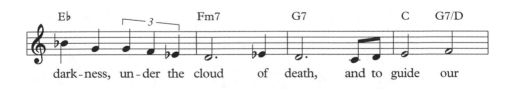

dark-ness, un - der the cloud of death, and to guide our

feet, to guide our feet in - to the way of peace.

WORDS: Luke 1:78-79
MUSIC: Elise S. Eslinger
Music © 1985 Upper Room Books

WAY OF PEACE
Irregular

12 Blest Be the God of Israel

1. Blest be the God of Is - rael, who comes to set us free,
2. Now from the house of Da - vid a child of grace is given;
3. Where once were fear and dark - ness the sun be - gins to rise —

who vis - its and re - deems us, and grants us lib - er - ty.
a Sav - ior comes a - mong us to raise us up to heaven.
the dawn - ing of for - give - ness up - on the sin - ner's eyes,

The proph - ets spoke of mer - cy, of free - dom and re - lease;
Be - fore him goes the her - ald — fore - run - ner in the way —
to guide the feet of pil - grims a - long the path of peace:

God shall ful - fill the prom - ise to bring our peo - ple peace.
the proph - et of sal - va - tion, the har - bin - ger of Day.
O bless our God and Sav - ior, with songs that nev - er cease!

WORDS: Michael Perry, alt. (Luke 1:68-79)
MUSIC: Hal H. Hopson

MERLE'S TUNE
76.76 D

A Liturgy for Midday Prayer   13

Stand or sit as indicated by the worship leader.

GATHERING AND SILENCE

CALL TO PRAYER
Jesus, our Savior, teach us your ways.
Our hope is in you, all the day long.

PRAYER AT MIDDAY
God be with you.
And also with you.
Let us pray.
**God of mercy, this midday moment of rest
    is your welcome gift.
Bless the work we have begun,
    make good its defects,
    and let us finish it in a way that pleases you.
Grant this through Christ we pray. Amen.**[1]

PSALM
May be recited or sung. Suggested psalms include 113; 119:105-112; 121; 122; 126; or 130.

HYMN VERSE *(this or other song or refrain)*
**Lord of all eagerness, Lord of all faith,
whose strong hands were skilled at the plane and the lathe:
Be there at our labors, and give us, we pray
your strength in our hearts, Lord, at the noon of the day.**[2]

BRIEF READING *(these scripture verses or other selection)*
"Those of steadfast mind you keep in peace—
    in peace because they trust in you.
In returning and rest you shall be saved;
    in quietness and trust shall be your strength."[3]

CLOSING AFFIRMATION
Strong is the love embracing us,
and faithful our God, from morning to night.

Here may follow a table blessing, dismissal prayer, or song of blessing.

1. *The Liturgy of the Hours*, International Commission on English in the Liturgy, 1974.
2. Jan Struther, "Lord of All Hopefulness," stanza 2 (New York: Oxford University Press, 1931).
    (See No. 179.)
3. Isaiah 26:3; 30:15 (NRSV).

14   A Liturgy for Evening Prayer

Stand or sit as indicated by the worship leader.

OPENING (*Light the vesper candle.*)

LIGHT PROCLAMATION

Light and peace in Je-sus Christ, our Lord.   Thanks be to God.

EVENING HYMN *or Phos Hileron (see No. 215)*
May process with the vesper candle.

EVENING PRAYER
May God be with you.
And also with you.
Let us pray.

We praise and thank you, O God,
    for you are without beginning and without end.
Through Christ, you created the whole world;
    through Christ, you preserve it.
You made the day for the works of light
    and the night for the refreshment of our minds and our bodies.
Keep us now in Christ, grant us a peaceful evening, a night free
    from sin, and bring us at last to eternal life.
Through Christ and in the Holy Spirit,
    we offer you all glory, honor, and worship, now and forever. Amen.[1]

or

Eternal Creator of light,
Yours is the morning and yours is the evening.
Draw us to yourself so there will be no darkness within us.
All praise to you, our holy and triune God. Amen.[2]

PSALM
May be recited or sung. Suggested psalms include 121; 141; 23; 27; 34:1-14; or 139.

Silence

Psalm Prayer

---

1. *Upper Room Worshipbook* (Nashville: Upper Room Books, 1985), No. 114, 2.
2. Richard Eslinger, *Alive Now!* July/August 1983 (Nashville, Tenn.: The Upper Room, 1983).

Scripture

After the reading:
The Word of Life.
Thanks be to God.

Silence for prayer and reflection.

Canticle of Mary ("Magnificat," Luke 1:46-55) (*See Nos. 17–20.*)

Prayers of Intercession
At the beginning, and after each petition:

(*The following or other litany may be chanted or spoken.*[3])

In peace, let us pray to the Lord.
Lord, have mercy.
For the peace of the world, that a spirit of respect and forbearance may grow among nations and peoples, let us pray to the Lord.
Lord, have mercy.
For those in positions of public trust, (especially *[insert names]*), that they may serve justice and promote the dignity and freedom of all people, let us pray to the Lord.
Lord, have mercy.
For a blessing upon the labors of all and for the right use of the riches of creation, let us pray to the Lord.
Lord, have mercy.
For the poor, the persecuted, the sick, and all who suffer; for refugees, prisoners, and all who are in danger: that they may be relieved and protected, let us pray to the Lord.
Lord, have mercy.
For this community: for those who are present and for those who are absent, that we may be delivered from hardness of heart and may show forth your glory in all that we do, we pray to the Lord.
Lord, have mercy.
For our enemies and those who wish us harm and for all whom we have injured or offended, let us pray to the Lord.
Lord, have mercy.

---

3. Prayers of the People Form V, The Book of Common Prayer (New York: The Church Hymnal Foundation, 1977), 390, adapted. See additional suggestions in *Upper Room Worshipbook Accompaniment and Worship Leader* edition, page 508, "Providing Variety in Communal Prayer."

For ourselves, for the forgiveness of our sins, and for the grace of the Holy Spirit to amend our lives, let us pray to the Lord.
Lord, have mercy.
For all who commended themselves to our prayers: for our families, friends, and neighbors; that being freed from anxiety, they may live in joy, peace, and health, let us pray to the Lord.
Lord, have mercy.
For all who have died in the faith of Christ, that with all the saints, they may have rest in that place where there is no pain or grief but life eternal, let us pray to the Lord.
Lord, have mercy.
Help, save, pity, and defend us, O God, by your grace.

(*Pause for silent prayer. Other petitions may be spoken by members of the community.*)

In the communion of the Holy Spirit and of all the saints, let us commend ourselves and one another to the living God through Christ our Lord.
Amen.

The Lord's Prayer *or* Prayer of Jesus
(*Sung or spoken. See Nos. 453–58 for musical and paraphrased alternatives.*)

Our Father in heaven,
   hallowed be your name,
   your kingdom come,
   your will be done on earth,
   as in heaven.
Give us today our daily bread.
Forgive us our sins
   as we forgive those who sin against us.
Save us from the time of trial
   and deliver us from evil.
For the kingdom, the power, and the glory are yours
   now and forever. Amen.[4]

Evening Song *or* Sung Blessing

Benediction
May God (the Father) bless us and keep us.
Amen.
May Jesus Christ make his face to shine upon us.
Amen.
May the Holy Spirit grant us peace.
Amen.

---

4. English translation of The Lord's Prayer © 1988 English Language Liturgical Consultation (ELLC).

My Soul Proclaims the Greatness of the Lord

Antiphon G   Am

My   soul proclaims the greatness of   the   Lord,

C   Em

and my spirit rejoices in   God,   my   Savior.

Verses

Em   C

1. God has remembered me, a   low – ly   servant.
2. God's name   is   holy.
3. Power is disclosed by the great deeds of   God's   arm.
4. The hungry are filled   with   good   things,
5. The promises made to our ances – tors   are   true.

C   D

From now on, people will   call   me blessed because of the
From one generation   to   the next the
The Holy has scattered the proud of heart and mind. Monarchs have been

————————————————————————————— but the
God comes to the aid of Israel, a   ser – vant people. For God has remembered

Bm   Em

(o)

wonderful things the mighty God   has done for me.
mercy of   the Lord is sure.
pulled from their thrones, but the humble, God has   lift – ed high. *(Antiphon)*
rich are sent   emp – ty a – way.
to show mercy to the descendants of Abraham for – ev – er. *(Antiphon)*

WORDS: Diedra Kriewald, alt. (Luke 1:46-55)
MUSIC: Elise S. Eslinger

18 Canticle of the Turning

1. My soul cries out with a joy - ful shout that the
2. Though I am small, my God, my all, you
3. From the halls of power to the for - tress tower, not a
4. Though the na - tions rage from age to age, we re -

God of my heart is great, and my spir - it sings of the
work great things in me, and your mer - cy will last from the
stone will be left on stone. Let the king be - ware for your
mem - ber who holds us fast: God's mer - cy must de -

won - drous things that you bring to the ones who
depths of the past to the end of the age to
jus - tice tears ev - ery ty - rant from his
liv - er us from the con - quer - or's crush - ing

wait. You fixed your sight on your ser - vant's plight, and my
be. Your ver - y name puts the proud to shame, and to
throne. The hun - gry poor shall weep no more, for the
grasp. This sav - ing word that our fore - bears heard is the

weak - ness you did not spurn, so from east to west shall my
those who would for you yearn, you will show your might, put the
food they can nev - er earn; there are ta - bles spread, ev - ery
prom - ise which holds us bound till the spear and rod can be

WORDS: Rory Cooney (Luke 1:46-55)
MUSIC: Trad. Irish; adapt. Rory Cooney
Words and adapt. © 1990 GIA Publications, Inc.

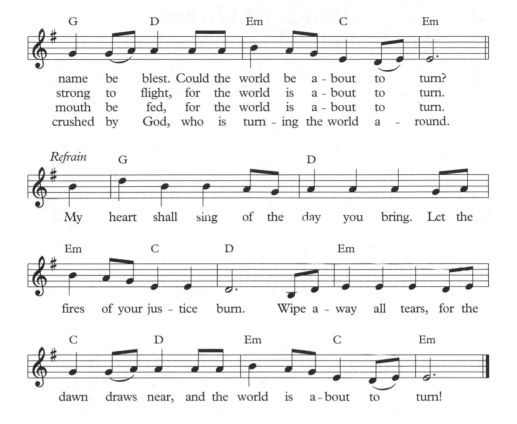

name   be   blest. Could the world   be   a - bout   to   turn?
strong   to   flight, for   the   world   is   a - bout   to   turn.
mouth   be   fed,   for   the   world   is   a - bout   to   turn.
crushed   by   God,   who   is   turn - ing the world   a -   round.

Refrain

My   heart   shall   sing   of the   day   you   bring.   Let the

fires   of your jus - tice   burn.   Wipe a - way   all   tears,   for the

dawn   draws   near,   and the   world   is   a - bout   to   turn!

My Soul Proclaims with Wonder   19

1. My soul proclaims with wonder the greatness of the Lord;
   rejoicing in God's goodness, my spirit is restored.
   To me has God shown favor, to one the world thought frail,
   and every age will echo the angel's first "All hail!"

2. God's mercy shields the faithful and saves them from defeat
   with strength that turns to scatter the proud in their conceit.
   The mighty have been vanquished, the lowly lifted up.
   The hungry find abundance, the rich, an empty cup.

3. To Abraham's descendants the Lord will steadfast prove,
   for God has made with Israel a covenant of love.
   My soul proclaims with wonder the greatness of the Lord;
   rejoicing in God's goodness, my spirit is restored.

Sing to MERLE'S TUNE, No. 12

Carl P. Daw, Jr. (Luke 1:46-55)

20 Holy Is Your Name

1. My soul is filled with joy as I
2. I am low - ly as a child, but I
3. I pro - claim the power of God, you do
4. To the hun - gry you give food, send the
5. In your love you now ful - fill what you

sing to God my Sav - ior: You have looked up - on your
know from this day for-ward that my name will be re -
mar - vels for your ser-vants: though you scat - ter the proud -
rich a - way emp - ty. In your mer - cy you are
prom - ised to your peo - ple. I will praise you, Lord, my

ser - vant, you have vis - i - ted your peo - ple.
mem-bered, for all will call me bless - ed.
heart - ed, and de - stroy the might of princ - es.
mind - ful of the peo - ple you have cho - sen.
Sav - ior, ev - er - last - ing is your mer - cy.

Refrain

And ho - ly is your name, through all gen - er -
a - tions! Ev - er - last - ing is your mer - cy to the
peo - ple you have cho - sen, and ho - ly is your name.

WORDS: David Haas (Luke 1:46-55)
MUSIC: Trad. Scottish; adapt. and arr. David Haas

WILD MOUNTAIN THYME
Irregular

Words, adapt., and arr. © 1989 GIA Publications, Inc.

A Liturgy for Night Prayer

Stand or sit as indicated by the worship leader.

OPENING
May God Almighty grant us a quiet night and peace at the last.
Amen.
It is good to give thanks to you, O God.
To sing praise to your name, O Most High;
To herald your love in the morning,
Your truth at the close of the day.[1]

EVENING HYMN

PRAYER OF CONFESSION, EXAMINATION OF CONSCIENCE, AND DECLARATION OF PARDON
Let us confess our sins in the presence of God and one another.
Silence for self-examination and confession
Let us pray. (*This or the Alternate Prayer of Confession on page 23*)
Holy and gracious God, I confess that I have sinned against you this day.
Some of my sin I know—
the thoughts and words and deeds of which I am ashamed—
but some is known only to you.
In the name of Jesus Christ, I ask forgiveness.
Deliver and restore me, that I may rest in peace.

By the mercy of God we are united with Jesus Christ,
and in Christ we are forgiven.
We rest now in peace
and rise in the morning to serve God.[2]

PSALM
Recited or sung. Suggested psalms include 4; 13; 31:1-5; 91; 121; or 134.

Silence

Psalm Prayer

SCRIPTURE

After the reading:
The Word of Life.
Thanks be to God.

1. Opening, Prayer at the Close of Day (Compline), *Lutheran Book of Worship* (Minneapolis, Minn.: Augsburg Publishing House, 1978), 154.
2. Ibid., 155.

RESPONSE

You have redeemed me, O Lord, God of truth.
Hear my prayer, O God; listen to my cry.
Keep me as the apple of your eye.
Hide me in the shadow of your wings.
In righteousness I shall see you;
When I awake, your presence will give me joy.
(pause)
You are my rock and my fortress.
Into your hands, O God, I commend my spirit.[3]

THE LORD'S PRAYER *or* PRAYER OF JESUS

(Sung or spoken. See Nos. 453–58 for musical and paraphrased alternatives.)
Our Father in heaven,
     hallowed be your name,
     your kingdom come,
     your will be done on earth,
     as in heaven.
Give us today our daily bread.
Forgive us our sins
     as we forgive those who sin against us.
Save us from the time of trial
     and deliver us from evil.
For the kingdom, the power, and the glory are yours
     now and forever. Amen.[4]

CANTICLE OF SIMEON ("Nunc Dimittis," Luke 2:29-32)

(Sung or spoken, see Nos. 24–27.)

DISMISSAL WITH BLESSING[5]

Guide us waking, O God, and guard us sleeping;
that awake we may watch with Christ,
and asleep we may rest in peace.

Let us bless the Lord.
Thanks be to God.
The almighty and merciful God bless us and keep us.
Amen.

Depart in silence.

---

3. Response, Prayer at the Close of Day (Compline), *Lutheran Book of Worship* (Minneapolis, Minn.: Augsburg Publishing House, 1978), 156–57, adapted.
4. English translation of The Lord's Prayer © 1988 English Language Liturgical Consultation (ELLC).
5. Gospel Canticle and Benediction, Prayer at the Close of Day (Compline), *Lutheran Book of Worship* (Minneapolis, Minn.: Augsburg Publishing House, 1978), 159–60.

Alternate Prayer of Confession

Let us pray.
Dear God, thank you for all that is good,
For our creation and our humanity,
for the stewardship you have given us of this planet earth,
for the gifts of life and of one another,
for your love which is unbounded and eternal.
O thou, most holy and beloved,
My Companion, my Guide upon the way,
my bright evening star.
We repent the wrongs we have done.

Silence

We have wounded your love.
O God, heal us.
We stumble in the darkness.
Light of the world, transfigure us.
We forget that we are your home.
Spirit of God, dwell in us.
Eternal Spirit, living God,
in whom we live and move and have our being,
all that we are, have been and shall be is known to you,
to the very secret of our hearts
and all that rises to trouble us.
Living flame, burn into us,
cleansing wind, blow through us,
fountain of water, well up within us,
that we may love and praise in deed and in truth.[6]

6. Prayer of Confession (Night Prayer), *A New Zealand Prayer Book—He Karakia Mihnare o Aotearoa* (New Zealand: William Collins Publishers Ltd., 1989), 168.

Song of Simeon

1. Now bid your ser - vant go in peace, your
2. This is the Sav - ior of the world, the

word is now ful - filled. These eyes have seen sal -
Gen - tiles' prom - ised light, God's glo - ry dwell - ing

va - tion's dawn, this child so long fore - told.
in our midst, the joy of Is - ra - el.

WORDS: *Nunc dimittis*; trans. by James Quinn, SJ, alt.
MUSIC: American folk hymn; arr. by Annabel Morris Buchanan
Trans. © 1969 James Quinn, SJ; admin. by Selah Publishing, Inc.

LAND OF REST
CM

Lord, Let Your Servant

Lord, let your ser- vant de-part in peace ac- cord-ing to your

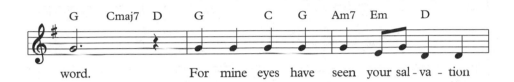

word. For mine eyes have seen your sal- va- tion

which you have pre- pared be- fore the face of all

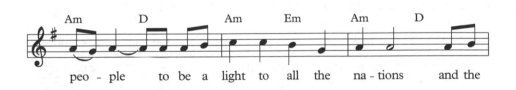

peo- ple to be a light to all the na- tions and the

glo- ry of your peo- ple Is- ra- el. A - men,

a - men, a - men. _____

WORDS: Jim Strathdee (Luke 2:29-32), alt.
MUSIC: Jim Strathdee
© 1977 Desert Flower Music

26 Now, Lord, You Have Kept Your Word

WORDS: Hal H. Hopson (Luke 2:29-32)
MUSIC: Hal H. Hopson

Now Let Your Servant Go

1. Now let your servant go in peace;
   let praise and blessing here increase;
   for in our midst your word is done
   and you have sent your Promised One.

2. Before the peoples you prepare
   your way of life which all may share.
   Your saving power is now made known;
   among the nations love is shown.

3. Child, you are chosen as a sign
   to test the human heart and mind;
   for secrets hidden in the night
   shall be revealed in piercing light.

4. Now let us sing our Savior's praise,
   and tell God's goodness all our days.
   While breath is ours, let praise be heard
   for God's own faithful, saving word.

Sing to CONDITOR ALME SIDERUM, No. 217, or TALLIS' CANON, No. 209

Ruth Duck (Luke 2:29-32)

© 1992 GIA Publications, Inc.

A Liturgy for Night Prayer
with Prayers for Healing

Stand or sit as indicated by the worship leader.

OPENING
May God Almighty grant us a quiet night and peace at the last.
Amen.
It is good to give thanks to you, O God,
To sing praise to your name, O Most High;
To herald your love in the morning.
Your truth at the close of the day.[1]

EVENING HYMN *or* SONG OF PRAISE[2]

PRAYER OF REFLECTION AND CONFESSION[3]
Gracious God,
    as darkness draws this day to a close,
    may we remember with gratitude your gifts and your presence,
    signs of your blessing.

Silence for reflection

Divine Healer,
    touch my memory so I may see your holy work
    in my life and in the world:
        the easing of pain,
        the healing of memories,
        the recovery from wounds.
    With loud alleluias or quiet thanks may I praise you.

Silence for reflection

Loving God,
    with the light of Christ as my guide,
    take me through this day
    and help me to see the sins of which I am ashamed.

Silence for reflection

---

1. Prayer at the Close of the Day (Compline), *Lutheran Book of Worship* (Minneapolis, Minn.: Augsburg Publishing House, 1978), 154, adapted.
2. All musical components for this service may, optionally, be chosen from the music of Taizé, Nos. 376–96. Further guidance for Taizé prayer and particular suggestions for the Night Prayer with Healing service are found in the *Upper Room Worshipbook Accompaniment and Worship Leader* edition, page 518, "Sung Prayer in the Spirit of Taizé."
3. Larry Peacock.

Holy and compassionate God,
    reconcile, renew, and restore me by your grace,
    that I may rest in peace.

WORDS OF ASSURANCE
By the mercy of God, we are united with Jesus Christ,
and in Christ we are forgiven and made whole.
We rest now in God's love and rise in the morning to serve our Creator.

PSALM
Recited or sung. Suggested psalms include 4; 13; 23; 31:1-5; 91; 103; or 134.

Silence

Psalm Prayer

READING(S) FROM SCRIPTURE
(James 5:13-16; Mark 5:21-34, or other healing stories may be chosen.)

Silence

PRAYER
Let us pray:
**Although there are wounds within us, O Christ, above all there is the miracle
of your mysterious and compassionate presence among us. Thus, made
lighter or even set free, we journey gratefully with you from one discovery to
another. Thanks be to God. Amen.**[4]

BLESSING OF THE OIL FOR ANOINTING
Let us pray:
O God, the giver of health and salvation,
    we give thanks to you for the gift of oil.
As your holy apostles anointed many who were sick and healed them,
    so pour out your Holy Spirit on us and on this gift,
    that those who in faith and repentance receive this anointing
        may be made whole;
through Jesus Christ our Lord. **Amen.**[5]

---

4. *Life from Within by Brother Roger of Taizé.* Geoffrey Chapman, Mowbray. Published in North
   America by Westminster/John Knox Press.
5. Thanksgiving over the Oil, *United Methodist Book of Worship* (Nashville, Tenn.: United
   Methodist Publishing House, 1992), 620.

LAYING ON OF HANDS AND ANOINTING WITH PRAYER
(Music of Taizé or other sung or instrumental selections may be offered during the prayers.)

Laying on of hands (with this or other prayer)
    Spirit of the Living God,
    Fall afresh on your servant *(insert name)*
    that he/she may be healed and strengthened
    in mind, body, and spirit;
    in the name of Jesus Christ.

Words of anointing
    God enfold you
    Christ embrace you
    Spirit surround you

        or

    Receive the sign of Christ's healing.
    Go in peace.[6]

CANTICLE OF SIMEON *(see Nos. 24–27)*
(May be prayed communally or as individual meditation before departing, if healing prayers are extended.)

CLOSING PRAYER WITH BLESSING
Watch now, dear Lord, with those who work or watch or weep tonight,
and give your angels charge over those who sleep.
Tend your sick ones, O Christ, rest your weary ones,
bless your dying ones, soothe your suffering ones,
pity your afflicted ones, shield the joyous,
and all for your love's sake.

May the love of Christ surround you as you go in peace.
Amen.[7]

---

6. Prayer at the Close of Day (Compline), *Lutheran Book of Worship* (Minneapolis, Minn.: Augsburg Publishing House, 1978), 154, adapted.
7. Closing Prayers (Compline), The Book of Common Prayer (New York: Church Hymnal Foundation, 1977), 134, by Don E. Saliers, adapted.

31 An Intercessory Prayer for Healing

O God,
   Here is my sister—
      overwhelmed with grief and pain—
      tearfully seeking your healing love.
   Here is my brother—
      anxious, lonely, and frightened—
      uncertain even how to pray.

Do not pass them by, Lord Jesus!

Send the light of your redeeming grace upon them.
Welcome them back into the arms of your loving embrace.
Comfort them in their grief and heal their infirmities;
Lead them in your way of Love.
By the power of the Holy Spirit we pray. **Amen.**

Jerry P. Haas
© 2006 Upper Room Books

32 A Prayer of Petition for Healing

Into the compassionate Womb of your love, O God,
   I bring my deepest needs, my strongest hopes, my greatest fears.

Give me tears for my grief, a voice that I might cry out to you.
Give me words that I might say what is most on my heart.
Give me courage, so that I will always seek the healing you have to give.
Let me always offer my suffering to you,
   So that when healing does not come,
   Wisdom, justice, and compassion may be its fruit,
      A life given to you,
      Abba God. **Amen.**

Jerry P. Haas
© 2006 Upper Room Books

Liturgies for Holy Communion

Living Eucharistically

From the beginning, Christians gathered around the risen Christ to receive his teachings and his saving life in a holy meal. Jesus, the incarnate life of God-with-us, was always breaking bread with friends and strangers. At that unforgettable meal with his disciples on the eve of his death, Jesus said the ancient blessing, broke and shared the bread, and offered the cup to them yet again. In so doing he also offered living bread and saving cup to all who would forever after gather about the table in his name. Hence the Book of Acts tells us that the earliest church in Jerusalem continued in the apostles' teachings, the fellowship, the breaking of bread and the ongoing prayers (Acts 2:42*ff*). At the end of the first century the *Didache* admonished Christians: "On the Lord's day . . . come together, break bread and give thanks [hold Eucharist]."

So when we gather to "do this in remembrance," we are taken up into the holy mystery of God's lavish grace made real. In doing his *anamnesis* (the remembering of Christ), we do far more than recall the dusty roads of Galilee. We are fed, healed, and empowered by his living presence here and now. This is the greatest gift of love the world knows. What Jesus Christ said and did he now says and does in this assembly, in this time and place. In the eucharistic meal we are remembered by God and transformed into Christ's body. Receiving who we are in Christ forms us in a eucharistic way of life.

This *Upper Room Worshipbook* provides a pattern for the holy meal that shapes us in the deepest traditions of Christ's church. Prayer at the Table blesses God for creation, redemption, and the hope of the world; but it also reveals who God is for us and for all creation. Participation in prayer, song, proclamation, and the ritual action around the table of the Lord gives us our identity as the people of God. Even more, when we celebrate Holy Communion by bringing our whole lives to God, we find ourselves being sent forth to love as God loves. The meaning of what we do in the eucharistic meal is inexhaustible, truly a "feast for all seasons." Whether quietly or robustly, we come to Christ's table to be embraced. God willing, we shall often be "lost in wonder, love, and praise."

Don E. Saliers
William R. Cannon Distinguished Professor of Theology and Worship
Candler School of Theology

34   A Celebration of Word and Table

MUSIC FOR GATHERING

*GREETING (*people standing as able*)
The grace of the Lord Jesus Christ be with you.
And also with you.
The risen Christ is with us.
Praise the Lord.

or

We gather in peace, graced by the living, risen Christ, who welcomes us!
We come with joy to meet our Savior. Alleluia!

or

Blessed be the one, holy and living God.
Glory to God forever and ever.

*OPENING HYMN OR SONG[1]

*OPENING PRAYER
Let us pray:
One of the following or an alternate prayer may be offered.

Almighty God,
to you all hearts are open, all desires known,
and from you no secrets are hidden.
Cleanse the thoughts of our hearts
by the inspiration of your Holy Spirit,
that we may perfectly love you,
and worthily magnify your holy name,
through Christ our Lord.
Amen.[2]

or

We praise and thank you, O God,
for you are without beginning and without end.
Through Christ, you created the whole world;

---

1. For evening celebration, the *Phos Hileron*, No. 215, or another evening hymn may be sung as the vesper candle is lit and processed.
2. Opening Prayer (A Service of Word and Table) *The United Methodist Hymnal* (Nashville, Tenn.: The United Methodist Publishing House, 1989), 6.

Through Christ you preserve it.
You made the day for the works of light
and the night for the refreshment of our minds and bodies.
Keep us now in Christ, grant us a peaceful evening,
a night free from sin, and bring us at last to eternal life.
Through Christ in the Holy Spirit,
we offer you all glory, honor and worship, now and forever. Amen.[3]

or

O God,
you have created the universe with such splendor
that all of it rises up to praise you.
We, the people you have called to be your own,
join with sun and moon, stars and mountains,
in singing hymns of glory to your wonderful Name.
Through Jesus Christ our Lord,
who lives and reigns with you and the Holy Spirit,
one God for ever and ever. Amen.[4]

MUSICAL RESPONSE (Kyrie *or other, see Global Songs and Responses, Nos. 410–12*)

PRAYER FOR ILLUMINATION
Let us pray:
God of Light, open our hearts and minds by the power of your Holy Spirit, that, as the Scriptures are read and your word proclaimed, we may hear with joy what you say to us today. **Amen.**[5]

or

Prepare our hearts, O Lord, to accept your word. Silence in us any voice but your own; that, hearing, we may also obey your will; through Jesus Christ our Lord. **Amen.**[6]

FIRST READING

After the reading:
The Word of Life.
Thanks be to God.

---

3. Liturgy of Evening Prayer, Syria, 4th c.
4. Timothy J. Crouch, OSL, *And Also with You,* Year C (Akron, Ohio: OSL Publications, 1994), 17 and 24.
5. Prayer for Illumination, *The United Methodist Hymnal* (Nashville, Tenn.: The United Methodist Publishing House, 1989), 6, adapted.
6. Prayer for Illumination, *The Worshipbook: Services and Hymns* (Philadelphia, Penn.: The Westminster Press, 1970, 1972), 28.

PSALM (*see Nos. 223–373*)

*GOSPEL ALLELUIA (*This, or another selection*)

MUSIC: Fintan O'Carroll and Christopher Walker

Music © 1985 Fintan O'Carroll and Christopher Walker, admin. by OCP Publications, Inc.

*GOSPEL READING

After the reading:
The Gospel of Jesus Christ
Praise to the living Word!

HOMILY

RESPONSE
Here may occur a time of silence, a song of response, prayers of intercession, or affirmation of faith.

and/or

CONFESSION
Let us confess our sin in the presence of God and of one another.

Silent confession

Let us pray together.
Gracious God, have mercy on us. In your compassion forgive us our sins, known and unknown, those things done and left undone. Uphold us by your Spirit so that we may live and serve you in newness of life, to the honor and glory of your holy name; through Jesus Christ our Lord. Amen.[7]

or

7. Don E. Saliers

Let us pray together.
God of all mercy,
we confess that we have sinned against you,
opposing your will in our lives.
We have denied your goodness in each other,
in ourselves, and in the world you have created.
We repent of the evil that enslaves us,
the evil we have done,
and the evil done on our behalf.
Forgive, restore, and strengthen us
through our Savior Jesus Christ,
that we may abide in your love
and serve only your will. Amen.[8]

or

Singing Triune God, we confess thick tongues
and awkward lives; we are slow to sing your praise.
Give us a longing for the gospel song:
the rhythm of hope, the harmony of love, the drumbeat of peace,
and the passionate joy of our Savior, Jesus Christ.[9]

DECLARATION OF PARDON
In the name of Jesus Christ, we are a forgiven people. Glory to God!
Alleluia! Amen.

THE PEACE
Let us offer one another signs of reconciliation and love.

OFFERING
As forgiven and reconciled children of God, let us now offer ourselves and our gifts.
A Communion song may be sung as the gifts are brought to the table.

TAKING THE BREAD AND THE CUP
The celebrant receives the bread and wine and prepares the table.

*THE GREAT THANKSGIVING[10] (*or an alternate Prayer at the Table. See Nos. 46A–C*)

The Lord be with you.
And also with you.
Lift up your hearts.

8. *Enriching our Worship*, Standing Liturgical Commission of the Episcopal Church, USA (New York: Church Publishing, Inc., 1998), 56.
9. Jerry P. Haas. © 2006 Upper Room Books.
10. The Great Thanksgiving, *The United Methodist Hymnal* (Nashville, Tenn.: The United Methodist Publishing House, 1989), 9–11, adapted.

We lift them up to the Lord.
Let us give thanks to the Lord our God.
It is right to give our thanks and praise.

It is right, and a good and joyful thing,
    always and everywhere to give thanks to you,
    Father Almighty (Almighty God), creator of heaven and earth.
You formed us in your image
    and breathed into us the breath of life.
When we turned away, and our love failed,
    your love remained steadfast.
You delivered us from captivity,
    made covenant to be our sovereign God,
    and spoke to us through the prophets.

Leader may invite the people to join as follows.

And so,
    with your people on earth
    and all the company of heaven
    we praise your name and join their unending hymn:

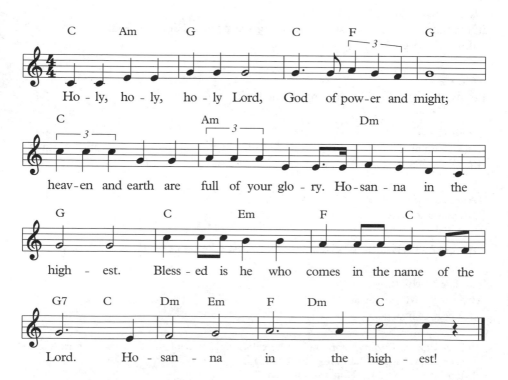

MUSIC: Elise S. Eslinger (based on NICAEA)
Music © 1985 The Upper Room

Holy are you, and blessed is your Son Jesus Christ.
Your Spirit anointed him
    to preach good news to the poor,
    to proclaim release to the captives
        and recovering of sight to the blind,
    to set at liberty those who are oppressed,
    and to announce that the time had come
        when you would save your people.
He healed the sick, fed the hungry, and ate with sinners.
By the baptism of his suffering, death, and resurrection
    you gave birth to your Church,
    delivered us from slavery to sin and death,
    and made with us a new covenant
        by water and the Spirit.
When the Lord Jesus ascended,
    he promised to be with us always,
        in the power of your Word and Holy Spirit.

On the night in which he gave himself up for us,
    he took bread, gave thanks to you, broke the bread,
    gave it to his disciples, and said:
"Take, eat; this is my body which is given for you.
Do this in remembrance of me."

When the supper was over, he took the cup,
    gave thanks to you, gave it to his disciples, and said:
"Drink from this, all of you;
    this is my blood of the new covenant,
    poured out for you and for many
        for the forgiveness of sins.
Do this, as often as you drink it,
In remembrance of me."

Leader may invite the people to join in the Memorial Acclamation as follows.

And so,
    in remembrance of these your mighty acts in Jesus Christ,
    we offer ourselves in praise and thanksgiving
        as a holy and living sacrifice,
        in union with Christ's offering for us,
    as we proclaim the mystery of faith.

Christ has died, Christ is ris - en, Christ will come a - gain!

MUSIC: Elise S. Eslinger
Music © 1985 The Upper Room

Pour out your Holy Spirit on us gathered here,
    and on these gifts of bread and wine.
Make them be for us the body and blood of Christ,
that we may be for the world the body of Christ,
    redeemed by his blood.

By your Spirit make us one with Christ,
    one with each other,
    and one in ministry to all the world,
until Christ comes in final victory
    and we feast at his heavenly banquet.

Leader may invite the people to join in the doxology as follows.

Through your Son Jesus Christ,
with the Holy Spirit in your holy Church,
all honor and glory is yours, almighty Father (God),
now and forever.

A - men,   a - men,   a - men.

MUSIC: Elise S. Eslinger
Music © 1985 The Upper Room

THE LORD'S PRAYER or PRAYER OF JESUS
(Sung or spoken. See Nos. 453–58 for musical and paraphrased alternatives.)
Our Father in heaven,
    hallowed be your name,
    your kingdom come,
    your will be done on earth,
        as in heaven.
Give us today our daily bread.
Forgive us our sins
    as we forgive those who sin against us.
Save us from the time of trial
    and deliver us from evil.
For the kingdom, the power, and the glory are yours
    now and forever. Amen.[11]

11. English translation of The Lord's Prayer © 1988 English Language Liturgical Consultation
    (ELLC).

*Breaking the Bread

The minister breaks the bread in silence or may say:
Because there is one loaf, we, who are many, are one body,
for we all partake of the one loaf.
The bread which we break is a sharing in the body of Christ.

The minister lifts the cup in silence, or may say:
The cup over which we give thanks is a sharing in the blood of Christ.

Here, the Agnus Dei *may be sung, see Nos. 413–14.*

Giving the Bread and the Cup

Communion songs, the music of Taizé, or instrumental music may be offered as the gifts are shared and prayer continues.

*Prayer after Receiving

Let us pray:
May be offered by the celebrant or prayed in unison.

Eternal God, we give you thanks for this holy mystery in which you have given yourself to us. Grant that we may go into the world in the strength of your Spirit, to give ourselves for others. In the name of Jesus Christ, our Lord. **Amen.**

or

We thank you, God, for inviting us to this table
where we have known the presence of Christ
and have received all Christ's gifts.
Strengthen our faith,
increase our love for one another,
and let us show forth your praise in our lives;
through Jesus Christ our Savior.
Amen.[12]

or

Having been consumed into your Body by your love, send us to all who hunger for your sustaining Presence that we may gratefully share the Feast. **Amen.**[13]

*Hymn *or* Song

---

12. Prayer of Thanksgiving, *Book of Worship United Church of Christ* (New York: United Church of Christ Office for Church Life and Leadership, 1986), 88.
13. Nancy Bryan Crouch, OSL

*Dismissal with Blessing

Go forth in peace.
The grace of the Lord Jesus Christ, and the love of God, and the communion of the
Holy Spirit be with you all. **Amen.**[14]

or

Go forth in hope and peace.
May the grace of Christ attend us, the love of God surround us, and the Holy Spirit
keep us, now and ever. **Amen.**[15]

or

God's blessing be with you,
Christ's peace be with you,
the Spirit's outpouring be with you,
now and always. **Amen.**[16]

---

14. The Great Thanksgiving, *The United Methodist Hymnal* (Nashville, Tenn.: The United
    Methodist Publishing House, 1989), 9–11, adapted.
15. Don E. Saliers
16. *Enriching Our Worship*, 70.

The pattern for this ecumenical liturgy is derived from the Service for Word and
Table 1 as found in *The United Methodist Hymnal* 1989. This adaptation was
prepared especially for this revision of the *Upper Room Worshipbook* and is intended
primarily for contexts in which daily Eucharist is celebrated. In addition to
alternate prayers provided within the liturgy itself, alternate versions of the Great
Thanksgiving are found on Nos. 46A–C. A variety of musical settings of the *Sanctus*,
Memorial Acclamation, and Great Amen are found on Nos. 43–45.

Alternate Setting A

Sanctus and *Benedictus*

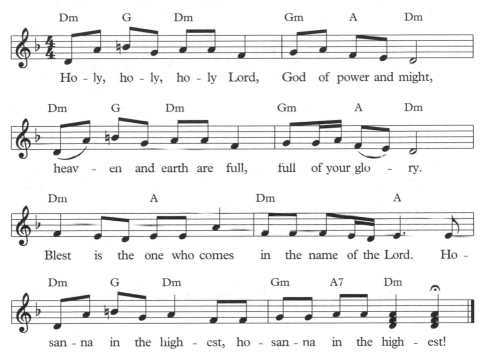

MUSIC: Elise S. Eslinger (based on EASTER CAROL)

Music © 2006 Upper Room Books

Memorial Acclamation

MUSIC: Elise S. Eslinger (based on EASTER CAROL)

Music © 2006 Upper Room Books

Great Amen

MUSIC: Elise S. Eslinger (based on EASTER CAROL)

Music © 2006 Upper Room Books

44 Alternate Setting B

Sanctus and *Benedictus*

Ho-ly, ho-ly, ho-ly Lord; Ho-ly, ho-ly, ho-ly Lord;

God of power and might. God of power and

might. Heaven and earth are full of your glo-ry.

Heaven and earth are full of your glo-ry. Ho-san-na

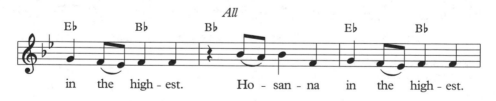

in the high-est. Ho-san-na in the high-est.

Blest is the One who comes, Blest is the One who

MUSIC: Gary Alan Smith (inspired by the anthem "Antiphonal Hosanna")
Music © 2005 Gamut Music Productions

Memorial Acclamation

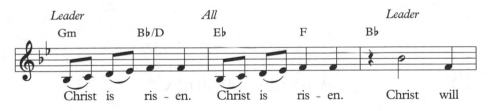

MUSIC: Gary Alan Smith (inspired by the anthem "Antiphonal Hosanna")

Great Amen

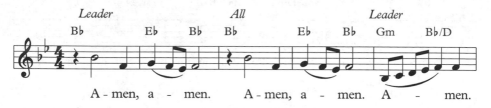

MUSIC: Gary Alan Smith (inspired by the anthem "Antiphonal Hosanna")

45   Alternate Setting C

Sanctus and *Benedictus*

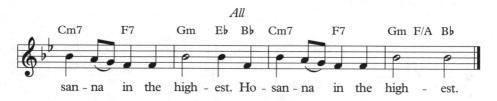

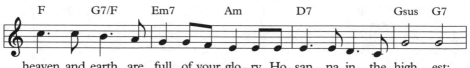

MUSIC: Dean McIntyre (based on SANTO)

Blest is he who comes in the name of the Lord. Ho -

san - na, ho - san - na in the high - est.

Memorial Acclamation

Christ has died. Christ is

ris - en. Christ will come a - gain.

MUSIC: Dean McIntyre (based on SANTO)
Music © 2000 The General Board of Discipleship of The United Methodist Church

Great Amen

A - men A - men. A - men.

MUSIC: Dean McIntyre (based on SANTO)
Music © 2000 The General Board of Discipleship of The United Methodist Church

46   Alternate Prayers at the Table

(Great Thanksgiving)
(*Select and announce the musical setting from Nos. 43–45.*)

A. THE GREAT THANKSGIVING

God be with you.
And also with you.
Lift up your hearts.
We lift them to our God.
Let us give thanks to the living God.
It is right to give our thanks and praise.

Blessed are you, God of all creation,
    Source of all mercies,
    Fount of love beyond all measure,
It is fitting and right to give you thanks and praise,
    and to adore you with grateful hearts and voices.
For wondrously you have created heaven and earth,
hovering in gracious care over all that you have made.
You formed us as your image of love in the world.
Yet even more wondrously, when we distorted your image
    you called us back again and again,
        forgiving us,
        delivering us from captivity to sin and death,
        feeding, healing, reconciling, making covenant,
        and setting before us the way which leads to life.
Therefore, with your people in all ages, in communion with the saints,
    and with the whole company of heaven,
    we join the glad song of unceasing praise:

(Sanctus, *as selected*)

Holy are you, and blessed be your name, gracious God,
    for you gave us Jesus, who emptied himself that we might be filled,
    who suffered and died that we might live.
He fed the hungry, healed the afflicted,
    and ate with the scorned and forgotten of this world.
He washed his disciples' feet and gave a holy meal
    as a feast of his ever-present love.

On the night he gave himself up for us and for the world,
    at table with those who would desert and deny him,
    he took bread, gave it to his disciples, saying:
        "Take, eat; this is my body which is given for you.
        Do this in remembrance of me."

When supper had ended, he took the cup, gave thanks to you,
gave it to his disciples, saying:
    "Drink from this, all of you;
    for this is my blood of the new covenant,
    poured out for you and for many, for the forgiveness of sins.
    Do this, as often as you drink it, in remembrance of me."

Therefore, remembering Christ's life of ministry and service, his suffering, death
and resurrection, his ascending to glory and his abiding presence through the power
of your Holy Spirit, we come in praise and thanksgiving with these gifts of your love,
as we proclaim the mystery of faith:

(Memorial Acclamation, *as selected*)

Pour out your Holy Spirit upon us gathered here in Christ's name,
    and upon these gifts, that they may be for us his body and blood;
    and so feed us with his grace that, in union with Christ,
    we may become a living offering to you.

(*Intercessions may be included here:* Remember, God of all mercy, those who suffer
this day from injustice or poverty, with no place to call home. Remember those who
are sick, imprisoned, or troubled, and those who face death with no one to comfort
them. Remember, also, we pray . . . *names may be offered.*)

Transform us into the image and likeness of Christ,
    that we may faithfully serve others in his name,
    and look forward to the final feast
    in which all shall be gathered as one at your table,
    and all manner of things shall be well.

Through Christ, with Christ, and in Christ, in the unity of the Holy Spirit,
    all honor and glory and blessing is yours, Almighty God (Father),
    now and forever.

(Great Amen, *as selected*)

(*Return to* The Lord's Prayer, *page 40, or select an alternative from Nos. 453–57.*)

Eucharistic Prayer by Don E. Saliers © 2006 Don E. Saliers.

B. THE GREAT THANKSGIVING

God be with you.
And also with you.
Lift up your hearts.
We lift them up to our God.
Let us give thanks to the living God.
It is right to give our thanks and praise.

Holy God,
 In the beginning was darkness, mystery, and you.
 By your own Word, you shattered the darkness with light.
 You set in the sky radiant beams of sunlight
 and punctured the night sky with sparkling jewels.
 You forever changed our darkness.

Holy God,
 Though there are shadows and worries,
 You have placed your Word in us to be a lamp for our feet.
 You have given your Spirit like a bright guiding star.
 You fill us with Your Love as glorious as the sun.
 You place your Truth like a crescent moon.
 Every darkness is overcome with Light.
 And every Light contains shafts of your Eternal Light.

God of the sun and stars, we praise you
 and with all the creatures of earth and
 all the company of heaven we join the unending hymn:

(Sanctus, *as selected*)

Ever-persistent and ever-loving God, you placed a star in the sky
 to guide people from far and near to your child.
 Jesus became the Light of the World,
 drawing the lost and forgotten, the hurt and the wounded,
 the oppressed and depressed to the wellsprings of life.
 He changed water into wine,
 called unheralded workers to be disciples,
 preached good news to the poor,
 healed the sick and beckoned people to love their neighbor.
 By his baptism, suffering, death and resurrection he revealed the depths
 of your love and the power of light over darkness.

On the night he gave himself up, Jesus gathered with his friends.
 He took bread, blessed it, broke it and gave it to his followers, saying,
 "Take, eat, this is my life broken for you."

Likewise, he took the cup, blessed it and gave it to his disciples.
"Drink this, all of you, for this is my life poured out for you and for all,
for the forgiveness of sins. Do this in remembrance of me."

Therefore, Holy God;
Grant that in praise and thanksgiving, we may be a living sacrifice, holy and
acceptable in your sight, and that our lives may proclaim the mystery of faith:

(Memorial Acclamation, *as selected*)

Pour out your Holy Spirit upon us
and upon these gifts of bread and wine,
that through Christ's presence we may become a beacon of holy light,
a source of joy, a witness for peace.
By your Spirit, make us one with Christ,
one with each other, one with seekers far and near,
and one in ministry to all the world
until we feast at the heavenly banquet.

Through your Son Jesus Christ,
with the Holy Spirit in your holy church,
all honor and glory is yours, almighty God,
now and forever.

(Great Amen, *as selected*)

(*Return to* The Lord's Prayer, *page 40, or select an alternative from Nos. 453–57.*)

C. The Great Thanksgiving

The Spirit of God be with you all.
And also with you.
Lift up your hearts;
We lift them to God.
Give thanks to our God!
All our thanks, all our praise!

Holy God, Holy One, Holy Three!

Before all that is, You were God.
  Outside all we know, You are God.
    After all is finished, You will be God.
Archangels sound the trumpets,
  Angels teach us their song,
    Saints pull us into your presence.

And this is our song:

> **Holy, Holy, Holy God,**
> **Our life, our mercy, our might.**
> **Heaven and earth are full of your glory.**
> **Save us, we pray, You beyond all.**
> **Blest is the One who comes in your name.**
> **Save us, we pray, You beyond all.**

Holy God, Holy One, Holy Three!

You beyond the galaxies,
  You under the oceans,
    You inside the leaves,
You pouring down rain,
  You opening the flowers,
    You feeding the insects,
You giving us your image,
  You carrying us through the waters,
    You holding us in the night,

Your smile on Sarah and Abraham,
  Your hand with Moses and Miriam,
    Your words through Deborah and Isaiah,
You lived as Jesus among us,
  Healing, teaching, dying, rising,
    Inviting us all to your feast.

In the night in which he was betrayed,
Jesus took bread, and gave thanks;
broke it, and gave it to his disciples, saying:
Take, eat; this is my body, given for you.
Do this for the remembrance of me.
Again, after supper he took the cup, gave thanks,
and gave it for all to drink, saying:
This cup is the new covenant in my blood,
shed for you and for all people
for the forgiveness of sin.
Do this for the remembrance of me.

Holy God, we remember your Son,

His life with the humble,
  His death among the wretched,
    His resurrection for us all:
Your wisdom our guide,
  Your justice our strength,
    Your grace our path to rebirth.

And so we cry, Mercy:
  Mercy!
And so we cry, Glory:
  Glory!
And so we cry, Blessing!
  Blessing!

Holy God, we beg for your Spirit:

Enliven this bread,
  Awaken this body,
    Pour us out for each other.
Transfigure our minds,
  Ignite your church,
    Nourish the life of the earth.
Make us, while many, united,
  Make us though broken, whole,
    Make us, despite death, alive.

And so we cry, Come, Holy Spirit:
  Come, Holy Spirit!
And so the church shouts, Come, Holy Spirit:
  Come, Holy Spirit!
And so the earth pleads, Come, Holy Spirit:
  Come, Holy Spirit!

You, Holy God, Holy One, Holy Three,

Our Life, our Mercy, our Might,
  Our Table, our Food, our Server,
    Our Rainbow, our Ark, our Dove,
Our Sovereign, our Water, our Wine,
  Our Light, our Treasure, our Tree,
    Our Way, our Truth, our Life.

You, Holy God, Holy One, Holy Three!

Praise now,
Praise tomorrow,
Praise forever.

And so we cry, Amen:
  Amen!

(*Return to* The Lord's Prayer, *page 40, or select an alternative from Nos. 453–57.*)

Eucharistic Prayer: Triple Praise by Gail Ramshaw © 2000 Gail Ramshaw. Used by permission.
gailramshaw@cs.com

52   A Brief Order for Evening Prayer with Eucharist

GREETING (*the vesper candle is lit*)
The Lord is my light and my salvation; whom shall I fear?
The Lord is the strength of my life; of whom then shall I be afraid?
Light and peace in Jesus Christ our Lord.
Thanks be to God.

EVENING HYMN (*the vesper candle may be processed*)

EVENING PRAYER (*see No. 14*)

PSALM

Silence

Psalm Prayer

READING OF SCRIPTURE

After the reading:
The Word of Life.
Thanks be to God.

HOMILY OR SILENCE FOR REFLECTION

SONG OF MARY (*or other song of praise*)

PRAYERS OF INTERCESSION

SHARING THE PEACE

OFFERING THE GIFTS

THE GREAT THANKSGIVING

THE LORD'S PRAYER

BREAKING THE BREAD

SHARING BREAD AND CUP

PRAYER AFTER COMMUNION

CLOSING SONG

BLESSING AND DISMISSAL

Note: This basic ordering suggests a way to combine the central elements of Holy Communion within a general pattern of Evening Prayer, for potential use when daily Eucharist takes place at the Vesper hour.

Hymns and Songs

Music and Communities of Transformation

Let the word of Christ dwell in you richly; teach and admonish one another in all wisdom; and with gratitude in your hearts sing psalms, hymns, and spiritual songs to God.—Colossians 3:16

Despite the cluttered, noisy confusions of our 21st-century world, we gather in praise as those who seek to be transformed by the Word who is Christ. We want to live as those who have beheld the glory of God! As the Colossians verse bids, these pages echo an urgent invitation: *to pay grace-filled attention to the Word-texts in which we immerse ourselves.* We are being invited to delight, indeed to bathe, in timeless narratives, images, and metaphors that call us to reflect upon and to abide in the Word.

What we say and sing when we gather for worship matters greatly. How our community itself articulates and embodies the word, song, and hospitality of God matters greatly. This intentional Christ-journey on which we embark needs silence, and it needs song: joyful and aching music that impresses sacred and reflective texts on our hearts; thoughtful and dynamic music that expresses our individual and communal "yes" to the One who calls us onward; meditative music that encourages listening; soulful rhythms that dance with the Word.

When we gather, we offer to God and one another an environment for the Spirit's holy work of transformation. As we connect through shared story and song, image and icon, sign and symbol, our isolated "I" is invited to become part of an organic "we." Having received profound gifts, we offer our thanks to the One who created us for such intimacy, companionship, and life together within the richly redemptive community of Christ's love. As theologians have observed, and scriptures and worshiping communities affirm in all times and places, *grace and gratitude go together.* The transformed community becomes its thanksgiving and bears the marks of the Son.

Through these pages, we invite hospitable attention to words that matter, sung to wonderful tunes that we may learn by heart. We urge patience in repeating the old and in exploring the new, that tunes and texts alike might become more and more your own. Varieties of musical forms and diverse sources encourage us to proclaim God's glory, to behold holy mystery, to rehearse and remember sacred story, and to evoke compassionate response to our Creator's invitation to become Christ's *shalom* for all the world. *May it be so!*

Elise S. Eslinger
Compiler and Editor

54

Gather Us In

1. Here in this place new light is stream-ing,
2. We are the young — our lives are a mys-t'ry,
3. Here we will take the wine and the wa-ter,
4. Not in the dark of build-ings con-fin-ing,

now is the dark - ness van-ished a - way,
we are the old — who yearn for your face,
here we will take the bread of new birth,
not in some heav - en, light-years a - way, but

see in this space our fears and our dream-ings,
we have been sung through-out all of his - t'ry,
here you shall call your sons and your daugh-ters,
here in this place the new light is shin - ing,

brought here to you in the light of this day. _____
called to be light to the whole hu-man race. _____
call us a - new to be salt for the earth. _____
now is the King-dom, now is the day. _____

Gath-er us in — the lost and for - sak - en, gath-er us in — the
Gath-er us in — the rich and the haugh-ty, gath-er us in — the
Give us to drink the wine of com - pas-sion, give us to eat the
Gath-er us in and hold us for - ev - er, gath-er us in and

WORDS: Marty Haugen (Matt. 5:13)
MUSIC: Marty Haugen

GATHER US IN

blind and the lame; call to us now, and we shall a-wak-en,
proud and the strong; give us a heart so meek and so low-ly,
bread that is you; nour-ish us well, and teach us to fash-ion
make us your own; gath-er us in — all peo-ples to-geth-er,

we shall a-rise at the sound of our name._____
give us the cour-age to en-ter the song._____
lives that are ho-ly and hearts that are true._____
fire of love in our flesh and our bone._____

Come to Us

55

1. Come to me, come to us, you who are bur-dened.
2. Come to me, come to us, pil-grim or stran-ger,
3. Come to me, come to us, bro-ken or build-ing,

Come to the Word, and come to the meal,
look-ing for change, or chal-lenge, or light.
come with your chil-dren, your choi-ces, your chains.

Come with-out ques-tion or pres-sure or price:
We all are peo-ple whose call-ing is care,
All are in-vit-ed to friend-ship or rest, to

Come, be em-braced by the bod-y of Christ._____
bear-ers of mer-cy, nour-ished in prayer._____
share in our strug-gle, our call, and our quest._____

WORDS: Rory Cooney
MUSIC: Rory Cooney
© 1986 OCP Publications, Inc.

COME TO US

56   Jesus Calls Us

Capo 3: D   Em7   D   Em7   F♯m7
     F   Gm7   F   Gm7   Am7

1. Je - sus calls us here to meet him as, through
2. Je - sus calls us to con - fess him Word of
3. Je - sus calls us to each oth - er: found in
4. Je - sus calls us to his ta - ble root - ed

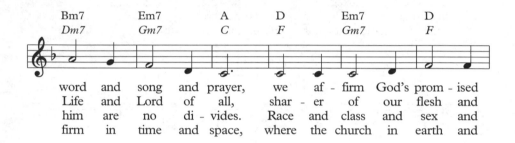

Bm7   Em7   A   D   Em7   D
Dm7   Gm7   C   F   Gm7   F

word and song and prayer, we af - firm God's prom - ised
Life and Lord of all, shar - er of our flesh and
him are no di - vides. Race and class and sex and
firm in time and space, where the church in earth and

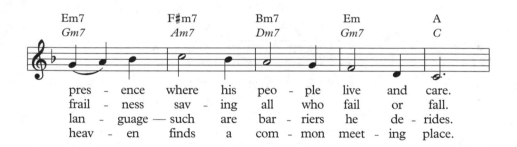

Em7   F♯m7   Bm7   Em   A
Gm7   Am7   Dm7   Gm7   C

pres - ence where his peo - ple live and care.
frail - ness sav - ing all who fail or fall.
lan - guage — such are bar - riers he de - rides.
heav - en finds a com - mon meet - ing place.

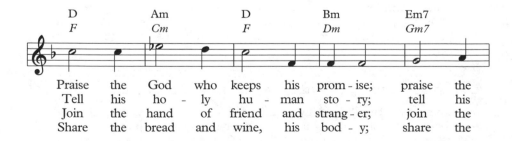

D   Am   D   Bm   Em7
F   Cm   F   Dm   Gm7

Praise the God who keeps his prom - ise; praise the
Tell his ho - ly hu - man sto - ry; tell his
Join the hand of friend and strang - er; join the
Share the bread and wine, his bod - y; share the

WORDS: John L. Bell and Graham Maule
MUSIC: Lewis folk melody; arr. by John L. Bell

JESUS CALLS US
87.87.D

Alternate tune: HOLY MANNA

Son who calls us friends; praise the Spir - it who, a -
tales that all may hear; tell the world that Christ in
hands of age and youth; join the faith - ful and the
love of which we sing; share the feast for saints and

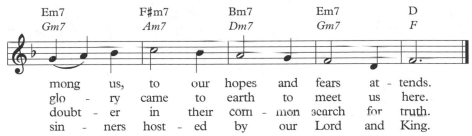

mong us, to our hopes and fears at - tends.
glo - ry came to earth to meet us here.
doubt - er in their com - mon search for truth.
sin - ners host - ed by our Lord and King.

Weave 57

Refrain

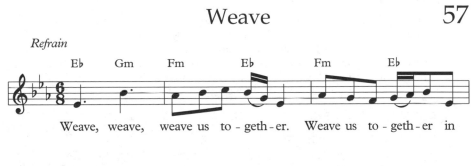

Weave, weave, weave us to - geth - er. Weave us to - geth - er in

u - ni - ty and love. Weave, weave, weave us to - geth - er,

Weave us to - geth - er, to - geth - er in love. ___

WORDS: Rosemary Crow
MUSIC: Rosemary Crow
© 1979 Rosemary Crow

58 All Are Welcome

1. Let us build a house where love can dwell and
2. Let us build a house where proph-ets speak, and
3. Let us build a house where love is found in
4. Let us build a house where hands will reach be-
5. Let us build a house where all are named, their

all can safe-ly live, a place where saints and
words are strong and true, where all God's chil-dren
wa-ter, wine, and wheat: A ban-quet hall on
yond the wood and stone to heal and strength-en,
songs and vi-sions heard and loved and treas-ured,

chil-dren tell how hearts learn to for-give. Built of
dare to seek to dream God's reign a-new. Here the
ho-ly ground, where peace and jus-tice meet. Here the
serve and teach, and live the Word they've known. Here the
taught and claimed as words with-in the Word. Built of

hopes and dreams and vi-sions, Rock of faith and vault of
cross shall stand as wit-ness and as sym-bol of God's
love of God, through Je-sus, is re-vealed in time and
out-cast and the stran-ger bear the im-age of God's
tears and cries and laugh-ter, prayers of faith and songs of

grace; here the love of Christ shall end di-vi-sions:
grace; here as one we claim the faith of Je-sus:
space; as we share in Christ the feast that frees us:
face; let us bring an end to fear and dan-ger:
grace, let this house pro-claim from floor to raft-er:

WORDS: Marty Haugen
MUSIC: Marty Haugen

TWO OAKS

Refrain

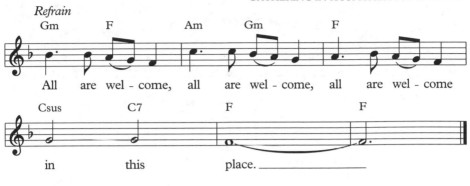

All are wel - come, all are wel - come, all are wel - come

in this place. _____

Come Away with Me 59

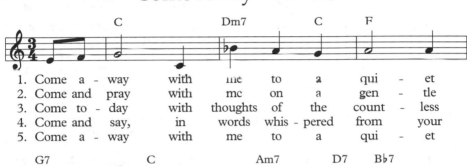

1. Come a - way with me to a qui - et
2. Come and pray with me on a gen - tle
3. Come to - day with thoughts of the count - less
4. Come and say, in words whis - pered from your
5. Come a - way with me to a qui - et

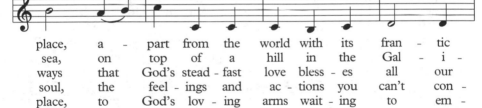

place, a - part from the world with its fran - tic
sea, on top of a hill in the Gal - i -
ways that God's stead - fast love bless - es all our
soul, the feel - ings and ac - tions you can't con -
place, to God's lov - ing arms wait - ing to em -

pace, to pray, re - flect, and seek God's grace.
lee, in gar - dens like Geth - se - ma - ne.
days, and join with me in si - lent praise.
trol. Your spir - it needs to be made whole.
brace all those who come in hope of grace.

Come a - way with me. Come a - way.

WORDS: Mary Nelson Keithahn
MUSIC: John D. Horman

RECREATION
10 10.88

60 The Summons

1. Will you come and fol-low me if I but call
2. Will you leave your-self be-hind if I but call
3. Will you let the blind-ed see if I but call
4. Will you love the "you" you hide if I but call
5. Lord, your sum-mons ech-oes true when you but call

your name?____ Will you go where you don't know and
your name?____ Will you care for cruel and kind and
your name?____ Will you set the pris-oners free and
your name?____ Will you quell the fear in-side and
my name.____ Let me turn and fol-low you and

nev-er be the same?____ Will you let my love be
nev-er be the same?____ Will you risk the hos-tile
nev-er be the same?____ Will you kiss the lep-er
nev-er be the same?____ Will you use the faith you've
nev-er be the same.____ In your com-pa-ny I'll

shown,____ will you let my name be known,____ will you
stare____ should your life at-tract or scare?____ Will you
clean,____ and do such as this un-seen,____ and ad-
found____ to re-shape the world a-round,____ through my
go____ where your love and foot-steps show.____ Thus I'll

let my life be grown in you and you in me?____
let me an-swer prayer in you and you in me?____
mit to what I mean in you and you in me?____
sight and touch and sound in you and you in me?____
move and live and grow in you and you in me.____

WORDS: John L. Bell
MUSIC: Traditional Scottish; arr. by John L. Bell

KELVINGROVE
13 13 7 7 13

Bring Us Home

Refrain

Bring us home on love's re - new - ing tide to the place of our be - long - ing. Bring us home to your re - deem - ing side. Bring your scat-tered peo-ple home.

1. From our wea - ry night bring us to the light,
2. From our closed-in fears, from our was - ted years,
3. From our self - ish views, learn - ings we re - fuse,

to the place of our be - long - ing;
to the place of our be - long - ing;
to the place of our be - long - ing;

with your warm em-brace, wa - ken us to grace,
to our high-est call, shar - ing love with all,
to the truth we are, to our ris - ing star,

bring your scat - tered peo - ple home.
bring your scat - tered peo - ple home.
bring your scat - tered peo - ple home. *(Repeat refrain.)*

WORDS: Rodney Romney
MUSIC: Peter Strauch

BRING US HOME
558 D with Refrain

Used by permission of Rodney Romney

62 Sing for God's Glory

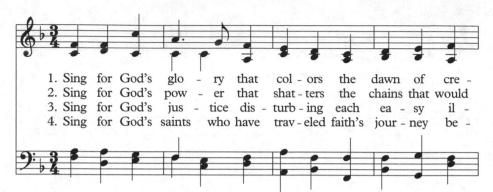

1. Sing for God's glo – ry that col – ors the dawn of cre –
2. Sing for God's pow – er that shat – ters the chains that would
3. Sing for God's jus – tice dis – turb – ing each ea – sy il –
4. Sing for God's saints who have trav – eled faith's jour – ney be –

a – tion, rac – ing a – cross the sky, trail – ing bright
bind us, sear – ing the dark – ness of fear and des –
lu – sion, tear – ing down ty – rants and put – ting our
fore us, who in our wear – i – ness give us their

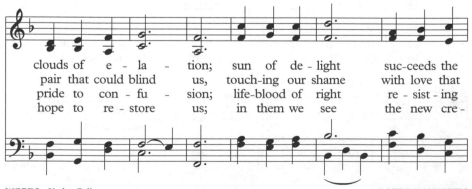

clouds of e – la – tion; sun of de – light suc – ceeds the
pair that could blind us, touch – ing our shame with love that
pride to con – fu – sion; life-blood of right re – sist – ing
hope to re – store us; in them we see the new cre –

WORDS: Kathy Galloway

MUSIC: *Erneuerten Gesangbuch;* harm. by William Sterndale Bennett

LOBE DEN HERREN
14 14.478

vel - vet of night,   warm-ing the earth's ex - ul - ta - tion.
will not lay blame,   reach-ing out gent - ly to find   us.
e - vil and slight,   of - fer-ing free-dom's trans - fu - sion.
a - tion to be,   spir - it of love made flesh for   us.

Praise Be to God, the Almighty   63

1. Praise be to God, the Almighty, who rules all creation!
   O my soul, worship the wellspring of health and salvation!
   Let all who hear now to God's temple draw near,
   joining in glad adoration!

2. Praise be to God, who o'er all things is wondrously reigning,
   bringing new life, in great mercy redeeming, sustaining.
   Ponder anew what the Almighty can do;
   ponder God's gracious ordaining.

3. Praise be to God, who works justice, who ends all oppressing!
   God's name most holy let Israel always be blessing!
   Rise up on wings! Healing and wholeness God brings!
   Always God's deeds be confessing!

4. Praise be to God! O forget not God's manifold graces!
   All that has life and breath, one song of gratitude raises!
   Let the amen sound from God's people again.
   Gladly forever sing praises.

Sing to LOBE DEN HERREN, No. 62

Joachim Neander; trans. by Catherine Winkworth, *et al.*; additional text by Ruth Duck

64   For the Music of Creation

1. For the mu - sic of cre - a - tion, for the song your
2. Psalms and sym - pho - nies ex - alt you, drum and trum - pet,
3. All the voic - es of the a - ges in tran - scen - dent

Spir - it sings, for your sound's di - vine ex - pres - sion,
string and reed, sim - ple mel - o - dies ac - claim you,
cho - rus meet, wor - ship lift - ing up the sens - es,

burst of joy in liv - ing things: God, our God, the
tunes that rise from deep - est need, hymns of long - ing
hands that praise and danc - ing feet; o - ver dis - cord

world's com - pos - er, hear us, ech - oes of your voice. Mu -
and be - long - ing, car - ols from a cheer - ful throat, lilt __
and di - vi - sion mu - sic speaks your joy and peace, har -

WORDS: Shirley Erena Murray
MUSIC: Ludwig van Beethoven; arr. by Edward Hodges

HYMN TO JOY

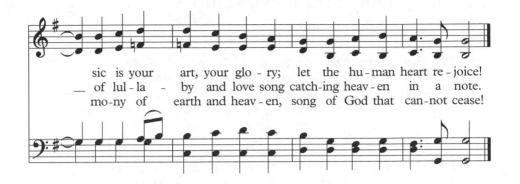

sic is your   art, your glo - ry;   let the hu - man heart re - joice!
_ of lul - la - by and love song catch-ing heav - en   in   a   note.
mo-ny of   earth and heav - en, song of God that can-not cease!

Joyful, Joyful, We Adore Thee   65

1. Joyful, joyful, we adore thee, God of glory, God of love;
    hearts unfold like flow'rs before thee, opening to the sun above.
    Melt the clouds of sin and sadness, drive the dark of doubt away;
    giver of immortal gladness, fill us with the light of day.

2. All thy works with joy surround thee, earth and heav'n reflect thy rays,
    stars and angels sing around thee, center of unbroken praise.
    Field and forest, vale and mountain, flowery meadow, flashing sea,
    chanting bird and flowing fountain, call us to rejoice in thee.

3. Thou art giving and forgiving, ever blessing, ever blest;
    wellspring of the joy of living, ocean depth of happy rest!
    God, Creator; Christ, Redeemer, all who live in love are thine;
    teach us how to love each other, lift us to the joy divine!

4. Mortals, join the mighty chorus; stars of morning, take your part;
    love divine is reigning o'er us, binding those of tender heart;
    ever singing, moving onward, loving in the midst of strife,
    joyful music leads us sunward in the triumph song of life.

Sing to HYMN TO JOY, No. 64

Henry Van Dyke, alt.
Alt. © 1974 Ecumenical Women's Center

66   Holy Spirit, Wind of Heaven

1. Holy Spirit, Wind of Heaven, Breath of Life, our warmth and light,
Power of creation, bringing hopeful dawn from darkest night:
you have birthed us, you have borne us, you have blessed us all our days,
Now you fill our lungs with singing; how you fill our hearts with praise!

2. Holy Spirit, flame of passion, you who brought the Church to be,
re-create us as your Body, holy in our unity.
Fill us with your fierce compassion, gentle courage, trust and peace;
Lead us all to love each other, make our sad divisions cease.

3. Holy Spirit, Dove descending, mind of Christ within us all;
speak your wisdom, move among us, help us hear your inner call.
Be the only pow'r that moves us; be our life, O singing Dove!
Holy Spirit, come! Revive us! Fill us with your heart of love!

Sing to HYMN TO JOY, No. 64

Steve Garnaas-Holmes
© 2006 Steve Garnaas-Holmes

67   Creating God, Your Fingers Trace

1. Cre - a - ting God, your fin - gers trace the
2. Sus - tain - ing God, your hands up - hold earth's
3. Re - deem - ing God, your arms em - brace all
4. In - dwell - ing God, your gos - pel claims one

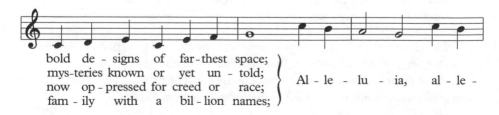

bold de - signs of far - thest space;
mys - teries known or yet un - told;
now op - pressed for creed or race;
fam - ily with a bil - lion names;
} Al - le - lu - ia, al - le -

WORDS: Jeffery Rowthorn, adapt.
MUSIC: *Geistliche Kirchengesänge*
Words © 1979 The Hymn Society, admin. by Hope Publishing Co.

LASST UNS ERFREUEN

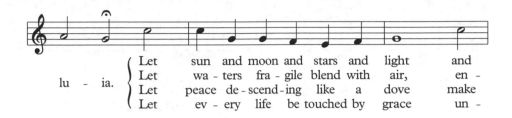

Let sun and moon and stars and light and
lu - ia. Let wa - ters fra - gile blend with air, en -
Let peace de - scend - ing like a dove make
Let ev - ery life be touched by grace un -

what lies hid - den praise your might.
a - bling life, pro - claim your care.
known on earth your heal ing love. Al - le - lu - ia, al - le -
til we praise you face to face.

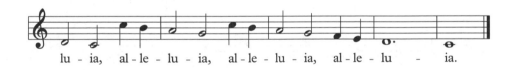

lu - ia, al - le - lu - ia, al - le - lu - ia, al - le - lu - ia.

Praise God, from Whom All Blessings Flow 68

Praise God, from whom all blessings flow;
praise God, all creatures here below:
Alleluia! Alleluia!
Praise God, the source of all our gifts!
Praise Jesus Christ, whose power uplifts!
Praise the Spirit, Holy Spirit! Alleluia! Alleluia! Alleluia!

Sing to LASST UNS ERFREUEN, No. 67

Thomas Ken; adapt. by Gilbert H. Vieira
Adapt. © 1989 The United Methodist Publishing House

69 Let All Creation Bless the Lord

1. Let all cre-a-tion bless the Lord, till
2. All liv-ing things up-on the earth, green
3. O men and wom-en ev-ery-where, lift

heaven with praise is ring - ing. Sun,
fer - tile hills and moun - tains, sing
up a hymn of glo - ry; let

moon, and stars, peal out a chord, stir
to the God who gave you birth; be
all who know God's stead - fast care tell

up the an - gels' sing - ing. Sing,
joy - ful, springs and foun - tains. Lithe
out sal - va - tion's sto - ry. No

WORDS: Carl P. Daw, Jr.   MIT FREUDEN ZART
MUSIC: Bohemian Brethren's *Kirchengesänge*; harm. by Heinrich Reinmann   87.87.887
Words © 1989 Hope Publishing Co.

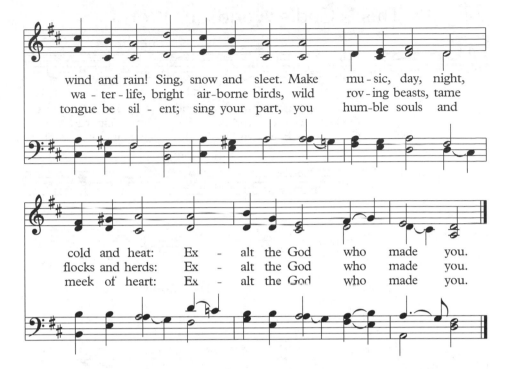

wind and rain! Sing, snow and sleet. Make mu - sic, day, night,
wa - ter - life, bright air-borne birds, wild rov - ing beasts, tame
tongue be sil - ent; sing your part, you hum-ble souls and

cold and heat: Ex - alt the God who made you.
flocks and herds: Ex - alt the God who made you.
meek of heart: Ex - alt the God who made you.

Sing Praise to God Who Reigns Above   70

1. Sing praise to God who reigns above, the God of all creation,
   the God of power, the God of love, the God of our salvation.
   With healing balm my soul is filled and every faithless murmur stilled:
   To God all praise and glory.

2. The Lord is never far away, but through all grief distressing,
   an ever present help and stay, our peace and joy and blessing.
   As with a mother's tender hand, God gently leads the chosen band:
   To God all praise and glory.

3. Thus, all my toilsome way along, I sing aloud thy praises,
   that earth may hear the grateful song my voice unwearied raises.
   Be joyful in the Lord, my heart, both soul and body, bear your part:
   To God all praise and glory.

4. Let all who name Christ's holy name give God all praise and glory;
   let all who own God's power proclaim aloud the wondrous story!
   Cast each false idol from its throne, for Christ is Lord, and Christ alone:
   To God all praise and glory.

Sing to MIT FREUDEN ZART, No. 69

Johann J. Schütz; trans. by Frances E. Cox (Deut. 32:3)

71 This Is God's Wondrous World

1. This is God's won-drous world, and to my lis-t'ning
2. This is God's won-drous world: The birds their car - ols
3. This is God's won-drous world: O let me ne'er for -

ears all na - ture sings, and round me rings the
raise; the morn - ing light, the li - ly white, de -
get that though the wrong seems oft so strong, God

mu - sic of the spheres. This is God's won-drous world, I
clare their Mak-er's praise. This is God's won-drous world: God
is the ru - ler yet. This is God's won-drous world: Why

rest me in the thought of rocks and trees, of
shines in all that's fair; in the rus - tling grass or
should my heart be sad? Let voic - es sing, let the

WORDS: Maltbie D. Babcock, alt.
MUSIC: Trad. English melody, adapt. by Franklin L. Sheppard

TERRA BEATA

skies and seas, God's hand the won - ders wrought.
moun - tain pass, God's voice speaks ev - ery - where.
heav - ens ring: God reigns, let earth be glad!

Shadow and Substance 72

1. Shad - ow and sub - stance, won - der and mys-ter - y,
2. We are your im - age, formed in com - mu - ni - ty,
3. Nam - ing the name - less Spir - it of u - ni - ty,

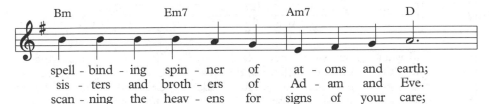

spell - bind - ing spin - ner of at - oms and earth;
sis - ters and broth - ers of Ad - am and Eve.
scan - ning the heav - ens for signs of your care;

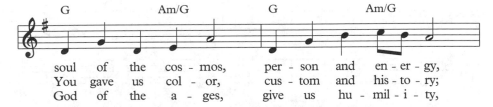

soul of the cos - mos, per - son and en - er - gy,
You gave us col - or, cus - tom and his - to - ry;
God of the a - ges, give us hu - mil - i - ty,

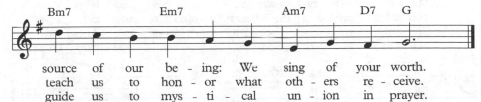

source of our be - ing: We sing of your worth.
teach us to hon - or what oth - ers re - ceive.
guide us to mys - ti - cal un - ion in prayer.

WORDS: Daniel Charles Damon
MUSIC: Daniel Charles Damon

TWILIGHT
5.6.10 D

Words © 1994, music © 1993 Hope Publishing Co.

73 Praise with Joy the World's Creator

1. Praise with joy the world's cre - at - or, God of jus - tice,
2. Praise to Christ who feeds the hun - gry, frees the cap - tive,
3. Praise the Spir - it sent a - mong us, lib - er - a - ting
4. Praise the Mak - er, Christ, and Spir - it, one God in com -

love, and peace, source and end of hu - man knowl - edge,
finds the lost, heals the sick, up - sets re - li - gion,
truth from pride, forg - ing bonds where race or gen - der,
mu - ni - ty, call - ing Chris - tians to em - bod - y

God whose grace shall nev - er cease. Cel - e - brate the
fear - less both of fate and cost. Cel - e - brate Christ's
age or na - tion dare di - vide. Cel - e - brate the
one - ness in di - ver - si - ty. This the world shall

Mak - er's glo - ry, power to res - cue and re - lease.
con - stant pres - ence: Friend and stran - ger, guest and host.
Spir - it's trea - sure: Fool - ish - ness none dare de - ride.
see re - flect - ed: God is One and One - in - Three.

WORDS: The Iona Community
MUSIC: John Goss

LAUDA ANIMA
87.87.87

God, Whose Love Is Reigning O'er Us   74

1. God, whose love is reigning o'er us, source of all, the ending true;
   hear the universal chorus raised in joyful praise to you:
   Alleluia! Alleluia! Worship ancient, worship new.

2. Word of God from nature bringing springtime green and autumn gold;
   mountain streams like children singing, ocean waves like thunder bold:
   Alleluia! Alleluia! As creation's tale is told.

3. Yahweh, God of ancient glory, choosing man and woman too;
   Abram's faith and Sarah's story formed a people bound to you:
   Alleluia! Alleluia! To your cov'nant keep us true.

4. Cov'nant, new again in Jesus, star-child born to set us free;
   sent to heal us, sent to teach us how love's children we might be:
   Alleluia! Alleluia! Risen Christ, our Savior he!

5. Lift we then our human voices, in the songs that faith would bring;
   live we then in human choices lives that, like our music, sing:
   Alleluia! Alleluia! Joined in love our praises ring!

Sing to LAUDA ANIMA, No. 73

William Boyd Grove
© 1980 William Boyd Grove

Praise, My Soul, the God of Heaven   75

1. Praise, my soul, the God of heaven, glad of heart your carols raise;
   ransomed, healed, restored, forgiven, who like me should sing God's praise?
   Alleluia! Alleluia! Praise the Maker all your days!

2. Praise God for the grace and favor shown our forebears in distress;
   God is still the same forever, slow to chide, and swift to bless.
   Alleluia! Alleluia! Sing our Maker's faithfulness.

3. Like a loving parent caring, God knows well our feeble frame;
   gladly all our burdens bearing, still to countless years the same.
   Alleluia! Alleluia! All within me, praise God's name!

4. Angels teach us adoration, you behold God face to face;
   sun and moon and all creation, dwellers all in time and space.
   Alleluia! Alleluia! Praise with us the God of grace!

Sing to LAUDA ANIMA, No. 73

Henry F. Lyte, adapt.
Adapt. © 1974 Ecumenical Women's Center

76

Song of Good News
(Open Your Ears, O Faithful People)

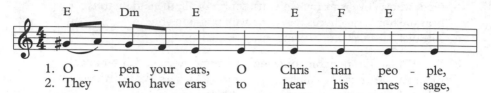

1. O-pen your ears, O Chris-tian peo-ple,
2. They who have ears to hear his mes-sage,

o-pen your ears and hear Good News! O-pen your hearts, O
they who have ears, now let them hear. They who would learn the

roy-al priest-hood, God has come to you.
way of wis-dom, let them hear God's word.

Refrain

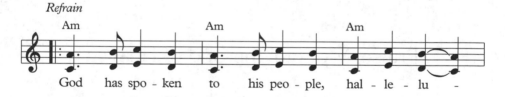

God has spo-ken to his peo-ple, hal-le-lu-

jah! And his words are words of wis-dom,

hal-le-lu- jah! Hal-le-lu- jah! jah!

WORDS: From *The Talmud:* "*Israel and the Torah are one,*" English by Willard F. Jabusch   YISRAEL V'ORAIT'A
MUSIC: Hasidic melody

Oh, the Life of the World

1. Oh, the life of the world is a joy and a
2. Oh, the life of the world is a foun - tain of
3. Oh, the life of the world is the source of our
4. So give thanks for the life and give love to the

trea - sure, un - fold - ing in beau - ty the green - grow - ing
good - ness ov - er - flow - ing in la - bor and pas - sion and
heal - ing. It ris - es in laugh - ter and wells up in
Mak - er, and re - joice in the gift of the bright ris - en

tree, the chang - ing of sea - sons in moun - tain and
pain, in the sound of the cit - y and the si - lence of
song; it springs from the care of the poor and the
Son, and walk in the peace and the power of the

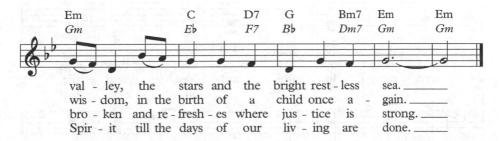

val - ley, the stars and the bright rest - less sea. _____
wis - dom, in the birth of a child once a - gain. _____
bro - ken and re - fresh - es where jus - tice is strong. _____
Spir - it till the days of our liv - ing are done. _____

WORDS: Kathy Galloway
MUSIC: Ian Galloway, arr. John L. Bell

LIFE OF THE WORLD
Irr.

78

The Word of God

1. The Word of God is source and seed;
2. The Word of God is breath and life;
3. The Word of God is flesh and grace

it comes to die and sprout and grow.
it comes to heal and wake and save.
who comes to sing, to laugh and cry.

So make your dark earth wel - come - warm;
So let the Spir - it touch and mend
So dare to be as Je - sus was,

root deep the grain God bent to sow.
and rouse your dry bones from their grave.
who came to live and love and die.

WORDS: Delores Dufner, OSB
MUSIC: Trier manuscript (15th cent.); adapt. by Michael Praetorius
PUER NOBIS
LM

Words © 1983, 2003 GIA Publications, Inc.

O Holy Spirit, Root of Life 79

1. O Holy Spirit, Root of life,
   Creator, cleanser of all things,
   anoint our wounds, awaken us
   with lustrous movement of your wings.

2. Eternal Vigor, saving One,
   you free us by your living Word,
   becoming flesh to wear our pain,
   and all creation is restored.

3. O Holy Wisdom, soaring power,
   encompass us with wings unfurled,
   and carry us, encircling all
   above, below, and through the world.

Sing to PUER NOBIS, No. 78

Jean Janzen, based on the writings of Hildegard of Bingen (12th cent.)
© 1991 Abingdon Press, admin. by The Copyright Co.

Great Lover, Calling Us to Share 80

1. Great Lover, calling us to share
   your joy in all created things,
   from atom-dance to eagles' wings,
   we come and go, to praise and care.

2. Though sure of resurrection grace,
   we ache for all earth's troubled lands
   and hold the planet in our hands,
   a fragile, unprotected place.

3. Your questing Spirit longs to gain
   no simple fishing-ground for souls,
   but as life's story onward rolls,
   a world more joyful and humane.

4. As midwives who assist at birth,
   we give our uttermost, yet grieve
   lest folly, greed, or hate should leave
   a spoiled, aborted, barren earth.

5. Self-giving Lover, since you dare
   to join us in our history,
   embracing all our destiny,
   we'll come and go with praise and care.

Sing to PUER NOBIS, No. 78

Brian Wren
© 1989 Hope Publishing Co.

81 Restless Weaver

1. Rest - less Weav - er, ev - er spin - ning
   threads of jus - tice and sha - lom; dream - ing pat - terns
   of cre - a - tion where all crea - tures
   find a home; gath - ering up life's var - ied fi - bers —
   ev - ery tex - ture, ev - ery hue: grant us your cre -

2. Where earth's fra - gile web is rav - eling,
   help us mend each bro - ken strand. Bless our ur - gent,
   bold en - deav - ors cleans - ing wa - ter,
   air, and land. Through the Spir - it's in - spir - a - tion —
   of - f'ring health where once was pain — strength - en us to

3. When our vio - lent lust for pow - er
   ends in lives a - bused and torn, from com - pas - sion's
   stur - dy fab - ric fash - ion hope and
   trust re - born. Where in - jus - tice rules as ty - rant,
   give us cour - age, God, to dare live our dreams of

4. Rest - less Weav - er, still con - ceiv - ing
   new life — now and yet to be — bind - ing all your
   vast cre - a - tion in one liv - ing
   tap - es - try: you have called us to be weav - ers.
   Let your love guide all we do. With your reign of

WORDS: O. I. Cricket Harrison
MUSIC: William Moore
Words © 1995 Chalice Press

HOLY MANNA
Alternate tune: HYMN TO JOY, No. 64

a - tive	vi - sion.	With	us	weave	your	world	a - new.
be	the	stew - ards	of	your	world	knit	whole	a - gain.
trans - for - ma - tion.	Make	our	lives	in - car - nate prayer.
peace	our	pat - tern,	we	will	weave	your	world	a - new.

For Your Generous Providing 82

1. For your generous providing which sustains us all our days,
for your Spirit here residing, we proclaim our heartfelt praise.
Through the depths of joy and sorrow, though the road be smooth or rough,
fearless, we can face tomorrow for your grace will be enough.

2. Hush our world's seductive voices tempting us to stand alone;
save us, then, from siren noises calling us to trust our own.
For those snared by earthly treasure, lured by false security,
Jesus, true and only measure, spring the trap to set folk free.

3. 'Round your table, through your giving, show us how to live and pray
till your kingdom's way of living is the bread we share each day:
Bread for us and for our neighbor; bread for body, mind, and soul,
bread of heav'n and human labor—broken bread that makes us whole.

Sing to HOLY MANNA, No. 81 or HYMN TO JOY, No. 64

Leith Fisher

Words © Panel on Worship

God, Who Spins the Whirling Planets 83

1. God, who spins the whirling planets, fills the seas and spreads the plain,
molds the mountains, fashions blossoms, calls forth sunshine, wind, and rain:
We, created in your image, would a true reflection be
of your justice, grace, and mercy, and the truth that makes us free.

2. You have called us to be faithful in our life and ministry.
We respond in grateful worship, joined in one community.
When we blur your gracious image, focus us and make us whole.
Healed and strengthened as your people, we move onward toward your goal.

3. God, your word is still creating, calling us to life made new.
Now reveal to us fresh vistas where there's work to dare and do.
Keep us clear of all distortion, polish us with loving care.
Thus new creatures in your image, we'll proclaim Christ everywhere.

Sing to HOLY MANNA, No. 81 or HYMN TO JOY, No. 64

Jane Parker Huber

Words © 1980 Jane Parker Huber

84   God, Who Stretched the Spangled Heavens

1. God, who stretched the spangled heavens, infinite in time and place,
   flung the suns in burning radiance through the silent fields of space;
   we, your children in your likeness, share inventive powers with you;
   great creator, still creating, show us what we yet may do.

2. Proudly rise our modern cities, stately buildings row on row;
   yet their windows, blank, unfeeling, stare on canyoned streets below,
   where the lonely drift unnoticed in the city's ebb and flow,
   lost to purpose and to meaning, scarcely caring where they go.

3. We have ventured worlds undreamed of since the childhood of our race,
   known the ecstasy of winging through untraveled realms of space;
   probed the secrets of the atom, yielding unimagined power,
   facing us with life's destruction or our most triumphant hour.

4. As each far horizon beckons, may it challenge us anew,
   children of creative purpose, serving others, honoring you.
   May our dreams prove rich with promise, each endeavor well begun.
   Great creator, give us guidance till our goals and yours are one.

Sing to HOLY MANNA, No. 81 or HYMN TO JOY, No. 64

Catherine Cameron

© 1967 Hope Publishing Co.

85   Jesus, Come! For We Invite You

1. Jesus, come! For we invite you, guest and master, friend and Lord;
   now as once at Cana's wedding, speak and let us hear your word:
   Lead us through our need or doubting, hope be born and joy restored.
   Jesus, come! For we invite you, guest and master, friend and Lord.

2. Jesus, come! Transform our pleasures, guide us into paths unknown;
   bring your gifts, command your servants, let us trust in you alone:
   Though your hand may work in secret, all shall see what you have done.
   Jesus, come! Transform our pleasures, guide us into paths unknown.

3. Jesus, come! In new creation, heav'n brought near in pow'r divine;
   give your unexpected glory changing water into wine:
   Rouse the faith of your disciples—come, our first and greatest sign!
   Jesus, come! In new creation, heav'n brought near in pow'r divine.

4. Jesus, come! Surprise our dullness, make us willing to receive
   more than we can yet imagine, all the best you have to give:
   Let us find your hidden riches, taste your love, believe, and live!
   Jesus, come! Surprise our dullness, make us willing to receive.

Sing to HOLY MANNA, No. 81 or HYMN TO JOY, No. 64

Christopher Idle

© 1982 Jubilaté Hymns, admin. by Hope Publishing Co.

Creation Sings! Each Plant and Tree 86

1. Cre - a - tion sings! Each plant and tree, each bird and beast in
2. Cre - a - tion speaks a mes - sage true, re - minds us we are
3. Cre - a - tion groans to see the day that ends all bond - age,

har - mo - ny; the bright - est star, the small - est cell, God's
crea - tures too. To serve as stew - ards is our role, de -
all de - cay. Frus - tra - ted now, it must a - wait the

ten - der care and glo - ry tell. From o - cean depths to
spite our dreams of full con - trol. When we dis - par - age
Lord who comes to re - cre - ate, till round the un - i -

moun - tain peaks, in praise of God, cre - a - tion speaks!
what God owns, in tur - moil, all cre - a - tion groans.
verse there rings the song God's new cre - a - tion sings!

WORDS: Martin E. Leckebusch
MUSIC: Attr. to Dimitri S. Bortnianski

ST. PETERSBURG
88.88.88

Words © 1999 Kevin Mayhew, Ltd.

87 Great God, Your Love Has Called Us Here

1. Great God, your love has called us here,
   as we, by love, for love were made.
   Your living likeness still we bear,
   though marred, dishonored, disobeyed.
   We come, with all our heart and mind
   your call to hear, your love to find.

2. We come with self-inflicted pains
   of broken trust and chosen wrong,
   half-free, half-bound by inner chains,
   by social forces swept along,
   by powers and systems close confined,
   yet seeking hope for humankind.

3. Great God, in Christ you call our name
   and then receive us as your own,
   not through some merit, right, or claim,
   but by your gracious love alone.
   We strain to glimpse your mercy seat
   and find you kneeling at our feet.

4. Then take the towel, and break the bread,
   and humble us, and call us friends.
   Suffer and serve till all are fed,
   and show how grandly love intends
   to work till all creation sings,
   to fill all worlds, to crown all things.

5. Great God, in Christ you set us free
   your life to live, your joy to share.
   Give us your Spirit's liberty
   to turn from guilt and dull despair
   and offer all that faith can do
   while love is making all things new.

Sing to ST. PETERSBURG, No. 86

Brian Wren
© 1975, 1995 Hope Publishing Co.

O God, Beyond All Face and Form 88

1. O God, beyond all face and form,
   you willed it that creation's night
   should blaze, and chaos still its storm,
   and birth a universe of light.
   All things below, all things above
   are formed of your eternal love.

2. The glory of the galaxies,
   the beauty of a baby's hand,
   the thundering of restless seas,
   and glory of a forest's stand,
   all things below, all things above
   are formed of your eternal love.

3. You gave our race both form and name,
   and love for us was your intent.
   Then to a woman's womb love came,
   and on a cross was wholly spent.
   All things below, all things above
   are formed of your eternal love.

4. Of this great love, all loves are born,
   of self or neighbor and of earth.
   By love shall night be turned to morn,
   and death shall never conquer birth.
   All things below, all things above
   are formed of your eternal love.

Sing to ST. PETERSBURG, No. 86

Herbert O'Driscoll
© 1993 Herbert O'Driscoll

Thou Hidden Source of Calm Repose 89

1. Thou hidden source of calm repose,
   thou all-sufficient love divine,
   my help and refuge from my foes,
   secure I am if thou art mine;
   and lo! from sin and grief and shame
   I hide me, Jesus, in thy name.

2. Thy mighty name salvation is,
   and keeps my happy soul above;
   comfort it brings, and power and peace,
   and joy and everlasting love;
   to me with thy dear name are given
   pardon and holiness and heaven.

3. Jesus, my all in all thou art,
   my rest in toil, my ease in pain,
   the healing of my broken heart,
   in war my peace, in loss my gain,
   my smile beneath the tyrant's frown,
   in shame my glory and my crown.

4. In want my plentiful supply,
   in weakness my almighty power,
   in bonds my perfect liberty,
   my light in Satan's darkest hour,
   in grief my joy unspeakable,
   my life in death, my heaven in hell.

Sing to ST. PETERSBURG, No. 86

Charles Wesley

90 Praise the One Who Breaks the Darkness

1. Praise the One who breaks the dark-ness with a lib - er - at - ing
2. Praise the One who blessed the chil-dren with a strong yet gen-tle
3. Praise the one true love in - car - nate: Christ who suf - fered in our

light. Praise the One who frees the pris - oners, turn - ing
word. Praise the One who drove out de - mons with a
place. Je - sus died and rose for man - y that we

blind - ness in - to sight. Praise the One who preached the
pierc - ing two-edged sword. Praise the One who brings cool
may know God by grace. Let us sing for joy and

gos - pel, heal - ing ev - ery dread dis - ease, calm - ing
wa - ter to the des - ert's burn - ing sand. From this
glad - ness, see - ing what our God has done. Praise the

WORDS: Rusty Edwards
MUSIC: John Wyeth's *Repository of Sacred Music*, 1813
NETTLETON
87.87 D

Words © 1987 Hope Publishing Co.

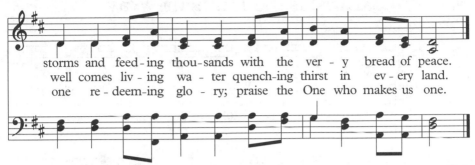

storms and feed-ing thou-sands with the ver - y bread of peace.
well comes liv - ing wa - ter quench-ing thirst in ev - ery land.
one re - deem-ing glo - ry; praise the One who makes us one.

God Whose Giving Knows No Ending 91

1. God whose giving knows no ending, from your rich and endless store;
   nature's wonder, Jesus' wisdom, costly cross, grave's shattered door.
   Gifted by you, we turn to you, offering up ourselves in praise;
   thankful songs shall rise forever, gracious donor of our days.

2. Skills and time are ours for pressing toward the goals of Christ, your Son:
   All at peace in health and freedom, races joined, the Church made one.
   Now direct our daily labor, lest we strive for self alone;
   born with talents, make us servants fit to answer at your throne.

3. Treasure, too, you have entrusted, gain through powers your grace conferred;
   ours to use for home and kindred, and to spread the Gospel Word.
   Open wide our hands in sharing, as we heed Christ's ageless call,
   healing, teaching, and reclaiming, serving you by loving all.

Sing to NETTLETON, No. 90

Robert L. Edwards, alt.

© 1961, renewed 1989 The Hymn Society in the United States and Canada, admin. by Hope Publishing Co.

Come, Thou Fount of Every Blessing 92

1. Come, thou Fount of every blessing, tune my heart to sing thy grace;
   streams of mercy, never ceasing, call for songs of loudest praise.
   Teach me some melodious sonnet, sung by flaming tongues above.
   Praise the mount! I'm fixed upon it, mount of thy redeeming love.

2. Here I raise mine Ebenezer; hither by thy help I'm come;
   and I hope, by thy good pleasure, safely to arrive at home.
   Jesus sought me when a stranger, wandering from the fold of God;
   he, to rescue me from danger, interposed his precious blood.

3. O to grace how great a debtor daily I'm constrained to be!
   Let thy goodness, like a fetter, bind my wandering heart to thee.
   Prone to wander, Lord, I feel it, prone to leave the God I love;
   here's my heart, O take and seal it, seal it for thy courts above.

Sing to NETTLETON, No. 90

Robert Robinson (1 Sam. 7:12)

93 Christ Is the Truth, the Way

1. Christ is the Truth, the Way, the Cen - ter of our life. Christ shares the strug - gles of our day, our earth - ly joy and strife. Re - deem - ing what is lost, and heal - ing those in pain, Christ walks the val - ley

2. Christ is the power of peace, of last - ing har - mo - ny. In Christ, the wars of earth shall cease; Christ is our u - ni - ty. The li - on shall lie down in peace be - side the lamb. The might - y shall lay

3. Christ is the Liv - ing Bread, the source of grace out - poured; our deep - est hun - gers shall be fed; in Christ, life is re - stored. Earth's hun - gry shall re - joice, for they shall all be filled. The good shall wel - come

4. Christ is the Liv - ing Head, our sole au - thor - i - ty. By Christ's own Spir - it we are led to serve hu - man - i - ty. We fol - low where Christ leads when oth - ers' pain we bear; re - spond - ing to our

WORDS: Ruth Duck
MUSIC: George J. Elvey
Words © 1981 Ruth Duck

DIADEMATA
SMD

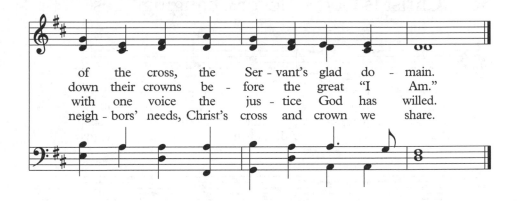

of   the   cross,   the   Ser - vant's glad   do - main.
down   their crowns   be - fore   the   great "I   Am."
with   one   voice   the   jus - tice   God   has   willed.
neigh - bors' needs, Christ's cross and   crown we   share.

Christ the Eternal Lord   94

1. Christ the eternal Lord whose promise here we claim,
   whose gifts of grace are freely poured on all who name your Name;
   with thankfulness and praise we stand before your throne,
   intent to serve you all our days and make your glory known.

2. Christ the unchanging Word to every passing age,
   whose timeless teachings still are heard set forth on scripture's page;
   transform our thought and mind, enlighten all who read,
   within your word by faith to find the bread of life indeed.

3. Christ the redeeming Son who shares our human birth,
   and by his death salvation won for every child of earth;
   inspire our hearts, we pray, to tell your love abroad,
   that all may honor Christ today and follow him as Lord.

4. Christ the unfading Light of everlasting day,
   our morning star in splendor bright, the Life, the Truth, the Way;
   that light of truth you give to servants as to friends,
   your way to walk, your life to live, till earth's brief journey ends.

5. Christ the ascended King exalted high above,
   whose praise unending ages sing, whom yet unseen we love;
   when mortal life is past your voice from heaven's throne
   shall call your children home at last to know as we are known.

Sing to DIADEMATA, No. 93

Timothy Dudley-Smith
© 1999 Hope Publishing Co.

95 Christ Is God's Never Changing "Yes"

C

1. Christ is God's nev - er chang - ing "Yes!"
2. Earth, cor - rupt - ed by sin and shame,
3. Je - sus, now, we are called to be
4. Love has con - quered, though Je - sus died;

F G

Dm

Ev - ery one of God's prom - is - es
scan - dal - ized the Cre - a - tor's name;
"Yes" our - selves to your vic - to - ry;
he is ris - en and glo - ri - fied;

C G

C

is con - firmed in the love that died,
now the Spir - it of God says "Yes!"
God a - noints us to serve with you;
this is prom - ised, and noth - ing less,

F G

Dm

by the one who was cru - ci - fied.
Christ has hon - ored God's ho - li - ness!
Yes, the Spir - it will keep us true.
all cre - a - tion will an - swer, "Yes!"

G7 C

Refrain Am C7 F Dm

"Yes" from God and then, "Yes" from Christ a - gain!

G C Dm7 C

In the Spir - it we say, "A - men!"

WORDS: Alan Gaunt
MUSIC: Jamaican folk tune; adapt. by Doreen Potter

LINSTEAD
LM with Refrain

Let Us Talents and Tongues Employ   96

1. Let us talents and tongues employ,
   reaching out with a shout of joy:
   bread is broken, the wine is poured,
   Christ is spoken and seen and heard.

Refrain Jesus lives again, earth can breathe again,
   pass the Word around: loaves abound! *(Repeat refrain.)*

2. Christ is able to make us one,
   at the table he set the tone,
   teaching people to live to bless,
   love in word and in deed express.   *Refrain (twice)*

3. Jesus calls us in, sends us out
   bearing fruit in a world of doubt,
   gives us love to tell, bread to share:
   God (Immanuel) everywhere!   *Refrain (twice)*

Sing to LINSTEAD, No. 95

Fred Kaan

© 1975 Hope Publishing Co.

All You Works of God, Bless the Lord!   97

1. All you works of God, bless the Lord!
   All you angels, now bless the Lord;
   come you heavens and powers that be,
   praise the Lord and God's majesty.

Refrain Raise your voices high, praise and magnify,
   all you works of God, praise the Lord! *(Repeat refrain.)*

2. Hills and mountains now sing God's worth,
   all you green things that grow on earth:
   seas and rivers, you springs and wells,
   beasts and cattle, you birds and whales. *Refrain (twice)*

3. Come humanity, sing along,
   sing, you people of God, a song;
   priests and servants, your Lord now bless,
   join, you spirits and souls at rest.   *Refrain (twice)*

4. Bless the Lord, all you pure of heart,
   All you humble, God's praises start;
   God in heaven and Son adore,
   bless the Spirit forevermore!   *Refrain (twice)*

Sing to LINSTEAD, No. 95

Stephen P. Starke (Ps. 148)

© 1995 Stephen P. Starke

98 You, Lord, Are Both Lamb and Shepherd

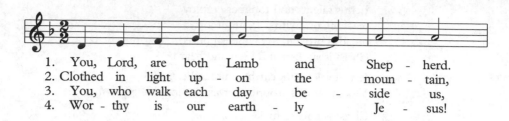

1. You, Lord, are both Lamb and Shep - herd.
2. Clothed in light up - on the moun - tain,
3. You, who walk each day be - side us,
4. Wor - thy is our earth - ly Je - sus!

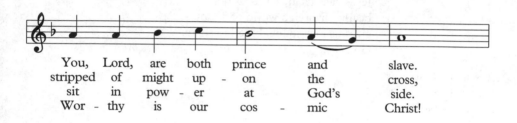

You, Lord, are both prince and slave.
stripped of might up - on the cross,
sit in pow - er at God's side.
Wor - thy is our cos - mic Christ!

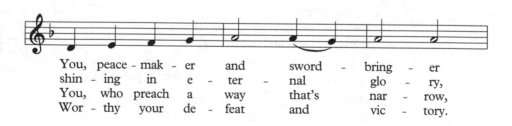

You, peace - mak - er and sword - bring - er
shin - ing in e - ter - nal glo - ry,
You, who preach a way that's nar - row,
Wor - thy your de - feat and vic - tory.

of the way you took and gave.
beg - gar'd by a sol - dier's toss,
have a love that reach - es wide.
Wor - thy still your peace and strife.

WORDS: Sylvia G. Dunstan
MUSIC: French carol melody
Words © 1991 GIA Publications, Inc.

PICARDY

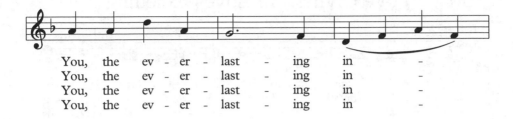

You, the ev - er - last - ing in -
You, the ev - er - last - ing in -
You, the ev - er - last - ing in -
You, the ev - er - last - ing in -

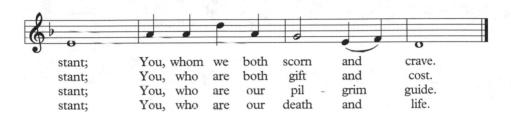

stant; You, whom we both scorn and crave.
stant; You, who are both gift and cost.
stant; You, who are our pil - grim guide.
stant; You, who are our death and life.

Come and Seek the Ways of Wisdom 99

1. Come and seek the ways of Wisdom,
   she who danced when earth was new.
   Follow closely what she teaches,
   for her words are right and true.
   Wisdom clears the path to justice,
   showing us what love must do.

2. Listen to the voice of Wisdom,
   crying in the marketplace.
   Hear the Word made flesh among us,
   full of glory, truth, and grace.
   When the word takes root and ripens,
   peace and righteousness embrace.

3. Sister Wisdom, come assist us;
   nurture all who seek rebirth.
   Spirit-guide and close companion
   bring to light our sacred worth.
   Free us to become your people,
   holy friends of God and earth.

Sing to PICARDY, No. 98

Ruth Duck

100 Love Divine, All Loves Excelling

1. Love divine, all loves ex-cell-ing, joy of
2. Breathe, O breathe thy lov-ing Spir-it in-to
3. Come, al-migh-ty to de-liv-er; let us
4. Fin-ish, then, thy new cre-a-tion; pure and

heaven to earth come down, fix in us thy hum-ble
ev-ery trou-bled breast! Let us all in thee in-
all thy grace re-ceive; sud-den-ly re-turn, and
spot-less let us be. Let us see thy great sal-

dwell-ing; all thy faith-ful mer-cies crown.
her-it; let us find that sec-ond rest.
nev-er, nev-er-more thy tem-ples leave.
va-tion per-fect-ly re-stored in thee,

Je-sus thou art all com-pas-sion, pure, un-
Take a-way our bent to sin-ning; Al-pha
Thee we would be al-ways bless-ing, serve thee
changed from glo-ry in-to glo-ry, till in

WORDS: Charles Wesley
MUSIC: Rowland H. Prichard; harm. from *The English Hymnal*, 1906

HYFRYDOL
87.87 D

bound - ed love thou art; vis - it us with
and O - me - ga be; end of faith, as
as thy hosts a - bove, pray, and praise thee,
heaven we take our place, till we cast our

thy sal - va - tion, en - ter ev - ery trem - bling heart.
its be - gin - ning, set our hearts at lib - er - ty.
with - out ceas - ing, glo - ry in thy per - fect love.
crowns be - fore thee, lost in won - der, love, and praise.

Come, Thou Long-Expected Jesus 101

1. Come, thou long-expected Jesus, born to set thy people free;
from our fears and sins release us, let us find our rest in thee.
Israel's strength and consolation, hope of all the earth thou art;
dear desire of every nation, joy of every longing heart.

2. Born thy people to deliver, born a child and yet a King,
born to reign in us forever, now thy gracious kingdom bring.
By thine own eternal spirit rule in all our hearts alone;
by thine all sufficient merit, raise us to thy glorious throne.

Sing to HYFRYDOL, No. 100; NETTLETON, No. 90; or HYMN TO JOY, No. 64

Charles Wesley

102 Hidden Christ, Alive for Ever

1. Hidden Christ, alive for ever,
   Savior, Servant, Friend and Lord,
   year by year, unseen, you offer
   life undying, love outpoured.
   Day by day, you walk among us,
   known and honored, or concealed,
   freeing, chiding, leading, guiding,
   till your glory is revealed.

2. Endless orbits by our planet
   spinning round its speeding star
   cannot trace creation's secret:
   why we live, and whose we are.
   Jesus, you alone uncover
   nature's rhythm, reason, rhyme,
   so your birthday is our center:
   hinge of history and time.

3. Still your life and way of living,
   God-revealing, Spirit-blown,
   teaching, healing, sins forgiving,
   measure and inspire our own;
   loving earth's despised, rejected,
   till with them you hang in pain,
   broken, buried, resurrected,
   life laid down, our life to gain.

4. Christ our hope, alive among us,
   take our love, our work, our prayer.
   We will trust and tell your purpose,
   braving evil and despair;
   in your name befriending, mending,
   making peace and setting free,
   showing, giving, and acclaiming
   signs of joy and jubilee.

Sing to HYFRYDOL, No. 100, or HOLY MANNA, No. 81

Brian Wren

Jesus, the Gift Divine I Know

103

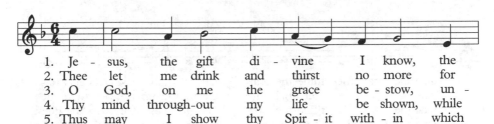

1. Je - sus, the gift di - vine I know, the
2. Thee let me drink and thirst no more for
3. O God, on me the grace be - stow, un -
4. Thy mind through-out my life be shown, while
5. Thus may I show thy Spir - it with - in which

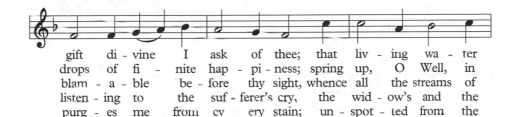

gift di - vine I ask of thee; that liv - ing wa - ter
drops of fi - nite hap - pi - ness; spring up, O Well, in
blam - a - ble be - fore thy sight, whence all the streams of
listen - ing to the suf - ferer's cry, the wid - ow's and the
purg - es me from ev - ery stain; un - spot - ted from the

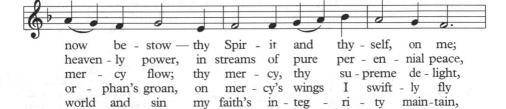

now be - stow — thy Spir - it and thy - self, on me;
heaven - ly power, in streams of pure per - en - nial peace,
mer - cy flow; thy mer - cy, thy su - preme de - light,
or - phan's groan, on mer - cy's wings I swift - ly fly
world and sin my faith's in - teg - ri - ty main - tain,

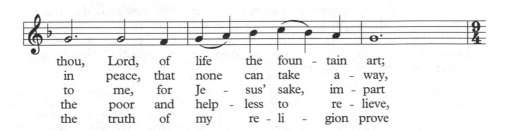

thou, Lord, of life the foun - tain art;
in peace, that none can take a - way,
to me, for Je - sus' sake, im - part
the poor and help - less to re - lieve,
the truth of my re - li - gion prove

now let me find thee in my heart.
in joy, which shall for - ev - er stay.
and plant thy na - ture in my heart.
my life, my all for them to give.
be per - fect pur - i - ty and love.

WORDS: Charles Wesley
MUSIC: Trad. English melody

SUSSEX CAROL
88.88.88

104   Thine the Amen, Thine the Praise

1. Thine the a - men thine the praise al - le - lu - ias an - gels raise
2. Thine the life e - ter - nal - ly thine the prom-ise let there be
3. Thine the tru - ly thine the yes thine the ta - ble we, the guest
4. Thine the king-dom thine the prize, thine the won - der - ful sur-prise
5. Thine the glo - ry in the night no more dy - ing on - ly light

thine the ev - er - last - ing head thine the break-ing of the bread
thine the vi - sion thine the tree all the earth on bend-ed knee
thine the mer - cy all from thee thine the glo - ry yet to be
thine the ban-quet then the praise then the jus - tice of thy ways
thine the riv - er thine the tree then the Lamb e - ter - nal - ly

thine the glo - ry thine the sto - ry thine the har - vest then the cup
gone the nail-ing gone the rail-ing gone the plead-ing gone the cry
then the ring-ing and the sing-ing then the end of all the war
thine the glo - ry thine the sto - ry then the wel-come to the least
then the ho - ly ho - ly ho - ly cel - e - bra - tion ju - bi - lee

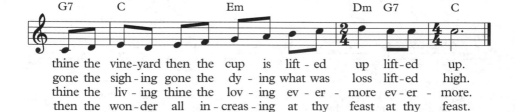

thine the vine-yard then the cup is lift - ed up lift-ed up.
gone the sigh-ing gone the dy - ing what was loss lift-ed high.
thine the liv - ing thine the lov - ing ev - er - more ev - er - more.
then the won-der all in - creas-ing at thy feast at thy feast.
thine the splen-dor thine the bright-ness on - ly thee on - ly thee.

WORDS: Herbert F. Brokering   THINE
MUSIC: Carl Schalk   14 14 15 14
© 1983 Augsburg Publishing House

Crashing Waters at Creation

1. Crash - ing wa - ters at cre - a - tion,
2. Part - ing wa - ter stood and trem - bled
3. Cleans - ing wa - ter once at Jor - dan
4. Liv - ing wa - ter, nev - er end - ing,

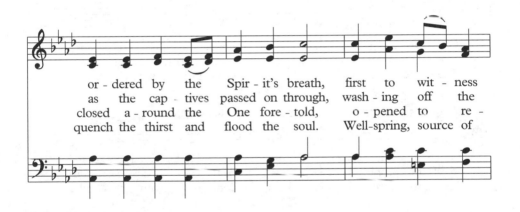

or - dered by the Spir - it's breath, first to wit - ness
as the cap - tives passed on through, wash - ing off the
closed a - round the One fore - told, o - pened to re -
quench the thirst and flood the soul. Well-spring, source of

day's be - gin - ning from the bright - ness of night's death.
chains of bon - dage, chan - nel to a life made new.
veal the glo - ry ev - er new and ev - er old.
life e - ter - nal, drench our dry - ness, make us whole.

WORDS: Sylvia G. Dunstan
MUSIC: William Walker's *Southern Harmony*

I WILL ARISE
87.87

Words © 1991 GIA Publications, Inc.

106 Here at Jordan's River

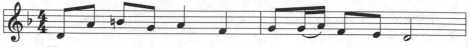

1. Here at Jor-dan's riv - er   all is washed a - way.
2. We at Jor-dan's riv - er   meet on lev - el ground.
3. God, re - form, re - new, us;   turn us toward your will.

As God's reign draws near - er,   noth - ing is the same.
Val - leys are up - lift - ed;   moun - tains fall to earth.
Till our hearts for learn - ing;   root us in your word.

Gone are class and stat - us;   gone, de - grees and fame.
None dare trust their lin - eage;   none need doubt their worth.
May the fruits of ac - tion   grow from all we've heard.

Grace a - lone can save us   on God's judg-ment day.
Still the proph - et asks us,   "Will you turn a - round?"
As we lose our old lives,   God, be with us still.

WORDS: Ruth Duck
MUSIC: 15th cent. French carol

NOEL NOUVELET

© 1987 GIA Publications, Inc.

107 Vine and Branches

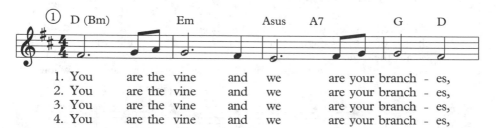

① D (Bm)   Em   Asus   A7   G   D

1. You   are the vine   and   we   are your branch - es,
2. You   are the vine   and   we   are your branch - es,
3. You   are the vine   and   we   are your branch - es,
4. You   are the vine   and   we   are your branch - es,

May be sung as a canon.

WORDS: Steve Garnaas-Holmes (John 15)
MUSIC: Steve Garnaas-Holmes

© 2005 Steve Garnaas-Holmes

② Bm   Em   Asus   A7   G   D

one   with your   life,   and   root - ed   in your heart.
flow - ing with pow - er   great - er   than our   own.
One   com-mon blood   flows through   all   of our   veins.
Deep   in our hearts   your   life   is   flow-ing through.

③ Bm   Em   Asus   A7   G   D

Flow - ing with grace,   with   life   you   fill   us,
You   grant us grace   to   love   each   oth - er,
We   all are   part   of   one   an - oth - er.
Root - ed in   you,   we   grow   and   flour - ish.

④ Bm   Em2   Asus   A7   G   D

strength - ened that noth - ing   can   break   us a - part.
Yours   are the   fruits   that with - in   us have grown.
We   are all branch - es   of   one   liv - ing vine.
You   live with - in   us, and   we   live in   you.

Transformation   108

The risen, living Christ calls us by our name;
    comes to the loneliness within us;
    heals that which is wounded within us;
    comforts that which grieves within us;
    releases us from that which has dominion over us;
    cleanses us of that which does not belong to us;
    renews that which feels drained within us;
    awakens that which is asleep in us;
    names that which is still formless within us;
    empowers that which is newborn within us;
    consecrates and guides that which is strong within us;
    restores us to this world which needs us;
    reaches out in endless love to others through us.
The risen, living Christ calls us by our name.

Musical setting for solo voice in Upper Room Worshipbook Accompaniment and Worship Leader *edition*

Flora Slosson Wuellner
© 1989 Upper Room Books

109

Traveling with God
(One More Step)

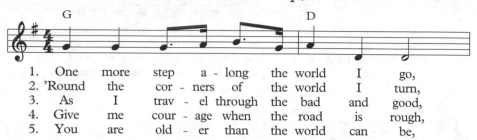

1. One more step a - long the world I go,
2. 'Round the cor - ners of the world I turn,
3. As I trav - el through the bad and good,
4. Give me cour - age when the road is rough,
5. You are old - er than the world can be,

one more step a - long the world I go. From the old things
more and more a - bout the world I learn. All the new things
keep me trav - el - ing the way I should. Where I see no
keep me lov - ing though the world is tough. Leap and sing in
you are young - er than the life in me. Ev - er old and

to the new keep me trav - el - ing a - long with you.
that I see you'll be look - ing at a - long with me.
way to go you'll be tell - ing me the way, I know.
all I do, keep me trav - el - ing a - long with you.
ev - er new, keep me trav - el - ing a - long with you.

Refrain

And it's from the old I trav - el to the new,

keep me trav - el - ing a - long with you.

WORDS: Sydney Carter
MUSIC: Sydney Carter

SOUTHCOTE
99.78 with Refrain

I Want Jesus to Walk with Me

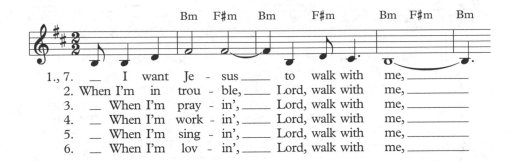

1., 7. __ I want Je - sus ____ to walk with me,
2. When I'm in trou - ble, ____ Lord, walk with me,
3. __ When I'm pray - in', ____ Lord, walk with me,
4. __ When I'm work - in', ____ Lord, walk with me,
5. __ When I'm sing - in', ____ Lord, walk with me,
6. __ When I'm lov - in', ____ Lord, walk with me,

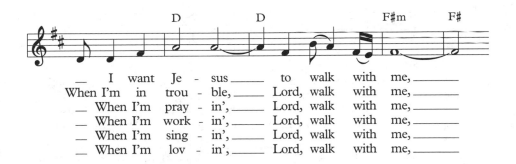

__ I want Je - sus ____ to walk with me,
When I'm in trou - ble, ____ Lord, walk with me,
__ When I'm pray - in', ____ Lord, walk with me,
__ When I'm work - in', ____ Lord, walk with me,
__ When I'm sing - in', ____ Lord, walk with me,
__ When I'm lov - in', ____ Lord, walk with me,

all a - long my ____ pil - grim jour - ney, ____
when my poor heart's __ al - most break - ing, ____
when my poor heart's __ o - ver - flow - ing, ____
when my hands are ____ build - ing your King - dom, ____
when I'm prais - ing ____ all of God's good - ness, ____
when I'm car - ing ____ for your chil - dren, ____

Lord, I want Je - sus ____ to walk with me. ____

WORDS: African American spiritual; stanzas 4–6 by Jim and Jean Strathdee
MUSIC: African American spiritual

SOJOURNER
888.9

111 Give Me Jesus

1. In the morn-ing when I rise, in the morn-ing when I
2. Dark mid-night was my cry, dark mid-night was my
3. Just a-bout the break of day, just a-bout the break of
4. Oh, when I come to die, oh, when I come to
5. And when I want to sing, and when I want to

rise, in the morn-ing when I rise, give me Je - sus.
cry, dark mid-night was my cry, give me Je - sus.
day, just a-bout the break of day, give me Je - sus.
die, oh, when I come to die, give me Je - sus.
sing, and when I want to sing, give me Je - sus.

Refrain

Give me Je - sus, give me Je - sus. You may

have all the rest, give me Je - sus.

WORDS: African American spiritual
MUSIC: African American spiritual; arr. by L. L. Fleming
Arr. © 1973 Augsburg Publishing House

GIVE ME JESUS
77.74 with Refrain

A Blessing 112

I pray that Christ may come to you early in the morning, as he came to Mary that morning in the garden. And I pray that you find Christ in the night when you need him as Nicodemus did. May Christ come to you while you are a child, for when disciples tried to stop them, Jesus insisted that the children come to him.

I pray that Christ may come to you when you are old, as he came to old Simeon's arms and made him cry: "Lord, now let your servant depart in peace, for my eyes have seen your salvation."

And may Christ come to you in your grief as he did for Mary and Martha when they lost their brother. May Christ come to you in joy as he did to the wedding in Cana. And may Christ visit you when you are sick, as he did for the daughter of Jairus, and for so many who could not walk, or stand straight, or see, or hear till he came.

May the Lord Jesus come in answer to your questions as he once did for a lawyer and a rich young ruler. And in your madness may he stand before you in all his power as he stood among the graves that day before Legion.

May Christ come to you in glory upon your dying day as he did to the thief hanging beside him that Good Friday. And though you seldom come to him, and though you often "make your bed in hell," as I do, may you find Christ descending there, where the apostles in their creed agreed he went—so you would know there is no place he would not come for you.

Chuck Wilhelm
© 2006 Chuck Wilhelm

Guidance 113

In our shepherding role to others—as parent, teacher, caregiver, counselor, listening friend—we begin to guide as we have been guided. Our faces and voices will change. The way we listen and respond will change, not through imitation but spontaneously through deep love. "When he is revealed, we will be like him, for we will see him as he is" (1 John 3:2).

A powerful way to pray when we find ourselves in a shepherding role would be something like this: "Living Christ, Shepherd of our lives, enfold me in your spirit, speak through my voice, touch through my hands. Give me your listening heart, the power of your silences, the compassion of your words. Let me be transformed and guided by you, even as I am helping to guide others."

Flora Slosson Wuellner
© 2004 Upper Room Books

Christ, Be Our Light

1. Long-ing for light, we wait in dark-ness.
2. Long-ing for peace, our world is trou-bled.
3. Long-ing for food, man-y are hun-gry.
4. Long-ing for shel-ter, man-y are home-less.
5. Man-y the gifts, man-y the peo-ple,

Long-ing for truth, we turn to you. Make us your
Long-ing for hope, man-y des-pair. Your word a-
Long-ing for wa-ter, man-y still thirst. Make us your
Long-ing for warmth, man-y are cold. Make us your
man-y the hearts that yearn to be-long. Let us be

own, your ho-ly peo-ple, light for the
lone has power to save us. Make us your
bread, bro-ken for oth-ers, shared un-til
build-ing, shel-ter-ing oth-ers, walls made of
ser-vants to one an-oth-er, mak-ing your

Refrain

world to see. _____
liv-ing voice. _____
all are fed. _____   Christ, be our
liv-ing stone. _____
king-dom come. _____

light! Shine in our hearts. Shine through the dark-

WORDS: Bernadette Farrell
MUSIC: Bernadette Farrell

LOOKING FOR LIGHT
Irregular with Refrain

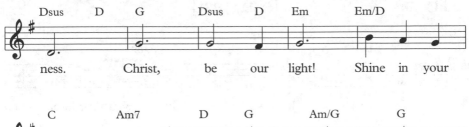

ness. Christ, be our light! Shine in your

church gath - ered to - day. _____

Stay with Us 115

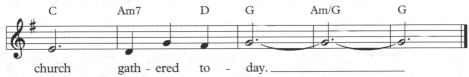

1. Stay with us, till night has come: Our praise to
2. Walk with us, our spir - its sigh: Hear when our
3. Walk with us, the road will bend: Make all our
4. Talk with us, till we be - hold a joy - ful
5. Stay with us, till day is done: No tears nor

you this day be sung. Bless our bread, o - pen our
wea - ry spir - its cry, feel a - gain our loss, our
weep - ing, wail - ing end. Wipe our tears, for - give our
life you will un - fold: Heal our eyes to see the
dark shall dim the sun. Cheer the heart, your grace im -

eyes: Je - sus, be our great sur - prise.
pain: Je - sus, take us to your side.
fears: Je - sus, lift the hea - vy cross.
prize: Je - sus, take us to the light.
part: Je - sus, bring e - ter - nal life.

WORDS: Herbert Brokering (Luke 24:13-35)
MUSIC: Walter L. Pelz
© 1980 Concordia Publishing House

STAY WITH US
78.77

Jesu, Jesu

Refrain

Je - su, Je - su, fill us with your love, show

us how to serve the neigh-bors we have from you.

1. Kneels at the feet of his friends,
2. Neigh - bors are rich and poor,
3. These are the ones we should serve,
4. Lov - ing puts us on our knees,
5. Kneel at the feet of our friends,

si – lent – ly wash – es their feet,
neigh – bors are black and white,
these are the ones we should love;
serv – ing as though we are slaves,
si – lent – ly wash – ing their feet,

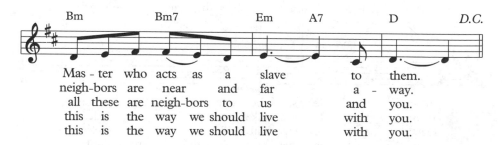

Mas – ter who acts as a slave to them.
neigh-bors are near and far a – way.
all these are neigh-bors to us and you.
this is the way we should live with you.
this is the way we should live with you.

Notes in Upper Room Worshipbook Accompaniment and Worship Leader *edition*

WORDS: Tom Colvin (John 13:1-17)
MUSIC: Ghana folk song; adapt. by Tom Colvin
© 1969, 1989 Hope Publishing Co.

CHEREPONI
Irr. with Refrain

Brother, Sister, Let Me Serve You
(The Servant Song)

117

1., 6. Broth-er, sis-ter, let me serve you, let me be as
2. We are pil-grims on a jour-ney; we're to-geth-er
3. I will hold the Christ-light for you in the night-time
4. I will weep when you are weep-ing; when you laugh, I'll
5. When we sing to God in heav-en, we shall find such

Christ to you; pray that I may have the grace to
on this road. We are here to help each oth-er
of your fear; I will hold my hand out to you,
laugh with you. I will share your joy and sor-row
har-mo-ny, born of all we've known to-geth-er

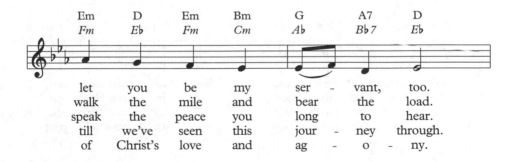

let you be my ser - vant, too.
walk the mile and bear the load.
speak the peace you long to hear.
till we've seen this jour - ney through.
of Christ's love and ag - o - ny.

Opt. extended ending

Let me be your ser - vant, let me be as Christ to you.

WORDS: Richard Gillard (Matt. 20:26)
MUSIC: Richard Gillard

THE SERVANT SONG
87.87

118

Walk with Me

Refrain

Walk with me, I will walk with you and

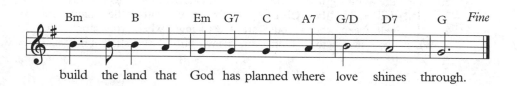

build the land that God has planned where love shines through. *Fine*

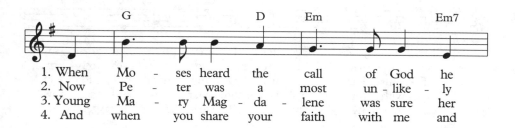

1. When Mo - ses heard the call of God he
2. Now Pe - ter was a most un - like - ly
3. Young Ma - ry Mag - da - lene was sure her
4. And when you share your faith with me and

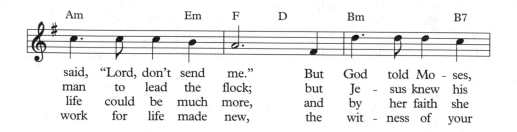

said, "Lord, don't send me." But God told Mo - ses,
man to lead the flock; but Je - sus knew his
life could be much more, and by her faith she
work for life made new, the wit - ness of your

D.C.

"You're the one to set my peo - ple free."
ho - li - ness and he be - came the Rock.
dared to let God's love un - lock the door.
faith - ful - ness calls me to walk with you.

WORDS: John S. Rice (Exod. 3:1–4:20; Matt. 16:13-20; Mark 16:9)
MUSIC: John S. Rice
© 1988 The Estate of John S. Rice

GLASER
CM with Refrain

What Feast of Love

1. What feast of love is of - fered here, what
2. What light of truth is of - fered here, what
3. What wine of love is of - fered here, what

ban - quet come from heav - en? What food of ev - er -
cov - e - nant from heav - en? What hope of ev - er -
crim - son drink from heav - en? What stream of ev - er -

last - ing life, what gra - cious gift is
last - ing life, what won - drous word is
last - ing life, what pre - cious blood is

giv - en? This, this is Christ the king, the
giv - en? This, this is Christ the king, the
giv - en? This, this is Christ the king, the

bread come down from heav - en. O taste and
sun come down from heav - en. O see and
sweet - est wine of heav - en. O taste and

see and sing! How sweet the man - na giv - en!
hear and sing! The Word of God is giv - en!
see and sing! The Son of God is giv - en!

WORDS: Delores Dufner, OSB
MUSIC: 16th cent. English melody

GREENSLEEVES
87.87 with Refrain

120

I Come with Joy

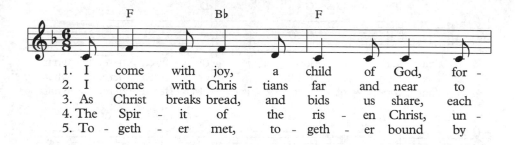

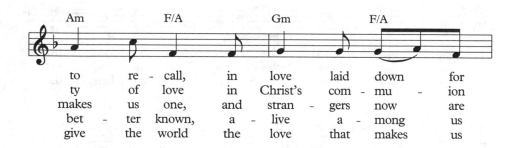

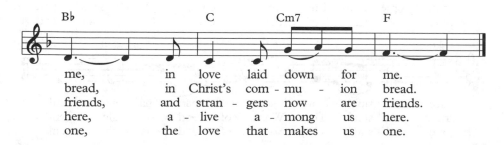

WORDS: Brian Wren
MUSIC: *Southern Harmony,* arr. by Austin C. Lovelace

DOVE OF PEACE
86.866

Words © 1971, 1995 Hope Publishing Co.; arr. © 1977 Hope Publishing Co.

Now in This Banquet

121

Refrain ① *   ②

Now in this ban-quet, Christ is our bread;
** God of our jour-neys, day-break to night;
** Lord, you can o - pen hearts that are stone;

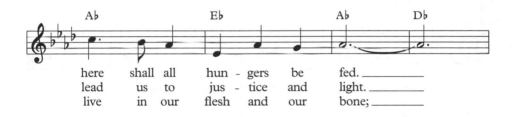

here shall all hun-gers be fed._____
lead us to jus - tice and light._____
live in our flesh and our bone;_____

Bread that is bro-ken, wine that is poured,
Grant us com-pas-sion, strength for the day,
lead us to won-der, mys - t'ry, and grace,

love is the sign of our Lord._____
wis - dom to walk in your way._____
one in your lov-ing em-brace._____

*May be sung as a canon.
**Optional refrains

Verses in Upper Room Worshipbook Accompaniment *and* Worship Leader *edition*

WORDS: Marty Haugen
MUSIC: Marty Haugen
© 1986 GIA Publications, Inc.

BANQUET
97.97

122 Eat This Bread and Never Hunger

Refrain

C · G/B · Am · Am/G

Eat this bread and nev-er hun-ger,

F · C/E · Dm · G · G7 · C · G/B

drink this cup and nev-er thirst; Christ in-vites us to the

Am · Am/G · Fmaj7 · G11 · C · *Fine*

ta-ble where the last be-come the first.

Verses

Abmaj7 · Ebmaj7

1. Ask - ing for a cup of wa - ter,
2. Walk - ing down a des - ert high - way,
3. Weep - ing for his friend at grave - side,

Abmaj7 · G · G7 · Am · Am/G♯

Je - sus touched for - bid - den ground; and the wom - an,
Je - sus healed a man born blind; soon the man be -
Je - sus felt the pain of death; yet he knew God's

D.C.

C/G · Am/F♯ · Fmaj7 · G7 · C · F · C/E · Dm

with a ques - tion, told the world what she had found.
came a wit - ness to the truth we seek and find.
power to wak - en: liv - ing wa - ter, liv - ing breath.

MUSIC: Daniel Charles Damon
WORDS: Daniel Charles Damon
© 1993 Hope Publishing Co.

MODESTO
87.87 with Refrain

On the Journey to Emmaus

123

1. On the jour - ney to Em - ma - us with our hearts cold as
2. And our hearts burned with - in us as we talked on the
3. And that eve - ning at the ta - ble as he blessed and broke
4. On the jour - ney to Em - ma - us, in our sto - ries and

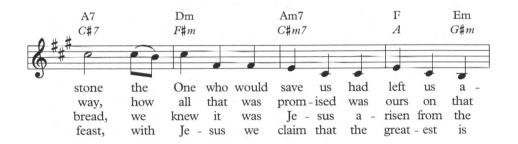

stone the One who would save us had left us a -
way, how all that was prom - ised was ours on that
bread, we knew it was Je - sus a - risen from the
feast, with Je - sus we claim that the great - est is

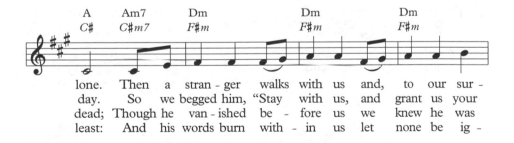

lone. Then a stran - ger walks with us and, to our sur -
day. So we begged him, "Stay with us, and grant us your
dead; Though he van - ished be - fore us we knew he was
least: And his words burn with - in us let none be ig -

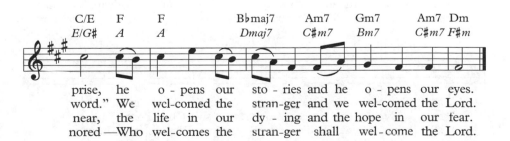

prise, he o - pens our sto - ries and he o - pens our eyes.
word." We wel - comed the stran - ger and we wel - comed the Lord.
near, the life in our dy - ing and the hope in our tear.
nored —Who wel - comes the stran - ger shall wel - come the Lord.

WORDS: Marty Haugen, based on Luke 24:13-35
MUSIC: Gaelic melody
Words © 1995 GIA Publications, Inc.

COLUMCILLE

124 The Hand of Heaven

1. We who live by sound and sym - bol, we who
2. Not just once with spe - cial peo - ple, not just
3. God, our Mak - er, send your Spir - it, to per -

learn from sight and word, find these mar - ried in the
hid - den deep in time, but wher - ev - er Christ is
vade the bread we break. Let it bring the life we

per - son of the one we call our Lord. Tak - ing
fol - lowed, earth - ly fare be-comes sub - lime. Though to
long for and the love which we for - sake. Bind us

bread to be his bod - y, tak - ing
sound this seems a mys - t'ry, though to
clo - ser to each oth - er, both for -

wine to be his blood, he let thought take flesh in
sense it seems ab - surd, yet in faith, which seems like
giv - ing and for - giv'n; give us grace in this and

ac - tion, he let faith take root in food.
fol - ly, we meet Je - sus Christ our Lord.
all things to dis - cern the hand of heav'n.

WORDS: John L. Bell and Graham Maule
MUSIC: French carol; arr. by John L. Bell

CHARTRES

Seed, Scattered and Sown

125

Refrain

Seed, scat-tered and sown; wheat, gath-ered and grown; bread, bro-ken and shared as one, the Liv - ing Bread of God. Vine, fruit of the land; wine, work of our hands; one cup that is shared by all; the Liv - ing Cup, the Liv - ing Bread of God.

1. Is not the bread we break a shar - ing in our Lord?
2. The seed which falls on rock will with - er and will die.
3. As wheat up - on the hills was gath-ered and was grown,

D.C.

Is not the cup we bless the blood of Christ out-poured?
The seed with - in good ground will flow - er and have life.
so may the church of God be gath-ered in - to one.

WORDS: Dan Feiten
MUSIC: Dan Feiten; arr. by Eric Gunnison and R. J. Miller
© 1987 Ekklesia Music, Inc.

SCATTERED SEED
12 12 with Refrain

126   Give Thanks to the Source

1. Give thanks to the Source who brings forth earth's
2. Re - mem - ber the Word, in - car - nate a -
3. We pray for the gift of life - giv - ing

good - ness: the bread on our ta - ble, the fruit of the
mong us, whose ta - ble is o - pen to all who draw
Spir - it that we may know Je - sus in shar - ing this

vine. Give thanks to the Love who wel - comes the
near. Re - call Je - sus Christ in liv - ing and
meal; so may we de - part re - freshed for the

wan-d'ring, in - vents new be - gin - nings, and calls us to dine.
dy - ing, in ris - ing to new life, set free from our fear.
jour - ney, to live by the Gos - pel, to love, and to heal.

WORDS: Ruth Duck
MUSIC: Jane Marshall

ANNIVERSARY SONG
11 11.11 11

What Gift Can We Bring

1. What gift can we bring, what present, what token?
   What words can convey it, the joy of this day?
   When grateful we come, remembering, rejoicing,
   what song can we offer in honor and praise?

2. Give thanks for the past, for those who had vision,
   who planted and watered so dreams could come true.
   Give thanks for the now, for study, for worship,
   for mission that bids us turn prayer into deed.

3. Give thanks for tomorrow, full of surprises,
   for knowing whatever tomorrow may bring,
   the Word is our promise always, forever;
   we rest in God's keeping and live in God's love.

4. This gift we now bring, this present, this token,
   these words can convey it, the joy of this day!
   When grateful we come, remembering, rejoicing,
   this song we now offer in honor and praise!

Sing to ANNIVERSARY SONG, No. 126

Jane Marshall

128 Within the Reign of God

Leader:

1. Come now, the feast is spread; in Je-sus' name we
2. Stand up and do not fear, for Christ is tru-ly
3. Wel-come the weak and poor, the sin-ner finds an
4. All fear and ha-tred ends and foes be-come our
5. Sing out the ju-bi-lee when those en-slaved are
6. One earth, one ho-ly band, one fam-ily as our

break the bread. Here shall we all be fed
pres-ent here. Heav-en is tru-ly near
o-pen door, none judged, and none ig-nored
faith-ful friends, just as our God in-tends
all set free, chil-dren of God are we
God has planned, will share the prom-ised land

All:

with-

Leader:

in the reign of God.

Come take this ho-ly food; re-
Now at the wed-ding feast, the
Here shall the wea-ry rest, the
All you who seek God's face are
No more can we for-get the
Come now, the feast is spread, in

ceive the bod-y and the blood. Grace is a
great-est here shall be the least. All bonds shall
stran-ger be a wel-come guest. So shall we
wel-come in this ho-ly place; Join in the
ones who bear life's crush-ing debt; God's jus-tice
Je-sus' name we break the bread; Here shall we

Additional performance notes in Upper Room Worshipbook Accompaniment and Worship Leader *edition*

WORDS: Marty Haugen
MUSIC: Marty Haugen

REIGN OF GOD

© 1999 GIA Publications, Inc.

All:

might - y flood
be re - leased
all be blest
feast of grace } with - in the reign of God.
guides us yet
all be fed

Refrain

Bless - ed are they who will feast in the reign of God.

Bless - ed are they who will share the bread of

life. Bless - ed are they who are least in the

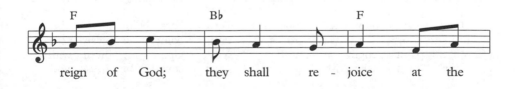

reign of God; they shall re - joice at the

feast of life. _____

129 We Gather at Your Table, Lord

*1. We gath-er at your ta-ble, Lord, be-cause you bid us
2. Re-mind us of our sa-cred past, our roots in Is-rael's
3. We gath-er as your peo-ple, Lord, you call, and we must
*4. In-to the world a-gain we take your cov-e-nant of

come. Our lives, though scat-tered through the week, we
soil. Re-fresh us with your pres-ence now as
heed. Our pow-er by it-self is weak; it
grace. Re-freshed by tak-ing time to pause from

now u-nite as one. Be-fore us is the
through to-day we toil, and point us toward your
is your strength we need. Your Spir-it dwell with-
our own self-ish pace. May love be ours and

Sing sts. 1–3 prior to Communion, st. 4 following.

WORDS: William Martin, alt.
MUSIC: 19th cent. USA camp meeting melody

CLEANSING FOUNTAIN
CMD

Words © 1980 The Hymn Society in the United States and Canada, admin. by Hope Publishing Co.

bread, the wine; pre - pare our souls to eat. Come
fu - ture, Lord, your King - dom we would know. And
in our hearts; your voice speak loud and clear, and
o - ver - flow that all the world may see, that

join us by your Spir - it, Lord, and make the feast com - plete.
for our friends a - round us here, our hearts in love would grow.
fill us with your power and might as we as - sem - ble here.
you will be our ho - ly God, and your peo - ple we will be.

We Meet as Friends at Table 130

1. We meet as friends at table,
   to listen, and be heard,
   united by the Spirit,
   attentive to the Word.
   Through prayer and conversation
   we tune our varied views
   to Christ, whose love has made us
   the bearers of good news.

2. With food and drink for sharing,
   the table soon is spread,
   the freedom–meal of Jesus
   is crowned with wine and bread,
   and all, without exception,
   may eat, and speak, and stay,
   for this is Christ's own table
   where none is turned away.

3. We share our lives and longings,
   and when the meal is done
   we pray as friends at table
   and promise to be one.
   To Christ, and to each other,
   we cheerfully belong:
   apart, our hope is fruitless;
   together, we are strong.

4. Fulfilled, and glad to follow
   wherever Christ may lead,
   we journey from the table
   to love a world in need
   with patience, truth, and kindness,
   that justice may increase
   and all may sit at table
   in freedom, joy, and peace.

Sing to MERLE'S TUNE, No. 12

Brian Wren
© 1996 Hope Publishing Co.

131 Give Thanks for Life

1. Give thanks for life, the meas-ure of our days, ___
2. Give thanks for those who made their life a light ___
3. And for our own, our liv-ing and our dead, ___
4. Give thanks for hope, that, like the wheat, the grain ___

___ mor-tal, we pass through beau-ty that de-cays, ___
___ caught from the Christ-flame, burst-ing through the night, ___
___ thanks for the love by which our life is fed, ___
___ ly-ing in dark-ness does its life re-tain, ___

___ yet sing to God our hope, our love, our praise: ___
___ who touched the truth, who burned for what is right: ___
___ a love not changed by time or death or dread: ___
___ in res-ur-rec-tion to grow green a-gain: ___

___ Al - le - lu - ia!
___

WORDS: Shirley Erena Murray
MUSIC: Charles Villiers Stanford
Words © 1987 Hope Publishing Co.

ENGELBERG
10 10 10 with Alleluias
Alternate tune: SINE NOMINE

132 Go to the World

1. Go to the world! Go into all the earth.
   Go preach the cross where Christ renews life's worth,
   baptizing as a sign of our rebirth.
      Alleluia!

Sing to ENGELBERG, No. 131

Sylvia G. Dunstan (Matt. 28)
© 1991 GIA Publications, Inc.

2. Go to the world! Go into every place.
   Go live the word of God's redeeming grace.
   Go seek God's presence in each time and space.
      Alleluia!

3. Go to the world! Go struggle, bless, and pray;
   the nights of tears give way to joyous day.
   As servant church, you follow Christ's own way.
      Alleluia!

4. Go to the world! Go as the ones I send,
   for I am with you till the age shall end,
   when all the hosts of glory cry, "Amen."
      Alleluia!

When All Is Ended   133

1. When all is ended, time and troubles past,
   shall all be mended, sin and death out-cast?
   in hope we sing, and hope to sing at last:
      Alleluia!

2. As in the night, when lightning flickers free,
   and gives a glimpse of distant hill and tree,
   each flash of good discloses what will be:
      Alleluia!

3. Against all hope, our weary times have known
   wars ended, peace declared, compassion shown,
   great days of freedom, tyrants overthrown:
      Alleluia!

4. Then do not cheat the poor who long for bread,
   with dream-worlds in the sky or in the head,
   but sing of slaves set free, and children fed:
      Alleluia!

5. With earthy faith we sing a song of heaven:
   all life fulfilled, all loved, all wrong forgiven.
   Christ is our sign of hope, for Christ is risen:
      Alleluia!

6. With all creation, pain and anger past,
   evil exhausted, love supreme at last,
   alive in God, we'll sing an unsurpassed
      Alleluia!

Sing to ENGELBERG, No. 131

Brian Wren
© 1989 Hope Publishing Co.

134 God Wills a Full Life for Us All

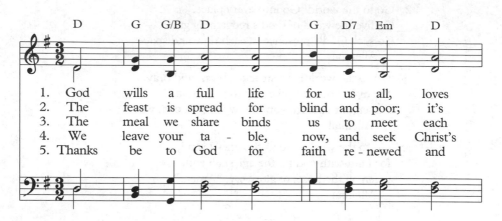

1. God wills a full life for us all, loves
2. The feast is spread for blind and poor; it's
3. The meal we share binds us to meet each
4. We leave your ta - ble, now, and seek Christ's
5. Thanks be to God for faith re - newed and

us with ten - der care, asks us to take the
spread for you and me. God's grace brings light and
cap - tive's deep - est need: For - give us, God, that
spir - it for our days; help us to live your
u - ni - ty re - stored. We go, one world, one

sac - ri - fice of bro - ken life to share.
strength, and sets life's bro - ken vic - tims free.
we have giv'n love's word but not love's deed.
word of love with deeds that sing your praise.
fam - i - ly, to live God's lov - ing Word.

WORDS: Paul R. Gregory
MUSIC: Carl G. Gläzer; arr. by Lowell Mason

AZMON
CM

Come, Let Us Use the Grace Divine 135

1. Come, let us use the grace divine, and all with one accord,
   in a perpetual cov'nant join ourselves to Christ the Lord.

2. Give up ourselves, through Jesus' power, his name to glorify;
   and promise, in this sacred hour, for God, to live and die.

3. The cov'nant we this moment make be ever kept in mind;
   we will no more our God forsake, or cast these words behind.

4. We never will throw off the fear of God who hears our vow;
   and if thou art well pleased to hear, come down and meet us now.

Sing to AZMON, No. 134 or AMAZING GRACE, No. 266

Charles Wesley

A Covenant Prayer in the Wesleyan Tradition 136

I am no longer my own, but thine.
Put me to what thou wilt, rank me with whom thou wilt.
Put me to doing, put me to suffering.
Let me be employed by thee or laid aside for thee,
    exalted for thee or brought low by thee.
Let me be full, let me be empty.
Let me have all things, let me have nothing.
I freely and heartily yield all things
    to thy pleasure and disposal.
And now, O glorious and blessed God,
    Father, Son, and Holy Spirit,
        thou art mine, and I am thine. So be it.
And the covenant which I have made on earth,
    let it be ratified in heaven. **Amen.**

From *The United Methodist Hymnal*

137   I Received the Living God

Refrain

B♭maj7   F   C   F   Dm

I re - ceived the liv - ing God, and my

Gm7   C7   F   B♭maj7   F   C

heart is full of joy. I re - ceived the liv - ing

Am   Dm   Gm7   C7   F   *Fine*

God, and my heart is full of joy.

F   C   Dm

1. Je - sus said: I am the bread knead - ed
2. Je - sus said: I am the way, and my
3. Je - sus said: I am the truth; if you
4. Je - sus said: I am the life far from

Am   B♭   F   Dm   Am   A7

long to give you life; you who will par - take of
Fa - ther longs for you; so I come to bring you
fol - low close to me, you will know me in your
whom no thing can grow, but re - ceive this liv - ing

Dm   B♭   Gm7   C7   *D.C.*

me need not ev - er fear to die.
home to be one with us a - new.
heart, and my word shall make you free.
bread, and my Spir - it you shall know.

WORDS: Anon.
MUSIC: Anon.; arr. by David Cherwien
Arr. © 1995 Augsburg Fortress

LIVING GOD
77.77 with Refrain

Arise, Your Light Is Come

138

1. A - rise, your light is come! The
2. A - rise, your light is come! Fling
3. A - rise, your light is come! All
4. A - rise, your light is come! The

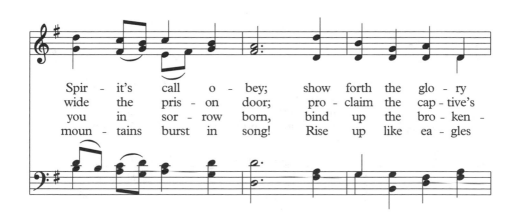

Spir - it's call o - bey; show forth the glo - ry
wide the pris - on door; pro - claim the cap - tive's
you in sor - row born, bind up the bro - ken -
moun - tains burst in song! Rise up like ea - gles

of your God which shines on you to - day.
lib - er - ty, good tid - ings to the poor.
heart - ed ones and com - fort those who mourn.
on the wing; God's pow'r will make us strong.

WORDS: Ruth Duck

ST. THOMAS

MUSIC: Williams's *New Universal Psalmodist*, 1770

SM

Words © 1992 GIA Publications, Inc.

139 We're Marching to Zion

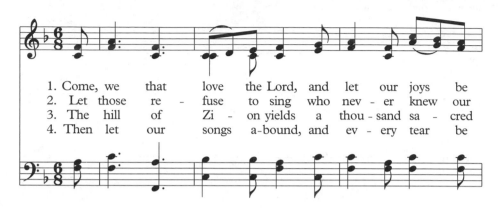

1. Come, we that love the Lord, and let our joys be
2. Let those re - fuse to sing who nev - er knew our
3. The hill of Zi - on yields a thou - sand sa - cred
4. Then let our songs a - bound, and ev - ery tear be

known. Join in a song with sweet ac - cord, join
God; but chil - dren of the heaven - ly King, but
sweets be - fore we reach the heaven - ly fields, be -
dry; we're march - ing through Em - man - uel's ground, we're

in a song with sweet ac - cord and
chil - dren of the heaven - ly King may
fore we reach the heaven - ly fields, or
march - ing through Em - man - uel's ground to

Note in Upper Room Worshipbook Accompaniment *and* Worship Leader *edition*

WORDS: Isaac Watts; refrain by Robert Lowry
MUSIC: Robert Lowry

MARCHING TO ZION
SM with Refrain

140   O Day of Peace

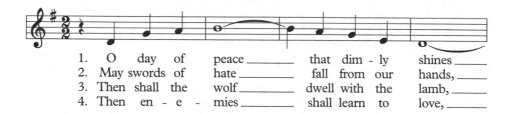

1. O day of peace   that dim - ly shines
2. May swords of hate   fall from our hands,
3. Then shall the wolf   dwell with the lamb,
4. Then en - e - mies   shall learn to love,

   through all our hopes   and prayers and dreams,
   our hearts from en - vy find re - lease,
   nor shall the fierce   de - vour the small;
   all crea - tures find   their true ac - cord;

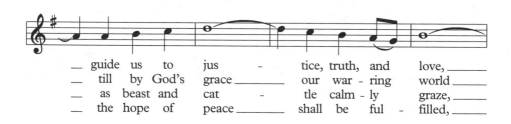

   guide us to jus - tice, truth, and love,
   till by God's grace   our war - ring world
   as beast and cat - tle calm - ly graze,
   the hope of peace   shall be ful - filled,

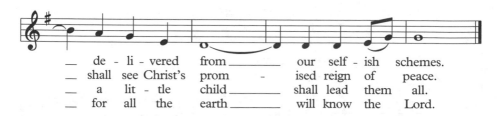

   de - li - vered from   our self - ish schemes.
   shall see Christ's prom - ised reign of peace.
   a lit - tle child   shall lead them all.
   for all the earth   will know the Lord.

WORDS: Carl P. Daw, Jr. (Isaiah 11)
MUSIC: Trad. English melody; adapt. by Hal H. Hopson
Adapt. © 1982, music © 1972 Hope Publishing Co.

THE GIFT OF LOVE
LM

The Gift of Love

141

1. Though I may speak with bravest fire,
   and have the gift to all inspire,
   and have not love; my words are vain,
   as sounding brass, and hopeless gain.

2. Though I may give all I possess,
   and striving so my love profess,
   but not be giv'n by love within,
   the profit soon turns strangely thin.

3. Come, Spirit, come, our hearts control,
   our spirits long to be made whole.
   Let inward love guide every deed;
   by this we worship, and are freed.

Sing to THE GIFT OF LOVE, No. 140

Hal H. Hopson (1 Cor. 13)
© 1972 Hope Publishing Co.

Before the Earth Had Yet Begun

142

1. Before the earth had yet begun
   its journey round the burning sun,
   before a seed of life had stirred,
   there sounded God's creating Word.

2. In that bright dawning of the world,
   e're ocean surged or wind unfurled,
   the vaults of heav'n with praises rang,
   the morning stars together sang.

3. Thus when creation's God did take
   the clay of earth our form to make,
   God willed that to our race belong
   the gifts of music, word, and song.

4. For mind can never comprehend,
   our noblest words can but pretend
   to grasp God's glory; praise alone
   is our companion by that throne.

Sing to THE GIFT OF LOVE, No. 140

Herbert O'Driscoll, alt.
© 1993 Herbert O'Driscoll

143
Come Follow Me

1. The grace of God is like a road
   that draws the heart from its first home;
   we long to go, but we hate to leave,
   and the Spirit calls, "Come follow me."

2. The voice of God is like the wind;
   it comes and goes and comes again.
   We read the signs in the bending trees,
   and the Spirit calls, "Come follow me."

3. The strength of God is like a stone;
   it firms the will of soul and bone;
   still soul and bone grow worn and weak,
   and the Spirit calls, "Come follow me."

4. The hope of God is like the sun;
   it shines until the day is done.
   And in the night, stars rise in the East,
   and the Spirit calls, "Come follow me."

5. The love of God is like a stream;
   it fills and feeds our deepest dreams;
   it finds a thirst and leaves a spring,
   and the Spirit calls, "Come follow me."

6. The peace of God is like a friend
   that sees us through the journey's end.
   The road is long and the talk is sweet,
   and the Spirit calls, "Come follow me."

Sing to THE GIFT OF LOVE, No. 140

Michael Hudson

Rain Down

Refrain

Rain down, rain down, rain down your
love on your peo — ple. Rain down, rain
down, rain down your love, God of life.

1. Faith - ful and true is the word of our God.
2. We who re - vere and find hope in our God
3. God of cre - a - tion, we long for your truth;

All of God's works are so wor - thy of trust.
live in the kind - ness and joy of God's wing.
you are the wa - ter of life that we thirst.

God's mer - cy falls on the just and the right;
God will pro - tect us from dark - ness and death;
Grant that your love and your peace touch our hearts,

D.C.

full of God's love is the earth.
God will not leave us to starve.
all of our hope lies in you.

WORDS: Jaime Cortez
MUSIC: Jaime Cortez

RAIN DOWN
10 10.10 8 with Refrain

145 Down by the Riverside

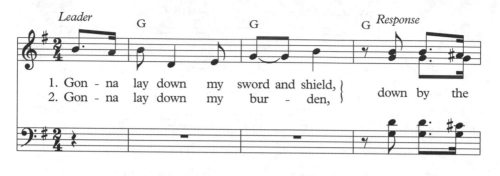

1. Gon - na lay down my sword and shield, ⎱
2. Gon - na lay down my bur - den, ⎰ down by the

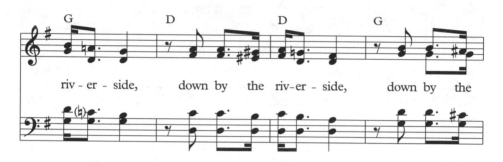

riv - er - side, down by the riv - er - side, down by the

riv - er - side; ⎰ gon - na lay down my sword and shield ⎱
                 ⎱ gon - na lay down my bur - den ⎰

down by the riv - er - side, gon - na stud - y war no

WORDS: African American spiritual
MUSIC: African American spiritual

STUDY WAR NO MORE
Irregular

146 We Cannot Measure How You Heal

| C | F | Gm7 | Am7 | Gm7 |

1. We can - not meas - ure how you heal
2. The pain that will not go a - way,
3. So some have come who need your help

| F | Bb | Gm7 | C |

or an - swer ev - ery suf - ferer's prayer,
the guilt that clings from things long past,
and some have come to make a - mends,

| C7 | F | Gm7 | Am7 | Gm7 |

yet we be - lieve your grace re - sponds
the fear of what the fu - ture holds,
as hands which shaped and saved the world

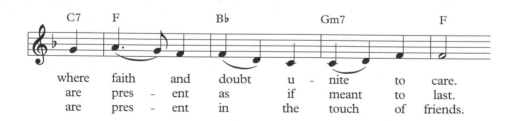

| C7 | F | Bb | Gm7 | F |

where faith and doubt u - nite to care.
are pres - ent as if meant to last.
are pres - ent in the touch of friends.

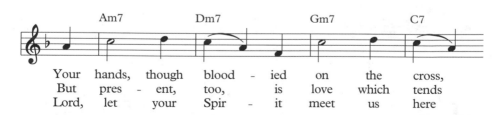

| Am7 | Dm7 | Gm7 | C7 |

Your hands, though blood - ied on the cross,
But pres - ent, too, is love which tends
Lord, let your Spir - it meet us here

WORDS: John L. Bell
MUSIC: Trad. Scottish melody

CANDLER
LMD

sur - vive to hold and heal and warm,
the hurt we nev - er hoped to find,
to mend the bod - y, mind, and soul,

to car - ry all through death to life
the pri - vate ag - o - nies in - side,
to dis - en - tan - gle peace from pain,

and cra - dle chil - dren yet un - born.
the mem - o - ries that haunt the mind.
and make your bro - ken peo - ple whole.

O World of God 147

1. O world of God, so vast and strange, profound and wonderful and fair,
beyond the utmost reach of thought but not beyond our Maker's care!
We are not strangers on this earth whirling amid the suns of space,
we are God's children, this our home, with those of every clime and race.

2. O world where human life is lived, so strangely mingling joy and pain,
so full of evil and of good, so needful that the good shall reign!
It is this world that God has loved, and goodness was its Maker's plan,
the promise of God's triumph is a humble birth in Bethlehem.

3. O world of time's far-stretching years! There was a day when time stood still,
a central moment when there rose a cross upon a cruel hill;
in pain and death love's pow'r was seen, the mystery of time revealed,
the wisdom of the ways of God, the grace through which our hurt is healed.

Sing to CANDLER, No. 146

R. B. Y. Scott, alt.

148   Come, O Thou Traveler Unknown

1. Come, O thou Traveler unknown, whom still I hold but cannot see!
My company before is gone, and I am left alone with thee.
With thee all night I mean to stay, and wrestle till the break of day;
with thee all night I mean to stay, and wrestle till the break of day.

2. I need not tell thee who I am, my misery and sin declare;
thyself hast called me by thy name, look on thy hands and read it there.
But who, I ask thee, who art thou? Tell me thy name, and tell me now.
But who, I ask thee, who art thou? Tell me thy name, and tell me now.

3. Yield to me now, for I am weak, but confident in self-despair!
Speak to my heart, in blessing speak, be conquered by my instant prayer.
Speak, or thou never hence shalt move, and tell me if thy name is Love.
Speak, or thou never hence shalt move, and tell me if thy name is Love.

4. 'Tis Love! 'tis Love! Thou diedst for me, I hear thy whisper in my heart.
The morning breaks, the shadows flee, pure Universal Love thou art.
To me, to all, thy mercies move; thy nature and thy name is Love.
To me, to all, thy mercies move; thy nature and thy name is Love.

Sing to CANDLER, No. 146

Charles Wesley (Gen. 32:24-32)

149   Your Song of Love

```
        G                                    Am
1. May  your  grace   make  me   whole    a - gain.
2. May  your  hands   touch the  poor     a - gain.
3. May  your  birth   make  me   live     a - gain.
4. May  your  feet    walk  the  road     a - gain.
5. Let  my    tears   wash  your feet     a - gain.
6. Let  me    give    you   your food     a - gain.
```

This song was dedicated by the composer to Mother Teresa and was sung by him at her funeral.

WORDS: Bob Fabing
MUSIC: Bob Fabing
© 1984 OCP Publications

SONG OF LOVE
888.4 D with Refrain

150   Spirit, Working in Creation

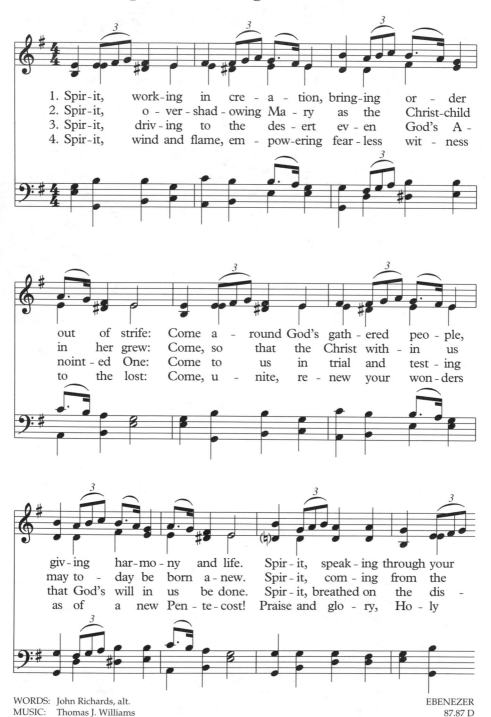

1. Spir-it, work-ing in cre - a - tion, bring-ing or - der out of strife: Come a - round God's gath - ered peo - ple, giv-ing har-mo - ny and life. Spir-it, speak-ing through your

2. Spir-it, o - ver-shad - owing Ma - ry as the Christ-child in her grew: Come, so that the Christ with - in us may to - day be born a-new. Spir-it, com-ing from the

3. Spir-it, driv-ing to the des - ert ev - en God's A - noint - ed One: Come to us in trial and test - ing that God's will in us be done. Spir-it, breathed on the dis -

4. Spir-it, wind and flame, em - pow-ering fear - less wit - ness to the lost: Come, u - nite, re - new your won - ders as of a new Pen - te-cost! Praise and glo - ry, Ho - ly

WORDS: John Richards, alt.
MUSIC: Thomas J. Williams

EBENEZER
87.87 D
Alternate tune: HYFRYDOL

proph-ets so the voice of God was heard: Come, in - spire, a -
heav-ens as a dove up - on our Lord: Come up - on your
ci - ples, giv-ing peace where there was fear: Come a - mong us,
Spir - it, for your love on us out-poured, giv - ing hon - or

lert your peo - ple to this day's pro - phe - tic word.
gath - ered peo - ple, and your bless-ings be out-poured.
touch us, send us, mak - ing Je - sus' pres - ence near.
to the Fa - ther and pro - claim-ing Je - sus, "Lord."

To Us All, to Every Nation 151

1. To us all, to every nation comes the moment to decide,
   in the strife of truth with falsehood, for the good or evil side;
   some great cause, God's new endeavor, off'ring each the bloom or blight,
   and the choice goes by forever 'twixt that darkness and that night.

2. By the light of burning martyrs, Jesus' bleeding feet I track,
   toiling up the Calvaries ever with the cross that turns not back.
   New occasions teach new duties, time makes ancient good uncouth;
   they must upward still and onward who would keep abreast of truth.

3. Though the cause of evil prosper, yet 'tis truth alone is strong,
   truth forever on the scaffold, wrong forever on the throne.
   Yet that scaffold sways the future, and, behind the dim unknown,
   God is standing in the shadow keeping watch beside God's own.

Sing to EBENEZER, No. 150 or HYFRYDOL, No. 100

James Russell Lowell; adapt. by W. Garrett Horder, alt.

152   O the Deep, Deep Love of Jesus

1. O the deep, deep love of Jesus, vast, unmeasured, boundless, free!
   Rolling as a mighty ocean in its fullness over me!
   Underneath me, all around me, is the current of thy love—
   leading onward, leading homeward, to thy glorious rest above.

2. O the deep, deep love of Jesus—spread his praise from shore to shore!
   How he loves us, ever loves us, changes never, nevermore!
   How he watches o'er his loved ones, dies to call them all his own;
   how for them he's interceding, watching o'er them from the throne!

3. O the deep, deep love of Jesus, love of every love the best!
   'Tis an ocean vast of blessing, 'tis a haven sweet of rest!
   O the deep, deep love of Jesus—'tis a heav'n of heav'ns to me;
   and it lifts me up to glory, for it lifts me up to thee!

Sing to EBENEZER, No. 150 or HYFRYDOL, No. 100

Samuel Trevor Francis

153   When from Bondage We Are Summoned

1. When from bondage we are summoned out of darkness into light,
   we must go in hope and patience, walk by faith and not by sight.
   Let us throw off all that hinders; let us run the race to win!
   Let us hasten to our homeland and, rejoicing, enter in.

2. When our God makes us a people, Jesus leads us by the hand
   through a lonely, barren desert, to a great and glorious land.
   Let us throw off all that hinders; let us run the race to win!
   Let us hasten to our homeland and, rejoicing, enter in.

3. At all stages of the journey God is with us, night and day,
   with compassion for our weakness ev'ry step along the way.
   Let us throw off all that hinders; let us run the race to win!
   Let us hasten to our homeland and, rejoicing, enter in.

4. We must not lose sight of Jesus, who accepted pain and loss,
   who, for joy of love unmeasured dared embrace the shameful cross.
   Let us throw off all that hinders; let us run the race to win!
   Let us hasten to our homeland and, rejoicing, enter in.

5. See the prize our God has promised: endless life with Christ the Lord.
   Now we fix our eyes on Jesus, walk by faith in Jesus' word.
   Let us throw off all that hinders; let us run the race to win!
   Let us hasten to our homeland and, rejoicing, enter in.

Sing to EBENEZER, No. 150 or HYFRYDOL, No. 100

Delores Dufner, OSB

Holy, Holy, Holy

154

(Sanctus from a Groaning Creation)

Refrain

Ho - ly, ho - ly, ho - ly, you are whole and ho - ly,

Fine

hear - ing, heal - ing, help - ing, O our God of hope.

1. God of heav - en, God of earth, God of Christ, our Sav - ior,
2. God of heav - en, God on high, God of help - ing Spir - it,

1. heal our world and give new birth to the world you love.
2. hear our groan - ing hear our cry. Save the world you love.

Additional stanzas and music in Upper Room Worshipbook Accompaniment and Worship Leader *edition*

WORDS: Per Harling
MUSIC: Per Harling
© 2000 General Board of Global Ministries, GBGMusik

GROANING CREATION
76.75 with Refrain

155   The Earth and All Who Breathe

1. The earth and all who breathe ex -
   ist through love di - vine, who formed the sea, the
   flow - 'ring tree, the wren, the fra - grant pine. Each
   wo - man, man, and child cre - at - ed from the

2. The good, a - bun - dant earth is
   ours to tend and keep, yet land lies waste, con -
   sumed in haste, and hun - gry chil - dren weep. The
   na - tions proud - ly build new Ba - bels to the

3. Cre - a - tion now a - waits hu -
   man - i - ty's re - birth at last to claim one
   com - mon aim: to nur - ture life on earth. A -
   wake, all hu - man - kind, the chal - lenge now em -

WORDS: Ruth Duck   ICH HALTE TREULICH STILL
MUSIC: Attr. to J. S. Bach   66.86 D
Words © 1992 GIA Publications, Inc.

dust   is   called   to   share   cre -
sky.   Their   bombs   de - stroy   cre -
brace,   ap - ply   your strength,   your

a - tion's   care,   a   sa - cred   liv - ing   trust.
a - tion's   joy;   their   mis - siles   ter - ri - fy!
voice,   your   means,   as   stew - ards   of   God's   grace.

We Lay Our Broken World   156

1. We lay our broken world
   in sorrow at your feet,
   haunted by hunger, war, and fear,
   oppressed by pow'r and hate.

   Here human life seems less
   than profit, might, and pride,
   though to unite us all in you,
   you lived and loved and died.

2. We bring our broken towns
   our neighbors hurt and bruised;
   you show us how old pain and wounds
   for new life can be used.

We bring our broken loves,
friends parted, fam'lies torn;
then in your life and death we see
that love must be re-born.

3. We bring our broken selves,
   confused and closed and tired;
   then through your gift of healing grace
   new purpose is inspired.

   O Spirit, on us breathe,
   with life and strength anew;
   find in us love, and hope, and trust,
   and lift us up to you.

Sing to ICH HALTE TREULICH STILL, No. 155

Anna Briggs

157 Fear Not, for I Have Redeemed You

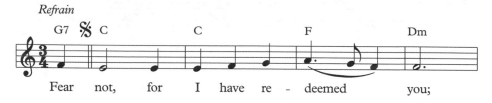

Refrain

Fear not, for I have re - deemed you;

I have called you by name.

I have called you by name. You

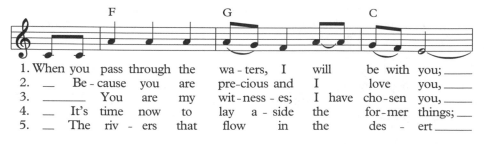

are mine. mine.

1. When you pass through the	wa - ters, I	will	be with you;
2. — Be - cause you are	pre - cious and I	love	you,
3. ——— You are my	wit - ness - es; I	have	cho - sen you,
4. — It's time now to	lay a - side the		for - mer things;
5. — The riv - ers that	flow in the		des - ert

WORDS: Jodi Page-Clark (Isa. 43)
MUSIC: Jodi Page-Clark; arr. by Patricia Allen

FEAR NOT
Irregular

| Am | | | Dm | | | G | |

_ and through riv - ers they will not o - ver -
_ _____ you whom I formed for my
_ _____ that you may know and be -
_ _ a new day has dawned, can you
_ give drink to my cho - sen

| C | | C7 | | F | | G | |

whelm you. _____ When you walk through the fire you will
glo - ry, _____ _____ you whom I call by my
lieve me. _____ _____ You are my ser-vants for the
see it? _____ _ I'm mak - ing a way in the
peo - ple; _____ _ to quench their thirst and to

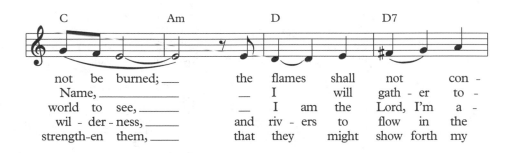

| C | | Am | | D | | D7 | |

not be burned; _ the flames shall not con -
Name, _____ _ I will gath - er to -
world to see, _____ _ I am the Lord, I'm a -
wil - der - ness, _____ and riv - ers to flow in the
strength-en them, _____ that they might show forth my

| 1-4 | | | | D.S. | 5 | | | D.S. |
| G | | G7 | | | G | | G7 | |

sume you. _____
geth - er. _____
mong you. _____   } Fear
des - ert. _____

praise. _____ Fear

158 You Are Mine

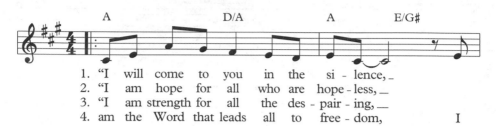

1. "I will come to you in the si - lence, __
2. "I am hope for all who are hope - less, __
3. "I am strength for all the des - pair - ing, __
4. am the Word that leads all to free - dom,   I

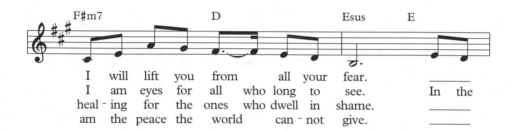

    I will lift you from all your fear. _____
    I am eyes for all who long to see.   In the
heal - ing for the ones who dwell in shame. _____
am the peace the world can - not give. _____

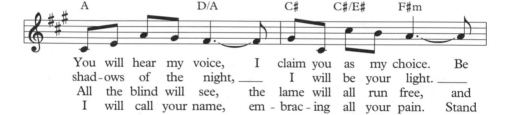

You will hear my voice, I claim you as my choice. Be
shad - ows of the night, ___ I will be your light. ___
All the blind will see, the lame will all run free, and
I will call your name, em - brac - ing all your pain. Stand

still and know I am here. _____ *(To Stanza 2)*
Come and rest in me. _____ *(To Refrain)*
all will know my name. _____ *(To Refrain)*
up, now walk, and live. _____ *(To Refrain)*

Refrain

Do not be a-fraid, I am with you. I have called you each by

WORDS: David Haas (Ps. 46:10; Isa. 43:1; John 14:27)
MUSIC: David Haas

YOU ARE MINE
Irregular with Refrain

name.   Come and fol-low me,   I will bring you

home;   I   love   you and you   are   mine."

3. —
4. "I

A Prayer for Healing Community   159

Bless your people, Lord,
    who have walked too long in this night of pain.
For the child has no more tears to cry
    and the old people no song of joy to sing,
    and the blood of our youth drains away in the gutters.
The cry from the cross is heard throughout the land.
The pain in your nailed hands is carried by the worker.
Terrible thirst is in the mouth of the farmer,
    too many women mourn the loss of their sons,
    and all the earth is turned into another Calvary.
With your spirit, Lord, we cry for peace.
With your spirit, we struggle to be free.

160 Make Us Holy, Make Us Whole

Refrain

In your love, make us whole. May we rest in your com-pas-sion. Calm the lost, wea-ry soul in the warmth of your love. May your peace fill our hearts. May we know the love of Je-sus. By your grace, you con-sole. Make us ho-ly, make us whole. whole.

1. Bind up the wounds of our soul. Com-fort the lone-ly and lost with the strength of your great Spir-it.
2. Nour-ish the hun-gry in need. Strength-en the faith of the poor with the hope of your sal-va-tion.
3. Care for the suf-fer-ing ones. Lift up the bro-ken in heart with the peace of your for-give-ness.

WORDS: Mark Friedman
MUSIC: Mark Friedman; arr. by Janet Vogt
© 1998 Lorenz Publishing Co.

MAKE US HOLY
7 15 with Refrain

Healer of Our Every Ill

Refrain

Heal - er of our ev - ery ill, light of each to - mor - row, give us peace be - yond our fear, and hope be - yond our sor - row.

1. You who know our fears and sad - ness, grace us with your peace and glad - ness, Spir - it of all com - fort: Fill our hearts. _____
2. In the pain and joy be - hold - ing, how your grace is still un - fold - ing, give us all your vi - sion: God of love. _____
3. Give us strength to love each oth - er, ev - ery sis - ter, ev - ery broth - er, Spir - it of all kind - ness: Be our guide. _____
4. You who know each thought and feel - ing, teach us all your way of heal - ing, Spir - it of com - pas - sion: Fill each heart. _____

WORDS: Marty Haugen
MUSIC: Marty Haugen
© 1987 GIA Publications, Inc.

HEALER OF OUR EVERY ILL
88.63 with Refrain

162 Healing River

WORDS: Fred Hellerman and Fran Minkoff
MUSIC: Fred Hellerman and Fran Minkoff
© 1964, renewed 1992 Appleseed Music, Inc.

HEALING RIVER
Irregular

163

Blest Are They

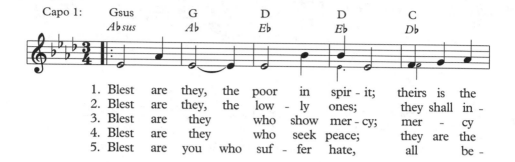

1. Blest are they, the poor in spir - it; theirs is the
2. Blest are they, the low - ly ones; they shall in -
3. Blest are they who show mer - cy; mer - cy
4. Blest are they who seek peace; they are the
5. Blest are you who suf - fer hate, all be -

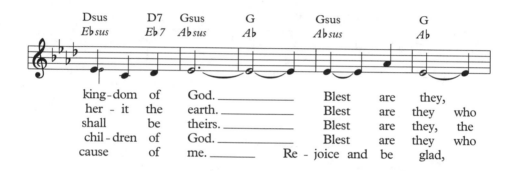

king - dom of God. _____ Blest are they,
her - it the earth. _____ Blest are they who
shall be theirs. _____ Blest are they, the
chil - dren of God. _____ Blest are they who
cause of me. _____ Re - joice and be glad,

full of sor - row; they shall be con - soled. ____
hun - ger and thirst; they shall have their fill. _____
pure of heart; they shall see God! ____
suf - fer in faith; the glo - ry of God is theirs. ___
yours is the king - dom. Shine for all to see. _____

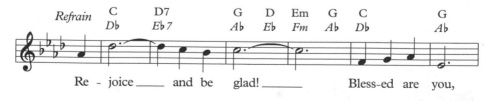

Re - joice ____ and be glad! _____ Bless - ed are you,

WORDS: David Haas (Matt. 5:3-16)
MUSIC: David Haas
© 1985 GIA Publications, Inc.

BLEST ARE THEY
Irregular with Refrain

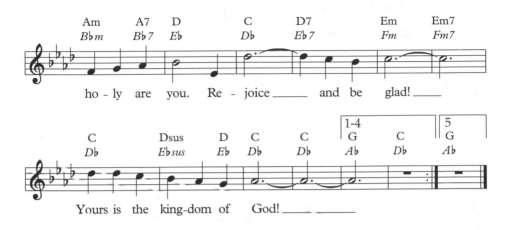

ho - ly are you. Re - joice_____ and be glad!_____

Yours is the king-dom of God!_____ _____

Spirit, Now Live in Me 164
(O Holy Dove)

1. O ho - ly Dove of God de - scend - ing,
2. O ho - ly Wind of God now blow - ing,
3. O ho - ly Rain of God now fall - ing,
4. O ho - ly Flame of God now burn - ing,

you are the love that knows no end - ing, all of our shat - tered
you are the seed that God is sow - ing, you are the life that
you make the Word of God en - thral - ling, you are the in - ner
you are the pow'r of Christ re - turn - ing, you are the an - swer

dreams you're mend - ing: Spir - it, now live in me.
starts us grow - ing: Spir - it, now live in me.
voice now call - ing: Spir - it, now live in me.
to our yearn - ing: Spir - it, now live in me.

WORDS: Bryan Jeffery Leech

MUSIC: Bryan Jeffery Leech

© 1976 Fred Bock Music Co., Inc.

HOLY DOVE
999.6

165 Enemy of Apathy

1. She sits like a bird,
(2. She) wings o-ver earth,
(3. She) danc-es in fire,
(4. For) she is the Spir-it,

brood-ing on the wa-ters, hov-'ring on the cha-os of the
rest-ing where she wish-es, light-ing close at hand or soar-ing
start-ling her spec-ta-tors, wak-ing tongues of ec-sta-sy where
one with God in es-sence, gift-ed by the Sav-ior in e-

world's first day; she sighs and she sings,
through the skies; she nests in the womb,
dumb-ness reigned; she weans and in-spires
ter-nal love; she is the ___ key

moth-er-ing cre-a-tion, wait-ing to give birth to all the
wel-com-ing each won-der, nour-ish-ing po-ten-tial hid-den
all whose hearts are o-pen, nor can she be cap-tured, si-lenced,
o-pen-ing the scrip-tures, en-e-my of ap-a-thy and

Word will say. 2. She
to our eyes. 3. She
or re-strained. 4. For
heav-en-ly dove.

WORDS: John L. Bell and Graham Maule
MUSIC: John L. Bell

THAINAKY
11 11 D

Come, God, and Hear My Cry 166

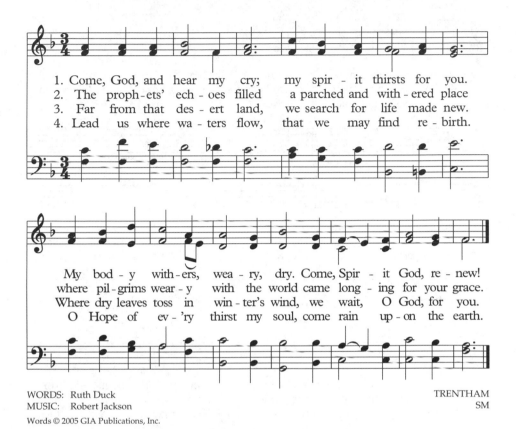

1. Come, God, and hear my cry; my spir - it thirsts for you.
2. The proph-ets' ech - oes filled a parched and with - ered place
3. Far from that des - ert land, we search for life made new.
4. Lead us where wa - ters flow, that we may find re - birth.

My bod - y with - ers, wea - ry, dry. Come, Spir - it God, re - new!
where pil - grims wear - y with the world came long - ing for your grace.
Where dry leaves toss in win - ter's wind, we wait, O God, for you.
O Hope of ev - 'ry thirst my soul, come rain up - on the earth.

WORDS: Ruth Duck
MUSIC: Robert Jackson
Words © 2005 GIA Publications, Inc.

TRENTHAM
SM

Breathe on Me, Breath of God 167

1. Breathe on me, Breath of God, fill me with life anew,
   that I may love what thou dost love, and do what thou wouldst do.

2. Breathe on me, Breath of God, until my heart is pure,
   until with thee I will one will, to do and to endure.

3. Breathe on me, Breath of God, till I am wholly thine,
   till all this earthly part of me glows with thy fire divine.

4. Breathe on me, Breath of God, so shall I never die,
   but live with thee the perfect life of thine eternity.

Sing to TRENTHAM, No. 166

Edwin Hatch (John 20:22)

168 We Humans Build to Frame a Life

Capo 3: D G D

1. We hu-mans build to frame a life with mean-ing, love, and
2. For ev-ery-thing our hands con-struct will one day fall and
3. We ded-i-cate our-selves to-day a-mid life's change and

A7 D G

feel-ing, but time or hate can bring col-lapse and
crum-ble. The God who is a car-pen-ter cre-
dan-ger to build with God a house of peace for

D A7 Dsus D D

loss can leave us reel-ing. Let faith-ful souls from
ates from scrap and jum-ble. And we can join the
friend and foe and strang-er. Here may the peo - ples

A7 Bm D D

rub-ble rise to find new ways from sor-row and
work of God to raise a new cre-a-tion that
come and go, de-light in shared en-deav-or, set

(Written in response to the disaster on September 11, 2001)

WORDS: Ruth Duck
MUSIC: Robert Lowry, arr. by John L. Bell

HOW CAN I KEEP FROM SINGING
87.87 with Refrain

slow - ly, slow - ly   form   a shape   to   wel-come God's to - mor-row.
what   we do will   long en-dure   up - on   a   firm foun - da - tion.
free from ter - ror,   hate, and war,   a - live   in   God for - ev - er.

Abundant Life   169

1. We cannot own the sunlit sky, the moon, the wild flow'rs growing,
   for we are part of all that is within life's river flowing.
   With open hands receive and share the gifts of God's creation,
   that all may have abundant life in every earthly nation.

2. When bodies shiver in the night and, weary, wait for morning,
   when children have no bread but tears, and war-horns sound their warning.
   God calls humanity to wake, to join in common labor,
   that all may have abundant life in oneness with their neighbor.

3. God calls humanity to join as partners in creating
   a future free from want and fear, life's goodness celebrating.
   That new world beckons from afar, invites our shared endeavor,
   that all may have abundant life and peace endure forever.

Sing to HOW CAN I KEEP FROM SINGING, No. 168

Ruth Duck

170　　How Can I Keep from Singing

1. My life flows on in endless song above earth's lamentation.
   I catch the sweet, though far-off, hymn that hails a new creation.
   No storm can shake my inmost calm while to that Rock I'm clinging.
   Since love is Lord of heav'n and earth, how can I keep from singing?

2. Through all the tumult and the strife, I hear that music ringing.
   It finds an echo in my soul. How can I keep from singing?
   No storm can shake my inmost calm while to that Rock I'm clinging.
   Since love is Lord of heav'n and earth, how can I keep from singing?

3. What though my joys and comforts die? The Lord, my Savior, liveth.
   What though the darkness round me close? Songs in the night he giveth.
   No storm can shake my inmost calm while to that Rock I'm clinging.
   Since love is Lord of heav'n and earth, how can I keep from singing?

4. The peace of Christ makes fresh my heart, a fountain ever springing.
   All things are mine since I am his! How can I keep from singing?
   No storm can shake my inmost calm while to that Rock I'm clinging.
   Since love is Lord of heav'n and earth, how can I keep from singing?

Sing to HOW CAN I KEEP FROM SINGING, No. 168

Robert Lowry

Sound a Mystic Bamboo Song 171

1. Dong dong ay si dong i - lay in - si - na - li

2. Sound a mys - tic bam - boo song, raise a chant - ing
3. See the Christ in tri - bal cloth, liv - ing in a
4. Free the Christ with - in the poor, break the chains of
5. May your live - ly Spir - it, God, blow through-out this

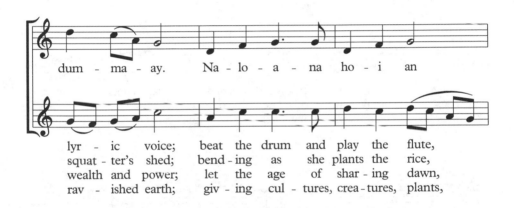

dum - ma - ay. Na - lo - a - na ho - i an

lyr - ic voice; beat the drum and play the flute,
squat - ter's shed; bend - ing as she plants the rice,
wealth and power; let the age of shar - ing dawn,
rav - ished earth; giv - ing cul - tures, crea - tures, plants,

in - ho yo in o hai an.

let the *church of God re - joice.
sleep - ing on a pave - ment bed.
sing the prom - ised gos - pel hour.
whole - ness, still - ness, growth, and worth.

*Original for "church of God" is "Asian church." Additional notes in Upper Room Worshipbook
Accompaniment and Worship Leader edition

WORDS: Bill Wallace   BAMBOO SONG
MUSIC: I-to Loh   77.77
© 2000 General Board of Global Ministries, GBGMusik

172 Dust and Ashes

1. Dust and ash - es touch our face,   mark our fail - ure and our
2. Dust and ash - es soil our hands —   greed of mar - ket, pride of
3. Dust and ash - es choke our tongue   in the waste-land of de -

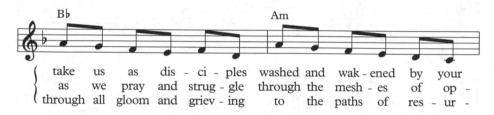

fall - ing.
na - tion.   Ho - ly Spir - it, come, walk with us to - mor - row,
pres - sion.

take us as dis - ci - ples washed and wak - ened by your
as we pray and strug - gle through the mesh - es of op -
through all gloom and griev - ing to the paths of res - ur -

Refrain

call - ing. ____
pres - sion. ____
rec - tion. ____   Take us by the hand and lead us,

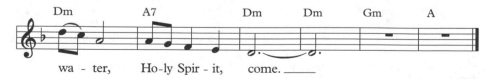

lead us through the des - ert sands,   bring us liv - ing

wa - ter, Ho - ly Spir - it, come. ____

WORDS: Brian Wren
MUSIC: David Haas

DUST AND ASHES
78.56.68 with Refrain

Wellspring of Wisdom

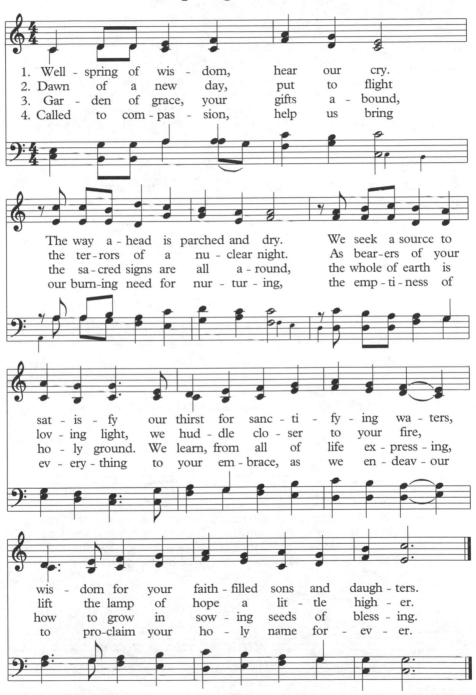

1. Well - spring of wis - dom, hear our cry.
2. Dawn of a new day, put to flight
3. Gar - den of grace, your gifts a - bound,
4. Called to com - pas - sion, help us bring

The way a - head is parched and dry. We seek a source to
the ter - rors of a nu - clear night. As bear-ers of your
the sa - cred signs are all a - round, the whole of earth is
our burn-ing need for nur - tur - ing, the emp - ti - ness of

sat - is - fy our thirst for sanc - ti - fy - ing wa - ters,
lov - ing light, we hud - dle clo - ser to your fire,
ho - ly ground. We learn, from all of life ex - press - ing,
ev - ery - thing to your em - brace, as we en - deav - our

wis - dom for your faith - filled sons and daugh - ters.
lift the lamp of hope a lit - tle high - er.
how to grow in sow - ing seeds of bless - ing.
to pro-claim your ho - ly name for - ev - er.

WORDS: Miriam Therese Winter
MUSIC: Miriam Therese Winter; harm. by Ruth Watson Henderson

WELLSPRING
888.9 10

174

Song of Shalom

D   Em   A7   D

1. When we are liv-ing____ it is in Christ Je-sus,____
2. God sent Christ Je-sus____ to be our Sha-lom.____
3. To pain and sor-row____ Christ brings Sha-lom.____
4. Sha-lom to you now,____ sha-lom, my friends.____

Bm   Em   A7   D

____ and when we're dy-ing.____ it is in the Lord.____
____ To show us mer-cy____ and heal-ing love.____
____ In peace and jus-tice____ Christ brings Sha-lom.____
____ May God's full mer-cies____ bless you, my friends.____

D7   G   Em   A   F#m

____ Both in our liv-ing____ and in our dy-ing,____
____ So in our liv-ing____ and in our dy-ing,____
____ So when we're liv-ing____ the ways of Je-sus,____
____ In all your liv-ing,____ and through your lov-ing,____

Bm   Em   A7   [1-3] D

____ we be-long to God,____ we be-long to God.
____ Christ is our Sha-lom,____ Christ is our Sha-lom.
____ we are God's Sha-lom,____ we are God's Sha-lom.
____ Christ be your Sha-lom,____ Christ be your Sha-

[4] D Bm   Em   A7   D

lom,____ Christ be your Sha-lom,____ Christ be your Sha-lom.

WORDS: St. 1 anon. (Rom. 14:8-9), trans. by Elise S. Eslinger; sts. 2–4 Elise S. Eslinger   SOMOS DEL SEÑOR
MUSIC: Mexican melody   Irregular

Trans. and sts. 2–4 © 1983 Elise S. Eslinger

When We Are Living

1. When we are living, it is in Christ Jesus,
   and when we're dying, it is in the Lord.
   Both in our living and in our dying,
   we belong to God, we belong to God.

2. Through all our living, we our fruits must give.
   Good works of service are for offering.
   When we are giving, or when receiving,
   we belong to God, we belong to God.

3. 'Mid times of sorrow and in times of pain,
   when sensing beauty or in love's embrace,
   whether we suffer, or sing rejoicing,
   we belong to God, we belong to God.

4. Across this wide world, we shall always find
   those who are crying with no peace of mind,
   but when we help them, or when we feed them,
   we belong to God, we belong to God.

Sing to SOMOS DEL SEÑOR, No. 174

St. 1 anon., trans. by Elise S. Eslinger; sts. 2–4 Roberto Escamilla, trans. by George Lockwood (Rom. 14:8)
Trans. st. 1 © 1983 Elise S. Eslinger; trans. sts. 2–4 © 1989 The United Methodist Publishing House

Pues si vivimos

1. Pues si vivimos, para Él vivimos
   y si morimos para Él morimos.
   Sea que vivamos o que muramos,
   somos del Señor, somos del Señor.

2. En esta vida, frutos hemos de dar.
   Las obras buenas son para ofrendar.
   Ya sea que demos o que recibamos,
   somos del Señor, somos del Señor.

3. En la tristeza y en el dolor,
   en la belleza y en el amor,
   sea que suframos o que gocemos,
   somos del Señor, somos del Señor.

4. En este mundo, hemos de encontrar
   gente que llora y sin consolar.
   Sea que ayudemos o que alimentemos,
   somos del Señor, somos del Señor.

Sing to SOMOS DEL SEÑOR, No. 174

St. 1 anon.; sts. 2–4 Roberto Escamilla

177   Till All the Jails Are Empty

1. Till all the jails are emp-ty and all the bell-ies filled; till
2. In ten-e-ment and man-sion, in fac-tory, farm, and mill, in
3. By sit-ting at a bed-side to hold pale trem-bling hands, by

no one hurts or steals or lies, and no more blood is spilled; till
board-room and in bill-iard-hall, in wards where time stands still, in
speak-ing for the pow-er-less a-gainst un-just de-mands, by

age and race and gen-der no long-er sep-a-rate; till
class-rooms, church, and of-fice, in shops or on the street; in
pray-ing through our do-ing and sing-ing though we fear, by

pul-pit, press, and pol-i-tics are free of greed and hate:
ev-ery place where peo-ple thrive or starve or hide or meet:
trust-ing that the seed we sow will bring God's har-vest near:

Refrain

God has work for us to do. _____

WORDS: Carl P. Daw, Jr.   WORK TO DO
MUSIC: John L. Bell   76.86 D with Refrain

Sing Your Joy

1. Sing your joy, pro - claim God's glo - ry!
2. All the earth is filled with re - joic - ing,
3. May we learn to be - come your King - dom.
4. Light our way, O God of the liv - ing,

Rise and sing, the morn - ing has come!
light and life, the won - der of God!
May we be your kind - ness and truth!
may we learn to see with new eyes!

Bless our God and praise all cre - a - tion;
Christ has tri - umphed! Ris - en for - ev - er!
Love is our call - ing, gift of your pres - ence;
Je - sus the Lord, our pow - er and prom - ise;

song of the earth, and light from heav - en:
Joy of our hearts, and hope of our dream - ing:
chil - dren of God, and spir - it of Je - sus:
light for the blind, and food for the hun - gry:

God is a - live! _____ Al - le - lu - ia!
God is a - live! _____ Al - le - lu - ia!
God is a - live! _____ Al - le - lu - ia!
God is a - live! _____ Al - le - lu - ia!

WORDS: David Haas
MUSIC: David Haas
© 1987 GIA Publications, Inc.

SUMMIT HILL
Irregular

179 Lord of All Hopefulness

1. Lord of all hope - ful - ness, Lord of all joy, whose
2. Lord of all eag - er - ness, Lord of all faith, whose
3. Lord of all kind - li - ness, Lord of all grace, your
4. Lord of all gen - tle - ness, Lord of all calm, whose

trust, ev - er child - like, no cares could de - stroy: Be
strong hands were skilled at the plane and the lathe: Be
hands swift to wel - come, your arms to em - brace: Be
voice is con - tent - ment, whose pres - ence is balm: Be

there at our wak - ing, and give us, we pray your
there at our la - bors, and give us, we pray your
there at our hom - ing, and give us, we pray your
there at our sleep - ing, and give us, we pray your

bliss in our hearts, Lord, at the break of the day. _____
strength in our hearts, Lord, at the noon of the day. _____
love in our hearts, Lord, at the eve of the day. _____
peace in our hearts, Lord, at the end of the day. _____

WORDS: Jan Struther (Joyce Placzek, née Torrens), from *Enlarged Songs of Praise*
MUSIC: Irish folk melody
Words © 1931 Oxford University Press

SLANE
10 10.9 10

180 Be Thou My Vision

1. Be thou my vision, O Lord of my heart;
   naught be all else to me, save that thou art.
   Thou my best thought, by day or by night,
   waking or sleeping, thy presence, my light.

Sing to SLANE, No. 179

Ancient Irish; trans. by Mary E. Byrne, versed by Eleanor H. Hull, alt.
Alt. © 1989 The United Methodist Publishing House

2. Be thou my wisdom, and thou my true word;
   I ever with thee and thou with me, Lord;
   thou and thou only, first in my heart,
   great God of heaven, my treasure thou art.

3. Great God of heaven, my victory won,
   may I reach heaven's joys, O bright heav'n's Sun!
   Heart of my own heart, whatever befall,
   still be my vision, O Ruler of all.

Today I Awake 181

1. To-day I a-wake and God is be-fore me. At
2. To-day I a-rise and Christ is be-side me. He
3. To-day I af-firm the Spir-it with-in me at
4. To-day I en-joy the Trin-i-ty 'round me, a-

night, as I dreamt, he sum-moned the day; for
walked through the dark to scat-ter new light. Yes,
wor-ship and work, in strug-gle and rest. The
bove and be-neath, be-fore and be-hind; the

God nev-er sleeps but pat-terns the morn - ing with
Christ is a-live, and beck-ons his peo - ple to
Spir-it in-spires all life which is chang - ing from
Mak-er, the Son, the Spir-it to-geth - er — they

slith-ers of gold or glo-ry in grey.
hope and to heal, re-sist and in - vite.
fear-ing to faith, from bro-ken to blest.
called me to life and call me their friend.

WORDS: John L. Bell and Graham Maule
MUSIC: John L. Bell

SLITHERS OF GOLD
56.55 D

© 1998 Wild Goose Resource Group, Iona Community, Scotland; GIA Publications, Inc., exclusive North American agent

182 God, We Praise You for the Morning

1. God, we praise you for the morn - ing,
2. God, we praise you for cre - a - tion,
3. God, we praise you for com - pas - sion,
4. God, we praise you for your Spir - it,
5. God, we praise you for the Sav - ior,
6. Al - le - lu - ia! Al - le - lu - ia!

hope springs forth with each new day, new be
moun - tains, seas, and des - ert land. Wak - ing
all the lov - ing that you show: Hu - man
com - for - ter and dai - ly friend, rest - less
come that we may know your ways. In his
Al - le - lu - ia! Al - le - lu - ia! Al - le -

gin - ning, prayer and prom - ise, joy in work and in
souls find joy and heal - ing in your boun - ti - ful
touch - ing, tears and laugh - ter help your chil - dren to
search - er, gen - tle teach - er, strength and cour - age you
lov - ing, dy - ing, ris - ing, Christ is Lord of our
lu - ia! Al - le - lu - ia! Christ is Lord of our

WORDS: Jim and Jean Strathdee
MUSIC: Jim Strathdee
© 1985 Desert Flower Music

WE PRAISE YOU
87.86

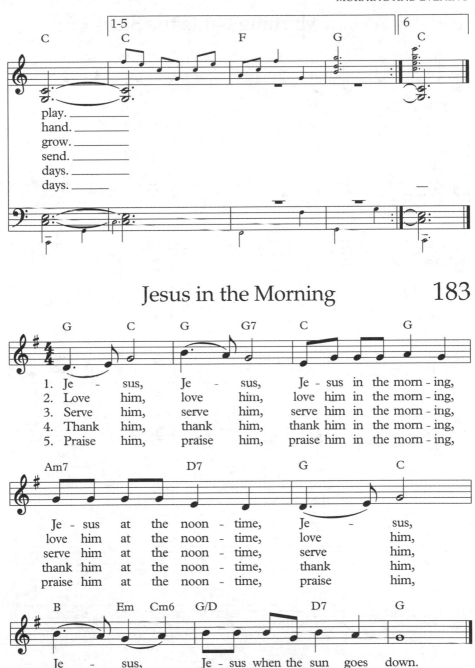

play. _____
hand. _____
grow. _____
send. _____
days. _____
days. _____

Jesus in the Morning   183

1. Je - sus, Je - sus, Je - sus in the morn - ing,
2. Love him, love him, love him in the morn - ing,
3. Serve him, serve him, serve him in the morn - ing,
4. Thank him, thank him, thank him in the morn - ing,
5. Praise him, praise him, praise him in the morn - ing,

Je - sus at the noon - time, Je - sus,
love him at the noon - time, love him,
serve him at the noon - time, serve him,
thank him at the noon - time, thank him,
praise him at the noon - time, praise him,

Je - sus, Je - sus when the sun goes down.
love him, love him when the sun goes down.
serve him, serve him when the sun goes down.
thank him, thank him when the sun goes down.
praise him, praise him when the sun goes down.

WORDS: Traditional
MUSIC: Traditional

SUNDOWN

184 When Morning Gilds the Skies

WORDS: *Katholisches Gesangbuch;* sts. 1, 2, 4 by Edward Caswall;
st. 3 by Robert S. Bridges
MUSIC: Joseph Barnby

LAUDES DOMINI
666.666

This Day God Gives Me

1. This day God gives me strength of high heav - ven,
2. This day God sends me strength as my guar - dian,
3. God's way is my way, God's shield is round me,
4. Ris - ing, I thank you, migh - ty and strong One,

sun and moon shin - ing, flame in my hearth, ___
might to up - hold me, wis - dom as guide. ___
God's host de - fends me, sav - ing from ill. ___
King of cre - a - tion, giv - er of rest, ___

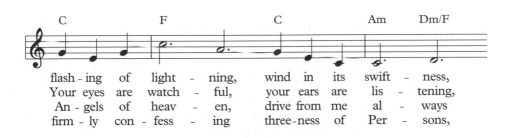

flash - ing of light - ning, wind in its swift - ness,
Your eyes are watch - ful, your ears are lis - tening,
An - gels of heav - en, drive from me al - ways
firm - ly con - fess - ing three-ness of Per - sons,

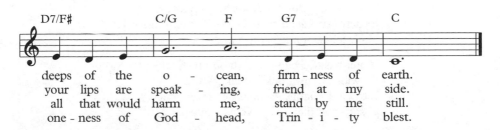

deeps of the o - cean, firm - ness of earth.
your lips are speak - ing, friend at my side.
all that would harm me, stand by me still.
one - ness of God - head, Trin - i - ty blest.

WORDS: Adapt. from "St. Patrick's Breastplate," by James Quinn, SJ
MUSIC: Trad. Gaelic melody

BUNESSAN
54.54 D

186 Morning Has Broken

1. Morning has broken like the first morning,
   blackbird has spoken like the first bird.
   Praise for the singing! Praise for the morning!
   Praise for them, springing fresh from the Word!

2. Sweet the rain's new fall sunlit from heaven,
   like the first dewfall on the first grass.
   Praise for the sweetness of the wet garden,
   sprung in completeness where his feet pass.

3. Mine is the sunlight! Mine is the morning
   born of the one light Eden saw play!
   Praise with elation, praise every morning,
   God's re-creation of the new day.

Sing to BUNESSAN, No. 185

Eleanor Farjeon

By permission of David Higham Associates Ltd.

187 Water Has Held Us
(A Song of Baptism)

1. Water has held us, moved by creation.
   Out of dark chaos, broke forth the light.
   Up from the deluge, showing God's promise,
   has come a rainbow, gladdening sight.

2. Water has saved us, as the sea parted
   for Israel's children, walled on each side.
   This love has led us, helped us in trouble,
   on far horizon, God's cloud our guide.

3. Water has cleansed us, bathed with forgiveness,
   has, with clear blessing, washed sin away.
   Jordan's strong currents God's Son announcing,
   made a beginning, baptismal day.

4. Water has touched us, fresh on our foreheads,
   showing an inward, spiritual grace.
   Into God's family we have been welcomed,
   as sons and daughters, we take our place.

Sing to BUNESSAN, No. 185

R. Deane Postlethwaite

© 1980 Marjean Postlethwaite

Praise and Thanksgiving   188

1. Praise and thanksgiving, now we would offer
   for all things living, created good:
   Harvest of sown fields, fruits of the orchard,
   hay from the mown fields, blossom and wood.

2. Bless, Lord, the labor we bring to serve you,
   that with our neighbor we may be fed.
   Sowing or tilling, we would work with you,
   harvesting, milling for daily bread.

3. You are providing food for your children,
   by your wise guiding, teach us to share
   one with another, so that, rejoicing
   with us, all others may know your care.

4. Then will your blessing reach ev'ry people,
   freely confessing your gracious hand.
   Where all obey you, no one will hunger;
   in your love's sway you nourish the land.

Sing to BUNESSAN, No. 185

Albert F. Bayly, alt.
© Oxford University Press

Touch the Earth Lightly   189

1. Touch the earth lightly, use the earth gently,
   nourish the life of the world in our care:
   gift of great wonder, ours to surrender,
   trust for the children tomorrow will bear.

2. We who endanger, who create hunger,
   agents of death for all creatures that live,
   we who would foster clouds of disaster,
   God of our planet, forestall and forgive!

3. Let there be greening, birth from the burning,
   water that blesses and air that is sweet,
   health in God's garden, hope in God's children,
   regeneration that peace will complete.

4. God of all living, God of all loving,
   God of the seedling, the snow and the sun,
   teach us, deflect us, Christ re-connect us,
   using us gently and making us one.

Sing to BUNESSAN, No. 185

Shirley Erena Murray
Words © 1992 Hope Publishing Co.

190 God, Who Made the Earth and Heaven

1. God, who made the earth and heav-en, dark-ness, and light,
2. When the con-stant sun re-turn-ing un-seals our eyes,

who the day for toil has giv-en, for rest the night,
may we, born a-new like morn-ing, to la-bor rise;

may your an-gels guard, de-fend us, slum-ber sweet your mer-cy send us,
fit us for the task that calls us, let not ease and self en-thrall us,

ho-ly dreams and hopes at-tend us, all through the night.
strong through you what-e'er be-fall us, O God, most wise!

WORDS: St. 1 by Reginald Heber; st. 2 by Frederick J. Hosmer
MUSIC: Trad. Welsh melody

AR HYD Y NOS

Day Is Done

1. Day is done, but Love unfailing dwells ever here;
   shadows fall, but hope prevailing calms every fear.
   Loving Parent, none forsaking, take our hearts, of Love's own making,
   watch our sleeping, guard our waking, be always near!

2. Dark descends, but Light unending shines through our night.
   You are with us, ever lending new strength to sight.
   One in love, your truth confessing, one in hope of heaven's blessing,
   may we see, in love's possessing, Love's endless light!

3. Eyes will close, but you, unsleeping, watch by our side.
   Death may come: In Love's safekeeping still we abide.
   God of love, all evil quelling, sin forgiving, fear dispelling,
   stay with us, our hearts indwelling, this eventide!

Sing to AR HYD Y NOS, No. 190

James Quinn, SJ
© James Quinn, SJ, admin. by Selah Publishing Co., Inc.

Morning Dawns and Love Awakens   192

1. Morning dawns and love awakens, new day is here.
   Tender blossoms, long forgotten, op'n without fear.
   Now we're graced and now forgiven, now we're blessed and joy is given,
   walking on in peace and beauty, God's radiance here.

2. Day unfolds with tasks and duties, God's presence near.
   People come and work accomplished, hope fashioned here.
   Work and play are weaved together, word and silence dance forever,
   each new day is filled with wonder, God's love made clear.

3. Let us gather 'round the table, touch holiness.
   Meals are shared and stories told now, through each we're blessed.
   Silent host is always near us, breaking bread to calm and feed us,
   ordinary gifts surround us, D'vine love expressed.

Sing to AR HYD Y NOS, No. 190

Larry J. Peacock
© 1992 Larry J. Peacock

193 For the Fruit of All Creation

1. For the fruit of all creation, thanks be to God.
   For the gifts of every nation, thanks be to God.
   For the plowing, sowing, reaping, silent growth while we are sleeping,
   future needs in earth's safekeeping, thanks be to God.

2. In the just reward of labor, God's will is done.
   In the help we give our neighbor, God's will is done.
   In our worldwide talk of caring for the hungry and despairing,
   in the harvests we are sharing, God's will is done.

3. For the harvests of the Spirit, thanks be to God.
   For the good we all inherit, thanks be to God.
   For the wonders that astound us, for the truths that still confound us,
   most of all, that love has found us, thanks be to God.

Sing to AR HYD Y NOS, No. 190

Fred Pratt Green
© 1970 Hope Publishing Co.

194 Go, My Children, with My Blessing

1. Go, my children, with my blessing, never alone.
   Waking, sleeping, I am with you; you are my own.
   In my love's baptismal river I have made you mine forever.
   Go, my children, with my blessing—you are my own.

2. Go, my children, sins forgiven, at peace and pure.
   Here you learned how much I love you, what I can cure.
   Here you heard my dear Son's story; here you touched him, saw his glory.
   Go, my children, sins forgiven, at peace and pure.

3. Go, my children, fed and nourished, closer to me;
   grow in love and love by serving, joyful and free.
   Here my Spirit's power filled you, here his tender comfort stilled you.
   Go, my children, fed and nourished, joyful and free.

4. I, the Lord, will bless and keep you and give you peace;
   I, the Lord, will smile upon you and give you peace:
   I, the Lord, will be your Savior, Comforter, and Friend, and Brother.
   Go, my children, I will keep you and give you peace.

Sing to AR HYD Y NOS, No. 190

Jaroslav J. Vajda, alt.
© 1983 Jaroslav J. Vajda

Through the Love of God Our Savior 195

1. Through the love of God our Savior all will be well.
   Free and changeless is God's favor; all, all is well.
   Precious is the blood that healed us, perfect is the grace that sealed us,
   strong the hand stretched forth to shield us; all must be well.

2. Though we pass through tribulation, all will be well.
   Ours is such a full salvation; all, all is well.
   Happy still in God confiding, fruitful, if in Christ abiding,
   holy, through the Spirit's guiding; all must be well.

3. We expect a bright tomorrow; all will be well.
   Faith can sing through days of sorrow, "All, all is well."
   On our Father's love relying, Jesus every need supplying,
   or in living or in dying, all must be well.

Sing to AR HYD Y NOS, No. 190

Mary B. Peters

Lord, We Come to Ask Your Healing 196

1. Lord, we come to ask your healing, teach us of love;
   all unspoken shame revealing, teach us of love.
   Take our selfish thoughts and actions, petty feuds, divisive factions,
   hear us now, to you appealing, teach us of love.

2. Soothe away our pain and sorrow, hold us in love;
   grace we cannot buy or borrow, hold us in love.
   Though we seek but dark and danger, though we spurn both friend and stranger,
   though we often dread tomorrow, hold us in love.

3. When the bread is raised and broken, fill us with love;
   words of consecration spoken, fill us with love.
   As our grateful prayers continue, make the faith that we have in you
   more than just an empty token, fill us with love.

4. Help us live for one another, bind us in love;
   stranger, neighbor, father, mother—bind us in love.
   All are equal at your table, through your Spirit make us able
   to embrace as sister, brother, bind us in love.

Sing to AR HYD Y NOS, No. 190

Jean Holloway
© 1995 Kevin Mayhew, Ltd.

197 O Christ, You Are the Light and Day

1. O Christ, you are the light and day that
2. As now the eve-ning shad-ows fall, please

drives a-way the night, the ev-er-shin-ing
grant us, Lord, we pray, a qui-et night to

Sun of God and pledge of fu-ture light.
rest in you un-til the break of day.

WORDS: Latin hymn; trans. by Frank C. Quinn
MUSIC: William Croft
Trans. © 1981 St. Dominic Priory

ST. ANNE
CM

198 Hymn to the Trinity
(Creator God, Creating Still)

1. Creator God, creating still, by will and word and deed,
   create a new humanity to meet the present need.

2. Redeemer God, redeeming still, with overflowing grace,
   pour out your love on us, through us, make this a holy place.

Sing to ST. ANNE, No. 197

Jane Parker Huber
© 1980 Jane Parker Huber

3. Sustainer God, sustaining still, with strength for every day,
   empow'r us now to do your will, correct us when we stray.

4. Great Trinity, for this new day we need your presence still.
   Create, redeem, sustain us now to do your work and will.

The Care the Eagle Gives Her Young 199

1. The care the eagle gives her young, safe in her lofty nest,
   is like the tender love of God for us made manifest.

2. As when the time to venture comes, she stirs them out to flight,
   so we are pressed to boldly try to strive for daring height.

3. And if we flutter helplessly, as fledgling eagles fall,
   beneath us lift God's mighty wings to bear us, one and all.

Sing to ST. ANNE, No. 197

R. Deane Postlethwaite (Deut. 32:11)
Words used by permission of Marjean Postlethwaite

O God, Our Help in Ages Past 200

1. O God, our help in ages past, our hope for years to come,
   our shelter from the stormy blast, and our eternal home!

2. Under the shadow of thy throne, still may we dwell secure;
   sufficient is thine arm alone, and our defense is sure.

3. Before the hills in order stood, or earth received her frame,
   from everlasting, thou art God, to endless years the same.

4. A thousand ages in thy sight, are like an evening gone;
   short as the watch that ends the night, before the rising sun.

5. Time, like an ever rolling stream, bears all who breathe away;
   they fly forgotten, as a dream dies at the opening day.

6. O God, our help in ages past, our hope for years to come;
   be thou our guide while life shall last, and our eternal home.

Sing to ST. ANNE, No. 197

Isaac Watts (Ps. 90)

201 God of Day and God of Darkness

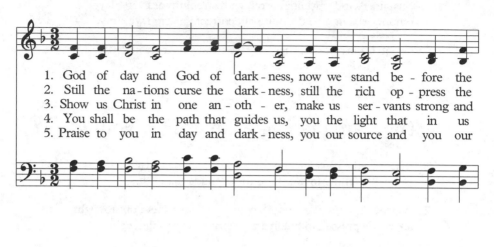

1. God of day and God of dark-ness, now we stand be-fore the
2. Still the na-tions curse the dark-ness, still the rich op-press the
3. Show us Christ in one an-oth-er, make us ser-vants strong and
4. You shall be the path that guides us, you the light that in us
5. Praise to you in day and dark-ness, you our source and you our

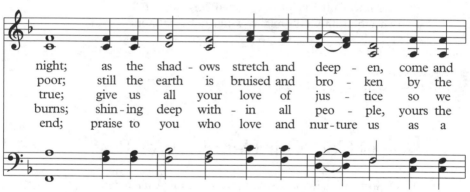

night;   as the shad-ows stretch and deep-en, come and
poor;   still the earth is bruised and bro-ken by the
true;   give us all your love of jus-tice so we
burns;   shin-ing deep with-in all peo-ple, yours the
end;   praise to you who love and nur-ture us as a

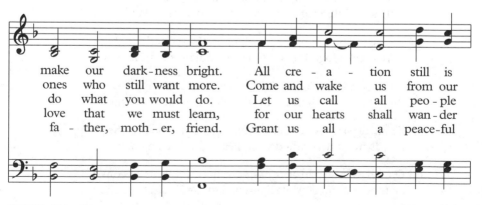

make our dark-ness bright.   All cre-a-tion still is
ones who still want more.   Come and wake us from our
do what you would do.   Let us call all peo-ple
love that we must learn,   for our hearts shall wan-der
fa-ther, moth-er, friend.   Grant us all a peace-ful

WORDS: Marty Haugen
MUSIC: Attr. to B. F. White; harm. by Ronald A. Nelson

BEACH SPRING
87.87 D

groan - ing for the dawn - ing of your might, when the
sleep - ing, so our hearts can - not ig - nore all your
ho - ly, let us pledge our hearts a - new, make us
rest - less 'til they safe to you re - turn; find - ing
rest - ing, let each mind and bod - y mend, so we

Sun of peace and jus - tice fills the earth with ra - diant light.
peo - ple lost and bro - ken, all your chil - dren at our door.
one with all the low - ly, let us all be one in you.
you in one an - oth - er, we shall all your face dis - cern.
rise re-freshed to - mor - row, hearts re-newed to King-dom tend.

Come Away from Rush and Hurry 202

1. Come away from rush and hurry to the stillness of God's peace;
   from our vain ambition's worry, come to Christ and find release.
   Come away from noise and clamor, life's demands and frenzied pace;
   come to join the people gathered here to seek and find God's face.

2. In the pastures of God's goodness we lie down to rest our soul.
   From the waters of God's mercy we drink deeply, are made whole.
   At the table of God's presence all the saints are richly fed.
   With the oil of God's anointing into service we are led.

3. Come, then, children, with your burdens—life's confusions, fears, and pain.
   Leave them at the cross of Jesus; take instead his kingdom's reign.
   Bring your thirsts, for Christ will quench them— Christ alone will satisfy,
   all our longings find attainment when to self we gladly die.

Sing to BEACH SPRING, No. 201

Marva J. Dawn
© 1999 Marva J. Dawn

203   Loving Spirit

1. Loving Spirit, loving Spirit,
   you have chosen me to be—
   you have drawn me to your wonder,
   you have set your sign on me.

2. Like a mother you enfold me,
   hold my life within your own,
   feed me with your very body,
   form me of your flesh and bone.

3. Like a father you protect me,
   teach me the discerning eye,
   hoist me up upon your shoulder,
   let me see the world from high.

4. Friend and lover, in your closeness
   I am known and held and blessed:
   In your promise is your comfort,
   in your presence I may rest.

5. Loving Spirit, loving Spirit,
   you have chosen me to be—
   you have drawn me to your wonder,
   you have set your sign on me.

May be sung to BEACH SPRING, No. 201, by combining sts. 1–2 and sts. 3–4, and omitting st. 5.

Shirley Erena Murray

© 1987 The Hymn Society, admin. by Hope Publishing Co.

204   Lord, Whose Love Through Humble Service

1. Lord, whose love through humble service bore the weight of human need,
   who upon the cross, forsaken, offered mercy's perfect deed:
   We, your servants, bring the worship not of voice alone, but heart,
   consecrating to your purpose every gift that you impart.

2. Still your children wander homeless; still the hungry cry for bread;
   still the captives long for freedom; still in grief we mourn our dead.
   As, O Lord, your deep compassion healed the sick and freed the soul,
   use the love your Spirit kindles still to save and make us whole.

3. As we worship, grant us vision, till your love's revealing light
   in its height and depth and greatness dawns upon our quickened sight,
   making known the needs and burdens your compassion bids us bear,
   stirring us to tireless striving your abundant life to share.

4. Called by worship to your service, forth in your dear name we go
   to the child, the youth, the aged, love in living deeds to show;
   hope and health, good will and comfort, counsel, aid, and peace we give,
   that your servants, Lord, in freedom may your mercy know, and live.

Sing to BEACH SPRING, No. 201

Albert F. Bayly, alt.

© 1961 Oxford University Press

Incarnation 205

1. Who is this whose silent advent summons mortals now to see?
   Word of God made flesh in secret, wisdom of eternity.
   Stand amazed as you behold him: Paradox of God's design.
   Lord transcendent, yet incarnate: Fully human and divine!

2. Reason cracks; it cannot hold him. God and man enfleshed as one!
   Faith alone, mind's transformation, leads us to embrace the Son.
   God's abode enclosed no longer, by the cult to temple tied.
   Holiness is loosed among us, all creation sanctified!

3. Harbinger of final triumph, infant born in Bethlehem;
   come in fullness now to save us, break into our lives again!
   Stand amazed as you behold him: Paradox of God's design.
   Lord transcendent, yet incarnate: Fully human and divine!

Sing to BEACH SPRING, No. 201

Lynn M. Labs
© 2004 Lynn M. Labs

Wisdom's Table 206

1. In her house there is a table, richly laid with bread and wine.
   All the foolish are invited; she calls to us, "Come and dine."
   Come and eat at Wisdom's table, come and lay your burdens down;
   come and learn the power of weakness—Wisdom's cross and Wisdom's crown.

2. In this world we will have trouble and our comforters will fail;
   all our answers will seem useless, all our hopes will seem unreal.
   Come and eat at Wisdom's table, come and lay your burdens down;
   come and learn the power of weakness—Wisdom's cross and Wisdom's crown.

3. There are roads which lead to danger, there are paths which lead to life:
   Wisdom's ways are filled with choices for the travelers she invites.
   Come and eat at Wisdom's table, come and lay your burdens down;
   come and learn the power of weakness—Wisdom's cross and Wisdom's crown.

4. There are those who search for reasons, there are those who look for signs;
   Wisdom dances on the tombstone of the fool who bled and died.
   Come and eat at Wisdom's table, come and lay your burdens down;
   come and learn the power of weakness—Wisdom's cross and Wisdom's crown.

Sing to BEACH SPRING, No. 201

Doug Gay
© 1998 Doug Gay

207 Now, on Land and Sea Descending

1. Now, on land and sea descending, brings the night its
peace profound; let our vesper hymn be blending
with the holy calm around. Jubilate!
Jubilate! Jubilate! Amen!

2. Soon as dies the sunset glory, stars of heaven shine
out above, telling still the ancient story,
their Creator's changeless love. Come rejoice now,
raise your voices, sing God's praises! Amen!

3. Now, our wants and burdens leaving to God's care who
cares for all, cease we fearing, cease we grieving:
touched by God our burdens fall. Come rejoice now,
raise your voices, sing God's praises! Amen!

4. As the darkness deepens o'er us, lo! eternal
stars arise; hope and faith and love rise glorious,
shining in the Spirit's skies. Jubilate!
Jubilate! Jubilate! Amen!

WORDS: Samuel Longfellow, alt.
MUSIC: *A Selection of Popular National Airs*

VESPER HYMN
87.87.86.87

Let our ves - per hymn be blend - ing
Tell - ing still the an - cient sto - ry,
Cease we fear - ing, cease we griev - ing:
Hope and faith and love rise glo - rious,

with the ho - ly calm a - round.
their Cre - a - tor's change - less love.
at God's touch our bur - dens fall.
shin - ing in the Spir - it's skies.

A Prayer at the End of the Day 208

O Lord, support us all the day long,
    until the shadows lengthen and the evening comes,
    and the busy world is hushed, and the fever of life is over,
    and our work is done.
Then, Lord, in your mercy grant us a safe lodging,
    and a holy rest, and peace at the last;
    through Jesus Christ our Lord.

Attr. to John Henry Cardinal Newman

209

New Every Morning

1. New ev - ery morn - ing is the love our
2. New mer - cies, each re - turn - ing day, hov -
3. The tri - vial round, the com - mon task, will
4. On - ly, O Lord, in thy dear love fit

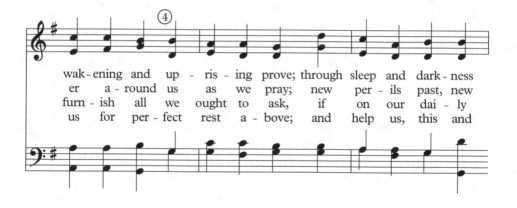

wak - ening and up - ris - ing prove; through sleep and dark - ness
er a - round us as we pray; new per - ils past, new
furn - ish all we ought to ask, if on our dai - ly
us for per - fect rest a - bove; and help us, this and

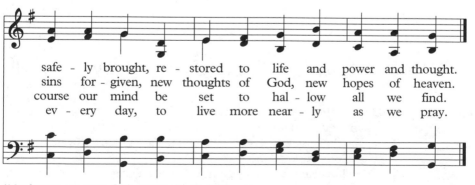

safe - ly brought, re - stored to life and power and thought.
sins for - given, new thoughts of God, new hopes of heaven.
course our mind be set to hal - low all we find.
ev - ery day, to live more near - ly as we pray.

May be sung as a canon. Omit accompaniment, singing unison.

WORDS: John Keble
MUSIC: Thomas Tallis

TALLIS' CANON
LM
Alternate tune: CONDITOR ALME SIDERUM, No. 217

As Pilgrims on Our Way 210

1. Can we, as pilgrims on our way,
   confess our faith in God today
   as we recall from journeys past
   the signs that held our purpose fast?

2. When we have used the gift of prayer
   we've known, in quiet, God was there.
   With others we have joined in praise
   and felt, with joy, our spirits blaze.

3. When we have seen compassion shown,
   we have believed it was God's own.
   Creative moments, bright and rare,
   made new beginnings everywhere.

4. Through scripture understanding grew;
   God's story was our story too.
   Glory we saw through other eyes.
   Examples came in splendid lives.

5. We will, as pilgrims on our way,
   confess our faith in God today;
   for we recall from journeys past
   the signs that held our purpose fast.

Sing to TALLIS' CANON, No. 209 or CONDITOR ALME SIDERUM, No. 217

R. Deane Postlethwaite

© 1980 Marjean Postlethwaite

O Splendor of God's Glory Bright 211

1. O Splendor of God's glory bright,
   from light eternal bringing light,
   O Light of life, life's living Spring,
   true Day, all days illumining.

2. Come, very Sun of heaven's love,
   in lasting radiance from above,
   and pour the Holy Spirit's ray
   on all we think or do today.

3. Confirm our will to do the right,
   and keep our hearts from envy's blight;
   let faith her eager fires renew,
   and hate the false, and love the true.

4. O joyful be the passing day
   with thoughts as clear as morning's ray,
   with faith like noontime shining bright,
   our souls unshadowed by the night.

5. Dawn's glory gilds the earth and skies,
   let him, our perfect Morn, arise,
   the Word in God Creator one,
   our Parent imaged in the Son.

Sing to TALLIS' CANON, No. 209 or CONDITOR ALME SIDERUM, No. 217

Ambrose of Milan, alt.

Happy the One 212

Happy the one, to whom 'tis given,
to eat the Bread of Life in heaven:
This happiness in Christ we prove,
who feed on his forgiving love.

Sing to TALLIS' CANON, No. 209 or CONDITOR ALME SIDERUM, No. 217

Charles Wesley

213

All Praise to You

1. All praise to you, O God, this night
   for all the blessings of the light,
   keep us, we pray, O King of kings,
   beneath your own almighty wings.

2. Forgive us, Lord, through Christ your Son,
   whatever wrong this day we've done;
   your peace, give to the world, O Lord,
   that all might live in one accord.

3. Enlighten us, O blessed Light,
   and give us rest throughout this night.
   O strengthen us, that for your sake,
   we all may serve you when we wake.

Sing to TALLIS' CANON, No. 209 or CONDITOR ALME SIDERUM, No. 217

Thomas Ken, alt.

214

O Holy One
(A Doxology)

1. O Holy One in whom we live,
   in whom we are, in whom we move,
   all glory, laud, and praise receive
   for your creating, steadfast love.

2. Come, Holy Spirit, and inspire,
   enlighten with celestial fire;
   impart your grace, our souls unite,
   renew the dullness of our sight.

3. All praise to God, the Three-in-One,
   all glory to our Christ, the Son,
   and to the Spirit, Holy Power,
   we give our thanks in this glad hour.

4. Alleluia, alleluia,
   alleluia, alleluia,
   alleluia, alleluia,
   alleluia, amen, amen.

Sing to TALLIS' CANON, No. 209 or CONDITOR ALME SIDERUM, No. 217

Compiled from various ancient sources by Elise S. Eslinger

O Radiant Light
(*Phos Hileron*)

215

1. O radiant light of Light, outpoured
   eternal brightness, blest, adored,
   from God the Father, holy Lord.
   Alleluia, alleluia.

2. The darkness falls, but here we see
   the evening lights; on bended knee
   we praise you, holy Trinity.
   Alleluia, alleluia.

3. Life-giving Son of God, your ways
   lighten the nations, thus we raise
   to you, Most Worthy, songs of praise.
   Alleluia, alleluia.

Sing to TALLIS' CANON, No. 209 or CONDITOR ALME SIDERUM, No. 217

Greek hymn, adapt. by Arlo Duba
Adapt. © 1983 Arlo Duba

God of the Morning and of Night

216

1. God of the morning and of night,
   we thank you for your gift of light;
   as in the dawn the shadows fly,
   we seem to find you now more nigh.

2. Fresh hopes have wakened in the heart,
   fresh force to do our daily part;
   in peaceful sleep our strength restore,
   throughout the day to serve you more.

3. O Lord of light, your love alone
   can make our human hearts your own;
   be ever with us, Lord, that we
   your blessed face one day may see.

4. Praise God, our maker and our friend;
   praise God, through time, till time shall end;
   till psalm and song Christ's name adore,
   through heav'n's great day of evermore.

Sing to TALLIS' CANON, No. 209 or CONDITOR ALME SIDERUM, No. 217

Francis Turner Palgrave, alt.

217 Now That the Daylight Fills the Sky

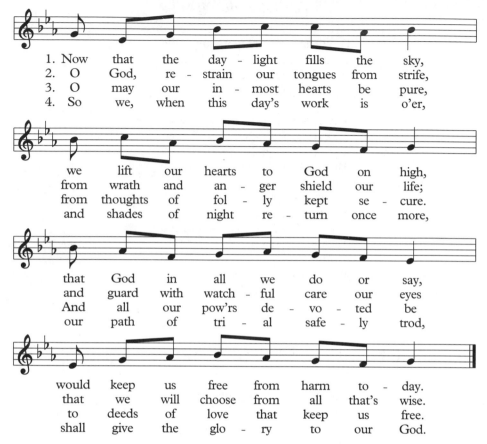

1. Now that the day-light fills the sky,
2. O God, re-strain our tongues from strife,
3. O may our in-most hearts be pure,
4. So we, when this day's work is o'er,

we lift our hearts to God on high,
from wrath and an-ger shield our life;
from thoughts of fol-ly kept se-cure.
and shades of night re-turn once more,

that God in all we do or say,
and guard with watch-ful care our eyes
And all our pow'rs de-vo-ted be
our path of tri-al safe-ly trod,

would keep us free from harm to-day.
that we will choose from all that's wise.
to deeds of love that keep us free.
shall give the glo-ry to our God.

WORDS: *Jam lucis orto sidere*, 8th cent.; trans. by John Mason Neale, et al.
MUSIC: Plainsong, Mode IV

CONDITOR ALME SIDERUM
LM

Trans. © 1981 International Committee on English in the Liturgy, Inc.; admin. by ELLC

Alternate tune: TALLIS' CANON

218 Creator of the Stars of Night

1. Creator of the stars of night,
   thy people's everlasting light,
   O Christ, the Savior of us all,
   we pray thee, hear us when we call.

2. Praise God from whom all blessings flow.
   Praise God, all creatures here below.
   Praise God, above, you heavenly hosts.
   Praise Father, Son, and Holy Ghost.

Sing to CONDITOR ALME SIDERUM, No. 217 or TALLIS' CANON, No. 209

WORDS: St. 1, 9th cent. Latin, trans. from *The Hymnal, 1940,* alt.; 2: Thomas Ken, alt.
Trans. © 1940 The Church Pension Fund

When Evening Falls and Labors Cease 219

1. When evening falls and labors cease,
   we turn to you in quiet peace,
   with grateful hearts for blessings past
   and hope for future joys that last.

2. As dawn will surely follow night,
   so shall you make our darkness light.
   New warmth will breathe upon our land;
   new life shall spring from Love's own hand.

3. Like birds returning to their nest,
   we find in your strong arms our rest.
   And as we sleep you will restore
   our health and strength and joy once more.

Sing to CONDITOR ALME SIDERUM, No. 217 or TALLIS' CANON, No. 209

Delores Dufner, OSB

A Prayer at Day's Beginning 220

Loving God, I desire only your will,
   nothing more, nothing less,
   and nothing else.
Guide my preparation and my actions
   so that my prayer can be answered. **Amen.**

Rueben P. Job

221 In the Quiet Curve of Evening

1. In the qui - et curve of eve - ning, in the sink - ing of the
2. In the rests be - tween the phras - es, in the cracks be - tween the
3. In the mys - tery of the hun - gers, in the si - lence of my

days, in the silk - y void of dark - ness, you are
stars, in the gaps be - tween the mean - ing, you are
rooms, in the cloud of my un - know - ing, you are

there._____ In the lap - ses of my
there._____ In the melt - ing down of
there._____ In the emp - ty cave of

breath - ing, in the space be - tween my ways, in the
end - ings, in the cool - ing of the sun, in the
griev - ing, in the des - ert of my dreams, in the

cra - ter carved by sad - ness, you are there._____
sol - stice of the win - ter, you are there._____ You are
tun - nel of my sor - row, you are there._____

there, you are there, you are there._____

WORDS: Juliana Howard
MUSIC: Juliana Howard
© 1993 Juliana Howard

YOU ARE THERE
Irregular with Refrain

Psalms

Deep and Wide: The Song of the Psalms

Each new generation of worshipers in the Judeo-Christian heritage is offered a unique, enduring gift that some have aptly named a "school" of prayer: the Psalter, an emotive range and depth that bring us near to the listening heart of God. Our prayer through the Psalms expresses personal thoughts and feelings, to be sure, but always, as well, wings its way toward God in solidarity with the human condition of countless neighbors of all times and places.

Such emotionally honest, ancient-new poetry undergirds and stretches our personal and communal vocabulary for articulating not only praise, thanks, trust, and hope but also longing, anger, confusion, loss, diminishment, and anguish. Joy and sorrow, ecstasy and despair—the poles of our human experience—are nevertheless held together by the Holy One whose steadfast love endures for all generations.

Christian pray-ers trying to live out a baptismal call to "become the Gospel" have yet another reason to receive and be immersed in this great gift of prayer in the Psalms: these prayers are the very ones in which Jesus himself was immersed. Some theologians have observed that the Lord's Prayer summarizes the message of the Psalms. We pray as Jesus did to his *Abba*—we sing with Christ, in the name of Christ, and for the sake of Christ and the world he was sent to save. We also join our Jewish brothers and sisters in praising the God of history who indeed created and redeemed, and most surely, sustains our hope in the fulfillment of the *shalom* intended for all creation.

Such prayer is contained in the poetic texts even if we do not sing them, but how deeply these prayers sink into our souls, touch our emotions, and form us together in praise and lament when they are sung. The *Upper Room Worshipbook Accompaniment and Worship Leader* edition provides special guidance for singing and chanting the Psalm texts, and it includes many cantor parts and all accompaniments. An abundance of psalm prayers are offered as well.

Whatever else might be said, the important word is this: You are invited to sing these prayers. Through praising and lamenting, rejoicing and weeping, confessing and experiencing grace in Christ, we approach the throne of God in humility but with confidence of a steadfast love that will never let us go. That is a deep and wide song.

Richard L. Eslinger
Professor of Homiletics and Worship
United Theological Seminary

Psalm 1
(Happy Are They)

Refrain 1

Hap-py are they who de-light, _____ who de - light in the Word of God.

Refrain 2

or

Like a tree that's plant-ed by the wa - ter, we shall not be moved.

Sung or read

1. Hap - py in-deed are they who re - fuse the way of the
2. Joy shall be in the hearts of those who de-light in the
3. They are like green trees that grow by clear flow-ing
4. Thus it is not so, not so with e - vil
5. God up - holds the just, God knows the way of the

e - vil; nor walk the road of the
Word of God; for they con - sume that
wa - ters, they bear their fruit in due
do - ers, they blow like chaff in the
righ - teous, but the e - vil ones shall

sin - ners, or join the mock - ers of God. *(To Vs. 2)*
Word, con - sume it day and night. *(Refrain)*
sea - son, their leaves fade not, they pros - per. *(To Vs. 4)*
wind, they fall by weight of the Truth. *(Refrain)*
per - ish, they per - ish by their deeds. *(Refrain)*

Stanzas of No. 224 may be substituted for these verses using either of the refrains.

WORDS: Verses and refrain 1 trans. by Hal H. Hopson, alt.; refrain 2 African American spiritual
MUSIC: Verses and refrain 1 by Hal H. Hopson; refrain 2 African American spiritual
Verses and refrain 1 © 1982 Hope Publishing Co.

Psalm 1
(Happy Is the One)

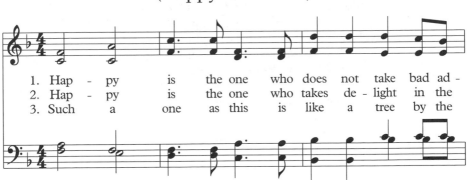

1. Hap - py   is   the one   who does   not   take   bad ad -
2. Hap - py   is   the one   who takes de - light in the
3. Such   a   one as this   is   like a   tree by the

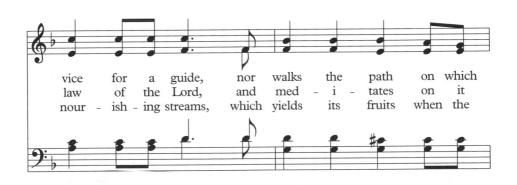

vice   for   a   guide,   nor   walks   the   path   on which
law   of   the Lord,   and   med - i - tates   on   it
nour - ish - ing streams, which yields its   fruits when the

sin - ners have trod,   nor sits where the   cy - nics mock.
both day and night,   and pros - pers in ev - ery way.
sea - son is right   and bears leaves that nev - er fade.

WORDS: John L. Bell
MUSIC: John L. Bell

© 1993 Iona Community, Scotland; by GIA Publications, Inc., exclusive North American agent

225

Psalm Prayer (Ps. 1)

Teach us your ways, God of Wisdom,
for you are righteous and just.
Plant your Word in our hearts, water it
from the streams of your everflowing mercy,
that it may bloom and produce in us
the fruit that is a blessing to you
and pleasing in your sight. **Amen.**

Ps. 1; adapt. by Douglas Mills
Adapt. © 2006 Upper Room Books

226

Psalm 5
(Lead Me, Lord)

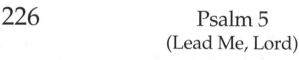

Lead me, Lord, lead me in thy righ-teous-ness;

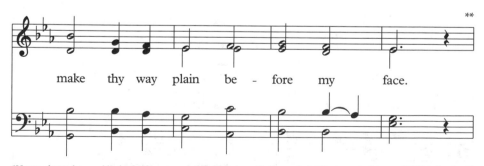

make thy way plain be - fore my face.

Verses chanted or read by leader from translation of choice; refrain may be used as a sung "prayer for illumination."
**Optional ending*

WORDS: Pss. 5:8; 4:8
MUSIC: Samuel Sebastian Wesley

For it is thou, Lord, thou, Lord, on - ly, that

mak - est me dwell in safe - ty.

Psalm Prayer (Ps. 5) 227

O Great Protector, watch over us this day,
    shield us from sin, and direct us toward your righteousness.
Showered with the abundance of your steadfast love,
    we will live for you. **Amen.**

Ps. 5; adapt. by Jo Hoover
Adapt. © 2006 Upper Room Books

Psalm Prayer (Ps. 5) 228

As the sun rises, so does our prayer, loving God.
With each new dawn, renew our trust in you,
    our delight to do justice,
    and our gladness to be in your presence. **Amen.**

Ps. 5; adapt. by Larry Peacock
Adapt. © 2006 Upper Room Books

Psalm 8
(God, Our God, Your Glorious Name)

1. God, our God, your glo - rious name
2. In - fant voic - es chant your praise,
3. Moon and stars in shin - ing height
4. Who are we that we should share
5. With do - min - ion crowned, we stand

all your won - drous works pro - claim; in the heav'ns with
tell - ing of your glo - rious ways; weak - est means work
night - ly tell their Ma - ker's might; when I view the
in your love and ten - der care, raised to an ex -
o'er the crea - tures of your hand; all to us de -

ra - diant signs ev - er - more your glo - ry shines.
out your will, might - y en - e - mies to still.
heav'ns a - far, then I know how small we are. ⎫
alt - ed height, crowned with hon - or in your sight! ⎬ How
vo - tion yield; in the sea and air and field. ⎭

Refrain may be used as response to alternate translations of Psalm 8 or as a response to other psalms of praise.

WORDS: *The Psalter* (1912), alt.
MUSIC: William F. Sherwin

Refrain

great your name. Ho - ly, ho - ly, ho - ly,

how great your name! Yours the name of match-less worth,

ex - cel-lent in all the earth. How great your name!

Psalm Prayer (Ps. 8)

230

Creator God, how great is your name!
All creation sings of your glory, and so do we.
You have exalted us and crowned us with honor—
 even the infants join stars and moon in singing your praise.
How great, O God, is your name in all the earth! **Amen.**

Ps. 8; adapt. by Richard Eslinger
Adapt. © 2006 Upper Room Books

231

Psalm 8
(O Lord, Our Lord)

1. O Lord, our Lord, throughout the earth how glorious is your name,
   and glorious, too, where unseen heav'ns your majesty proclaim.
   On infant lips, in children's song a strong defense you raise
   to counter enemy and threat, and foil the rebel's ways.

2. When I look up and see the stars which your own fingers made,
   and wonder at the moon and stars, each perfectly displayed,
   then must I ask, "Why do you care? Why love humanity?
   And why keep ev'ry mortal name fixed in your memory?"

3. Yet such as us you made and meant just less than gods to be;
   with honor and with glory, Lord, you crowned humanity.
   And then dominion you bestowed for all made by your hand,
   all sheep and cattle, birds and fish, that move through sea or land.

Sing to RESIGNATION, No. 244

The Iona Community

232

Many and Great

Many and great, O God, are thy things,
Maker of earth and sky.
Thy hands have set the heavens with stars;
thy fingers spread the mountains and plains.
Lo, at thy word the waters were formed;
deep seas obey thy voice.

Grant unto us communion with thee,
thou star abiding one;
come unto us and dwell with us;
with thee are found the gifts of life.
Bless us with life that has no end,
eternal life with thee.

May be sung to LAQUIPARLE, *The United Methodist Hymnal*, No. 148

Joseph R. Renville, para. by Philip Frazier

Psalm 13
(How Long, O Lord)

1. How long, O Lord, will you quite for-get
2. How long, O Lord, must this grief pos-sess my
3. Look now, look now, and an-swer me, my

me? How long, O Lord, will you turn your face from
heart? How long, O Lord, must I lan-guish night and
God; give light, give light lest I sleep the sleep of

me? How long, O Lord, must I suf-fer in my
day? How long, O Lord, shall my en-e-my op-
death. Lest my en - e-mies re - joice at my down-

soul? How long, how long, O Lord?_____
press? How long, how long, O Lord?_____
fall. Look now, look now, O Lord._____

WORDS: John L. Bell (Ps. 13)
MUSIC: John L. Bell

Psalm Prayer (Ps. 13)

O God, though I know that you love me,
    I ache, not feeling your love.
When your presence seems remote,
    I find it hard to believe that you care for me.
In the midst of my pain, give me light, I pray,
    light to see your bountiful goodness. **Amen.**

Ps. 13; adapt. by Jo Hoover

Psalm 16
(You Will Show Me the Path of Life)

Refrain 1

You will show me the path of life, you, my hope and my shel - ter; in your pres - ence is

To Verses

end - less joy, at your side is my home for - ev - er.

or

Refrain 2   *To Verses*

Keep me safe, O God, I take ref - uge in you.

or

Refrain 3   *To Verses*

You are my in - her - i - tance, O Lord.

Verses

1. Faith - ful God   I look to you,   you a - lone my life and
2. From of old you are my her - i - tage,   you, my wis - dom and my
3. So my heart   shall sing for joy,   in your arms I rest se -

WORDS: Marty Haugen (Ps. 16:1-2, 6-8, 9-10); refrain 3 trans. ICEL
MUSIC: Marty Haugen; refrains 2 and 3 adapt. by Diana Kodner

Words © 1988, and music © 1988, 1994 GIA Publications, Inc.; refrain 3 trans. © 1969 ICEL

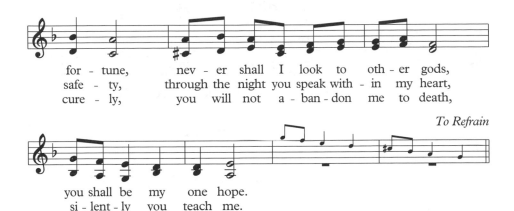

for - tune, | nev - er shall I look to oth - er gods,
safe - ty, | through the night you speak with - in my heart,
cure - ly, | you will not a - ban - don me to death,

To Refrain

you shall be | my | one hope.
si - lent - ly | you | teach me.
you shall not | de - sert | me.

Psalm Prayer (Ps. 16)   236

Indeed, faithful God, you have shown us the path of life
and given us a heritage of unspeakable richness.
You call us now into joyful trust of the future you bring.
We abide in you. **Amen.**

Ps. 16; adapt. by Elise S. Eslinger
Adapt. © 2006 Upper Room Books

We Will Not Keep Silent   237

We are people who must sing you,
　　for the sake of our very lives.
You are a God who must be sung by us,
　　for the sake of your majesty and honor.
And so we thank you,
　　for lyrics that push us past our reasons,
　　for melodies that break open our givens,
　　for cadences that locate us home,
　　　　beyond all our safe places,
　　for tones and tunes that open our lives beyond control
　　　　and our futures beyond despair.

We thank you for the long parade of mothers and fathers
　　who have sung you deep and true;
We thank you for the good company
　　of artists, poets, musicians, cantors, and instruments
　　that sing for us and with us, toward you.
We are witnesses to your mercy and splendor;
We will not keep silent...ever again. Amen.

Walter Brueggemann
© 2003 Augsburg Fortress Publishers

238   Psalm 17

Response

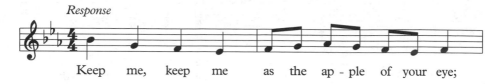

Keep me, keep me as the ap-ple of your eye;

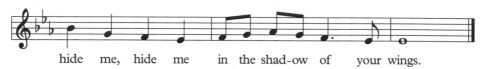

hide me, hide me in the shad-ow of your wings.

Response

(Read responsively)

Hear a just cause, O Lord; attend to my cry.
    Give ear to my prayer from lips free of deceit!
From you let my vindication come!
    Let your eyes see the right!
If you try my heart, if you visit me by night,
    if you test me, you will find no wickedness in me;
    my mouth does not transgress.
Concerning what others do:
    I have avoided the ways of the violent
    by following your word.
My steps have held fast to your paths,
    my feet have not slipped.   *Response*

I call upon you, for you will answer me, O God;
    incline your ear to me, hear my words.
Wondrously show your steadfast love,
    O savior of those who seek refuge
    from their adversaries at your right hand.
As for me, I shall behold your face in righteousness;
    when I awake I shall be satisfied with beholding your presence. *Response*

WORDS: Ps. 17:1-7, 15; response Ps. 17:8
MUSIC: Jane Marshall
Music © 1986 Choristers Guild

239   Psalm Prayer (Ps. 17)

We rest, dear God, in the hope of your love and protection,
    for our help comes from you.
You will not let our feet slip,
    you watch over us day and night,
    you keep us in the safety of your eternal love,
Now and forevermore. **Amen.**

Ps. 17; adapt. by Sheri Daylong
Adapt. © 2006 Upper Room Books

Psalm 19:1-6

Refrain

Glo - ry and praise to God whose word brings life.

Verses

1. The heavens declare the glory of God, re-veal - ing God's handiwork;

one day speaks to another, and night shares its know - ledge with night,

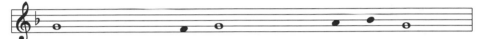

and this without speech or language, their voices are not heard.

To Refrain

But their sound goes out to all the lands, their words to the ends of the earth.

2. In the heavens God has pitched a tent for the sun,

which comes out like a bridegroom from un - der the canopy.

Like an athlete eager for the race it runs its course to the other,

To Refrain

and there is nothing hid from its heat.

WORDS: Ps. 19:1-6
MUSIC: Refrain by Geoffrey Shaw; psalm tones by Elise S. Eslinger

241

Psalm 19:7-14

Refrain

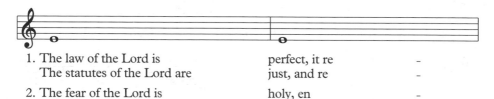

The stat-utes of the Lord are just, and re - joice the heart.

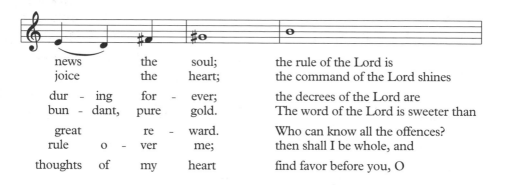

1. The law of the Lord is	perfect, it re -
The statutes of the Lord are	just, and re -
2. The fear of the Lord is	holy, en -
They are more precious than	gold, more than a -
3. By them your servant is guided, in	keeping them there is
Above all, keep your servant from foolish	pride, let it not
4. Let the words of my	mouth, the

news	the	soul;	the rule of the Lord is
joice	the	heart;	the command of the Lord shines
dur - ing	for -	ever;	the decrees of the Lord are
bun - dant,	pure	gold.	The word of the Lord is sweeter than
great	re -	ward.	Who can know all the offences?
rule	o - ver	me;	then shall I be whole, and
thoughts	of	my	heart	find favor before you, O

sure, it makes	wise	the	simple.
clear, it	light - ens	the	eyes. *(to Refrain)*
true, and	all	of	them	righteous.
honey, than honey	fresh	from	the	comb. *(to Refrain)*
Wash me from my	se - cret	wrong -	doing.
innocent of	all	my	trans -	gression. *(to Refrain)*
Lord, my re -	deem - er	and	rock. *(to Refrain)*

WORDS: Ps. 19:7-14
MUSIC: Refrain and psalm tone Hal H. Hopson, alt.
© 1985 Hope Publishing Co.

Psalm Prayer (Ps. 19)

Night and day, all creation declares your glory, holy God.
Yet you call us into covenant
    and reveal your will for our lives.
Your perfect instruction renews life;
    your commands can be trusted.
In humility may we serve you, O Lord,
    our rock and our redeemer. **Amen.**

Ps. 19; adapt. by Richard Eslinger
Adapt. © 2006 Upper Room Books

Why the Psalms Today?

Perhaps,
    if we allow age-old poetry to become personal prayer;
    if we join ourselves to the communion of saints who
        have prayed the psalms throughout the history of the church;
    if we accept the psalter as both proclamation and response;
    if we begin to hear the song of the universe, echoing back
        our own new song;
then,
    we may encounter the God whose *Yes* is contemporary and
        whose goodness overpowers the *No* of the worlds perceived
        without the eyes and ears of the Eternal Singer;
    we may empathize with neighbor, with those who suffer, even
        with Jesus Christ, whose prayer was the psalms
        and in whose name we pray;
    we may recover a grammar of praise, a renewed language
        of sung joy at the goodness of creation;
    we may be startled by a vision of what life totally
        related to God might mean;
    we may discover in songs of trust a God whose *Yes* message
        is answered when we *choose* life over death;
and ultimately,
    we may find radical conversion in ourselves and in our community.

Elise S. Eslinger
© 1981 The Upper Room

Psalm 23
(My Shepherd, You Supply My Need)

1. My shep - herd, you sup - ply my need; and
2. When I walk through the shades of death, your
3. The sure pro - vi - sions of my God at -

Yah - weh is your name. _____ In pas - tures fresh you
pres - ence is my stay; _____ one word of your sup -
tend me all my days; _____ O may your house be

make me feed, be - side the liv - ing stream. _____ You
port - ing breath drives all my fears a - way. _____ Your
my a - bode, and all my work be praise! _____ There

bring my wan - dering spir - it back when I for -
hand, in sight of all my foes, does still my
would I find a set - tled rest (while oth - ers

sake your ways, _____ and lead me for your
ta - ble spread; _____ my cup with bless - ings
go and come), _____ no more a stran - ger

mer - cy's sake in paths of truth and grace. _____
o - ver - flows, your oil a - noints my head. _____
nor a guest; but like a child at home. _____

May be sung to the tune, AMAZING GRACE, No. 135. Each verse requires that the melody be sung through twice.

WORDS: Isaac Watts; adapt. by Mary Ruth Coffman
MUSIC: William Walker's *Southern Harmony*
Words adapt. © 1981 The Upper Room

RESIGNATION
CMD

Psalm 23
(Your Goodness and Love)

Refrain

Your good-ness and love pur-sue me, my shep-herd, my Lord.

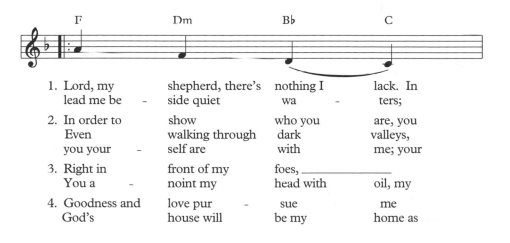

1. Lord, my   shepherd, there's   nothing I   lack. In
   lead me be   –   side quiet   wa   –   ters;

2. In order to   show   who you   are, you
   Even   walking through   dark   valleys,
   you your   –   self are   with   me; your

3. Right in   front of my   foes, _____
   You a   –   noint my   head with   oil, my

4. Goodness and   love pur   –   sue   me
   God's   house will   be my   home as

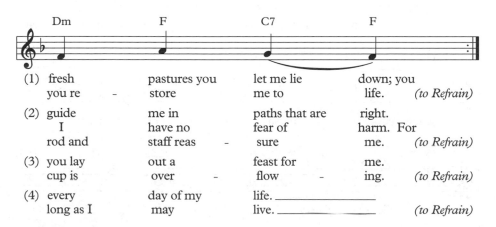

(1) fresh   pastures you   let me lie   down; you
     you re   –   store   me to   life.   *(to Refrain)*

(2) guide   me in   paths that are   right.
     I   have no   fear of   harm. For
     rod and   staff reas   –   sure   me.   *(to Refrain)*

(3) you lay   out a   feast for   me.
     cup is   over   –   flow   –   ing.   *(to Refrain)*

(4) every   day of my   life. _____
     long as I   may   live. _____   *(to Refrain)*

WORDS: Trans. by Gary Chamberlain
MUSIC: Jane Marshall

Trans. and music © 1984 The Upper Room

Psalm 23
(Gentle Shepherd)

WORDS: Fr. Tobias Colgan
MUSIC: Fr. Tobias Colgan
© 1979 St. Meinrad Archabbey

2. You have pre-pared me a ban-quet in the sight of my foes. _____ My head you have a-noint-ed with pre - cious oil, and my cup is o - ver-flow-ing. O

3. Sure-ly good-ness and kind-ness shall fol-low me all my days. _____ In the Lord's own house shall I dwell _____ for - ev - er and ev - er. O

Psalm Prayer (Ps. 23) 247

Blessed are you, Lord Jesus Christ, Good Shepherd of your Church!
In our baptism you anointed us with the oil of salvation,
    and in the Eucharist you spread before us the table of your heavenly bread.
Lead us by your goodness and kindness through the dark valley of death
    to the day that we will dwell forever in the house of your Father. **Amen.**

Ps. 23; adapt. by Lucien Deiss

248

Psalm 25
(To You, O Lord)

Refrain

To you, O Lord, I lift my

soul; to you, I lift my soul. _____

Psalm verses in Upper Room Worshipbook Accompaniment and Worship Leader *edition*

WORDS: Marty Haugen
MUSIC: Marty Haugen
Words © 1969 ICEL; music © 1982 GIA Publications, Inc.

249

Psalm Prayer (Ps. 25)

O God, in you there is shelter and comfort.
Lead us in your truth and teach us your ways.
Your path is steady and sure.
Be our companion, our protector, and our deliverer. **Amen.**

Ps. 25; adapt. by Judy Holloway
Adapt. © 2006 Upper Room Books

Psalm 27
(The Lord Is My Light)

Psalm verses in Upper Room Worshipbook Accompaniment and Worship Leader edition

WORDS: David Haas
MUSIC: David Haas
© 1983 GIA Publications, Inc.

Psalm Prayer (Ps. 27)

251

O God, source of light, salvation, and strength,
    we seek to know you and to serve you, day by day.
Keep us safe from all that would hinder
    as we try to walk in your way.
When difficulties come,
    give us courage to wait for you.
Help us to see your goodness, displayed every day.
Thank you for love beyond comprehension. **Amen.**

Ps. 27; adapt. by Jo Hoover
Adapt. © 2006 Upper Room Books

252

Psalm Prayer (Ps. 27)

Find us, searching God, wherever we hide.
Find us at prayer, sheltered in your grace,
    singing of your light and salvation.
Then, take us with a strong hand
    and lead us on the right path. **Amen.**

Ps. 27; adapt. by Larry Peacock
Adapt. © 2006 Upper Room Books

253

Psalm Prayer (Ps. 30)

Almighty God,
    free us from anxiety over what we cannot control.
Restore our deep trust in you so that we can always rejoice
    and be thankful. **Amen.**

Ps. 30; adapt. by Kyunglim Shin Lee
Adapt. © 2006 Upper Room Books

254

Psalm Prayer (Ps. 30)

Loving God, you have always been our help.
We cry to you and you hear us.
You bring healing to your people
    and deliver us from death.
Our grief you have turned to dancing
    and our sorrow to joy.
Our hearts sing to you, gracious God;
    we will praise you forever. **Amen.**

Ps. 30; adapt. by Richard Eslinger
Adapt. © 1985 The Upper Room

Psalm 30
(You Have Turned Our Sadness)

Refrain

You have turned our sad - ness in - to a joy - ful

1, 2   *To Verses*   3

dance, you are our Lord, our God. God.

Verses

I.*   Lord, I exalt you, for you lift me up,
       and keep my foes from rejoicing over me.
   My God, I cry to you for help,
       it is you who heals me, Lord.
   You brought me up from the grave;
       you restored me to life from among the dead.

II.   Let faithful people sing to the Lord;
       let them praise the holy God,
   whose anger is brief, whose grace is lifelong—
       we weep in the evening but laugh at dawn.   *Refrain*

I.   I, unconcerned, said to myself,
       "I will never stumble."
   You allowed me to stand like a splendid mountain;
       but you hid your face, and I was in terror.

II.   I cried out to you, Lord;
       I sought my Lord's mercy —
   "What will you gain if I die in tears?
       Does dust declare your faithful love?"

I., II.   Lord, you heard, and were gracious to me;
       O Lord, you were my helper.
   You turned my grief into dancing,
       stripped me of sorrow and clothed me with joy.
   So my heart will sing to you, not weep;
       Lord, my God, I will praise you forever.   *Refrain*

*I and II may be read alternately by two leaders, leader and congregation, men and women, etc.

WORDS: Refrain Ps. 30:11*a*; verses trans. by Gary Chamberlain
MUSIC: Elise S. Eslinger

Refrain text adapt. from *Good News Bible*, © American Bible Society; verses trans. © 1984 and music © 1985 The Upper Room

Psalm 31:1-5, 9-16

Refrain

In you, O God, I seek refuge;
do not let me ever be put to shame;
in your righteousness deliver me.
Incline your ear to me;
rescue me speedily.
Be a rock of refuge for me,
a strong fortress to save me.

You are indeed my rock and my fortress;
for your name's sake lead me and
guide me,
take me out of the net that is hidden
for me, for you are my refuge.
Into your hand I commit my spirit;
you have redeemed me, O God,
faithful God. *Refrain*

Be gracious to me, O God, for I am
in distress;
my eye wastes away from grief,
my soul and body also.

For my life is spent with sorrow,
and my years with sighing;
my strength fails because of my
misery, and my bones waste away.

I am the scorn of all my adversaries,
a horror to my neighbors,
an object of dread to my acquaintances;
those who see me in the street flee
from me. *Refrain*

I have passed out of mind like one
who is dead;
I have become like a broken vessel.
For I hear the whispering of many—
terror all around—
as they scheme together against me,
as they plot to take my life.

But I trust in you, O God;
I say, "You are my God."
My times are in your hand;
deliver me from the hand of my
enemies and persecutors.

Let your face shine upon your servant;
save me in your steadfast love. *Refrain*

Refrain 1

Make your face to shine up - on your ser - vant, and

in your lov - ing kind - ness save me.

WORDS: Psalm text, NRSV; Refrain 1, Jay Wilkey; Refrain 2, AnnaMae Meyer Bush
MUSIC: Refrain 1, Jay Wilkey; Refrain 2, AnnaMae Meyer Bush, arr. Kathleen Hart Brumm

CODA *(sung last time only)*

But as for me, I have trust - ed in you, O God.

I have said, "You are my God." My times are in your

hand, O God. You de - liv - er me.

or

Refrain 2

My times are in your hands. You strength-en me in

My times are in your hands. You

strife. My hope is in your Word. Your

strength-en me in strife. My hope is in your

love pre - serves my life. _____

word. Your love pre - serves my life.

257

Psalm 34
(The Cry of the Poor)

Refrain (Melody is in alto part.)

The Lord hears the cry of the poor. Bless-ed be the Lord.

Slightly faster

1. I will bless the Lord at all times, ___ with praise ev-er in my mouth. ___ Let my soul glo-ry in the Lord, ___ who will hear the cry of the poor. ___
2. Let the low-ly hear and be glad: ___ the Lord lis-tens to their pleas; ___ and to hearts bro-ken God is near, ___ who will hear the cry of the poor. ___
3. Ev-ery spir-it crushed, God will save; ___ will be ran-som for their lives; ___ will be safe shel-ter for their fears, ___ and will hear the cry of the poor. ___
4. We pro-claim your great-ness, O God, ___ your praise ev-er in our mouth; ___ ev-ery face bright-ened in God's light, ___ for you hear the cry of the poor. ___

The

WORDS: John Foley, SJ (Ps. 34:2, 3, 17–19, 23)
MUSIC: John Foley, SJ

Psalm 34
(Taste and See)

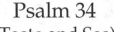

Refrain

Taste and see, taste and see the good-ness of the Lord.___ O taste and see, taste and see the good-ness of the Lord,___ of the Lord.

Verses in Upper Room Worshipbook Accompaniment and Worship Leader *edition*

WORDS: James E. Moore, Jr. (Ps. 34:1-10)
MUSIC: James E. Moore, Jr.

© 1983 GIA Publications, Inc.

Psalm 34

Refrain

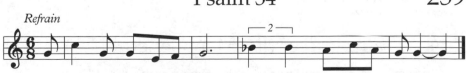

Re-joice, all saints in the Lord; look towards God and be ra-diant!

Cantor verses and accompaniment in Upper Room Worshipbook Accompaniment and Worship Leader *edition*

WORDS: Don E. Saliers (Ps. 34)
MUSIC: Don E. Saliers

© 2005 Don E. Saliers

260   Psalm Prayer (Ps. 34 *or* General Use)

In your compassion, gracious God,
    you hear the cry of the poor, the needy, and the lonely ones.
May we also hear the cries of our brothers and sisters,
    responding in love as you have shown us in your Son,
    our Savior, Jesus Christ. **Amen.**

Ps. 34; adapt. by Elise S. Eslinger
Adapt. © 2006 Upper Room Books

261   Psalm Prayer (Ps. 34 *or* General Use)

We magnify and exalt your name, O God.
We cry to you for help in the midst of suffering,
    brokenness, despair, and fear.
Fill us with an awareness of your redeeming love,
    so that we may taste and see that you are good. **Amen.**

Ps. 34; adapt. by Jo Hoover
Adapt. © 2006 Upper Room Books

262   Psalm Prayer (Ps. 34 *or* General Use)

Gracious God, you hear our prayers, lift our burdens,
    free us from fear and guard us through the day and night.
So shall we praise you, resting in your strength,
    living in your brightness and dwelling in your bounty. **Amen.**

Ps. 34; adapt. by Larry Peacock
Adapt. © 2006 Upper Room Books

263   Psalm Prayer (Ps. 34 *or* General Use)

O God, we turn to you in the time of trouble.
In your presence we find the promise of deliverance
    and the assurance of your redeeming love.
For this we give you thanks and praise. **Amen.**

Ps. 34; adapt. by Judy Holloway
Adapt. © 2006 Upper Room Books

264   Psalm Prayer (Ps. 34 *or* General Use)

O listening God, ever gentle with your children, we exalt you.
You call us to take refuge in you and to find happiness and peace through you.
Redeem us, your servants, with your grace.
May praise always be on our lips. **Amen.**

Ps. 34; adapt. by Jerry Oakland
Adapt. © 2006 Upper Room Books

Psalm Prayer (Ps. 34)

O God, you are worthy of our praise.
With humble hearts we bow in awe
   of your great mercy toward us.
You are near to the brokenhearted.
You save us from all our troubles.
Holy is your name. **Amen.**

Ps. 34; adapt. by Ginger Howl

Adapt. © 2006 Upper Room Books

Psalm 40
(I Waited Patiently for God)

266

1. I waited patiently for God,
2. God raised me from a miry pit,
3. And on my lips a song was put,
4. Great wonders you have done, O Lord,

for God to hear my prayer;
from mud and sinking sand,
a new song to the Lord.
all purposed for our good.

and God bent down to where I sank
and set my feet upon a rock
Many will marvel o-pen-eyed
Unable every one to name,

and listened to me there.
where I can firmly stand.
and put their trust in God.
I bow in gratitude.

WORDS: John L. Bell

MUSIC: Trad. Scottish adapt. of 19th cent. USA melody

AMAZING GRACE
CM

Words and arr. © 1993 Wild Goose Resource Group, Iona Community, Scotland; GIA Publications, Inc., exclusive
North American agent

As the Deer

As the deer pants for the wa-ter, so my soul longs af-ter you.

You a-lone are my heart's de-sire and I long to wor-ship you.

You a-lone are my strength, my shield; to

you a-lone may my spir-it yield. You a-lone are my

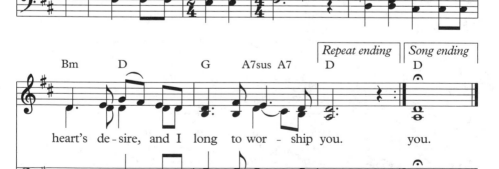

Repeat ending | *Song ending*

heart's de-sire, and I long to wor-ship you. you.

WORDS: Martin Nystrom (Ps. 42:1)
MUSIC: Martin Nystrom

Psalm 42
(As the Deer Longs)

As the deer longs for run - ning streams, so I long, so I long, so I long for you.

Cantor verses in Upper Room Worshipbook Accompaniment and Worship Leader *edition*

WORDS: Bob Hurd
MUSIC: Bob Hurd

© 1988 Bob Hurd, published by OCP Publications

Psalm Prayer (Ps. 42)

269

O God, I taste my thirst for you in my tears.
In the midst of my anguish, I long for the days
 when I sang your praises and shouted your glory.
Held in your steadfast love, I will again rejoice in you,
 my help and my hope. **Amen.**

Ps. 42; adapt. by Jo Hoover
Adapt. © 2006 Upper Room Books

Psalm Prayer (Ps. 42)

270

Quench the thirst of my heart, O God.
Sing the song of your love deep within me.
Lead me to the waters of mercy,
 for my hope is in you. **Amen.**

Ps. 42; adapt. by Judy Holloway
Adapt. © 2006 Upper Room Books

Psalm 46
(A Mighty Fortress Is Our God)

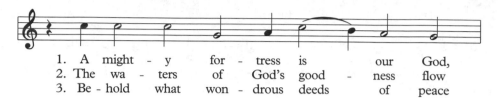

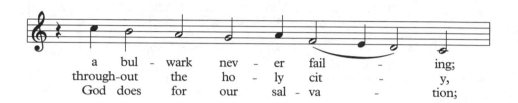

1. A might - y   for - tress is   our   God,
2. The wa - ters of   God's good - ness flow
3. Be - hold what won - drous deeds of   peace

a   bul - wark nev - er fail - ing;
through-out the   ho - ly cit - y,
God does for   our sal - va - tion;

pro - tect - ing us   with staff and   rod,
and glad - den hearts of   those who know
God knows our   wars and makes them cease

and pow - er all - pre - vail - ing.
God's ten - der - ness and pit - y.
in   ev - ery land and na - tion.

What if   the   na - tions rage
Though na - tions stand un - sure,
The war - rior's spear and lance

Accompaniment in Upper Room Worshipbook Accompaniment and Worship Leader *edition*

WORDS: Omer Westendorf; st. 1, lines 1–2, Martin Luther
        trans. by Frederick Henry Hedge
MUSIC: Martin Luther (based on original rhythmic pattern of chorale)

and surg - ing seas ram - page; what though the moun - tains fall,
God's king - dom shall en - dure; God's pow - er shall re - main,
are splin - tered by God's glance; the guns and nu - clear might

the Lord is God of all;
and peace is shall ev - er reign;
stand with - ered in God's sight;

the Lord of hosts is with us.
the Lord of hosts is with us.
the Lord of hosts is with us.

Psalm Prayer (Ps. 46)   272

Though the world shakes us and life overwhelms us,
    you are our help, our strength.
You still our hearts and turn us
    and the whole earth toward peace.
You are our refuge, O God. **Amen.**

Ps. 46; adapt. by Larry Peacock
Adapt. © 2006 Upper Room Books

Psalm Prayer (Ps. 46)   273

God of refuge, we come to you,
    placing our trust in you
    and seeking your protection.
In your tenderness and mercy you gather us close,
    sustaining us in the midst of trial
    and encouraging us in the midst of terror.
Bless us always in the shelter of your abiding grace. **Amen.**

Ps. 46; adapt. by Jerry Oakland
Adapt. © 2006 Upper Room Books

Psalm 51
(Create in Me a Clean Heart)

Leader

Group

Capo 2:

| Am | G6 | Am | | Em | D | Em |
| Cm | Bb6 | Cm | | Gm | F | Gm |

Cre - ate in me a clean heart, O God, And re -

| Am | G6 | F | Em7 | Am |
| Cm | Bb6 | Ab | Gm7 | Cm |

new a right spir - it with - in me.

Leader

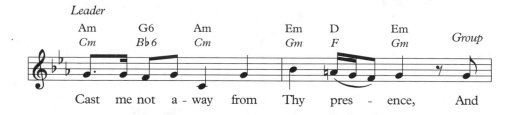

| Am | G6 | Am | | Em | D | Em |
| Cm | Bb6 | Cm | | Gm | F | Gm |

Group

Cast me not a - way from Thy pres - ence, And

| Am | G6 | F | Em7 | Am |
| Cm | Bb6 | Ab | Gm7 | Cm |

Leader

take not Thy ho - ly spir - it from me. Re -

| Em | D | Em | | Em | D | Em |
| Gm | F | Gm | | Gm | F | Gm |

Group

store to me the joy of Thy sal - va - tion And up -

WORDS: Ps. 51; adapt. by Jim Strathdee
MUSIC: Jim Strathdee

hold me with a will - ing spir - it.

Leader

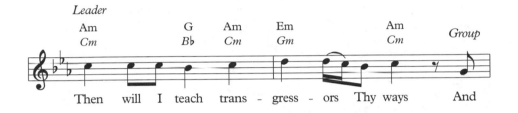

Then will I teach trans - gress - ors Thy ways And

sin - ners will re - turn to Thee. Cre -

ate in me a clean heart, O God, And re -

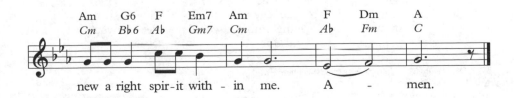

new a right spir-it with - in me. A - men.

275

Psalm 51
(Create in Me)

Refrains

1. Cre - ate in me a clean heart, O God.
2. I will a - rise and go to my God.

Cantor verses in Upper Room Worshipbook Accompaniment and Worship Leader *edition*

WORDS: David Haas (Ps. 51:3-4, 12-13, 14-15); ref. 1 by ICEL
MUSIC: David Haas

© 1987 GIA Publications, Inc.; ref. 1 trans. © 1969 ICEL

276

Psalm 51
(The Sacrifice You Accept)

Refrain

The sac - ri-fice you ac-cept, O God, is a hum - ble spir-it.

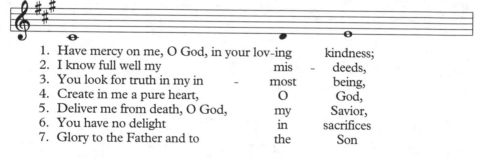

1. Have mercy on me, O God, in your lov-ing   kindness;
2. I know full well my   mis - deeds,
3. You look for truth in my in - most   being,
4. Create in me a pure heart,   O   God,
5. Deliver me from death, O God,   my   Savior,
6. You have no delight   in   sacrifices
7. Glory to the Father and to   the   Son

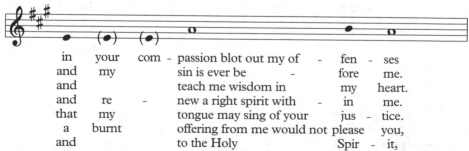

in   your   com - passion blot out my of - fen - ses
and   my   sin is ever be - fore   me.
and   teach me wisdom in   my   heart.
and   re -   new a right spirit with - in   me.
that   my   tongue may sing of your   jus - tice.
a   burnt   offering from me would not please   you,
and   to the Holy   Spir - it,

WORDS: Psalm 51:1-17; trans. Massey H. Shepherd, Jr.
MUSIC: David Clark Isele

Trans. © 1976 Massey H. Shepherd, Jr.; music © 1979 GIA Publications, Inc.

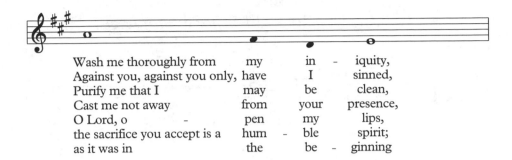

Wash me thoroughly from my in - iquity,
Against you, against you only, have I sinned,
Purify me that I may be clean,
Cast me not away from your presence,
O Lord, o - pen my lips,
the sacrifice you accept is a hum - ble spirit;
as it was in the be - ginning

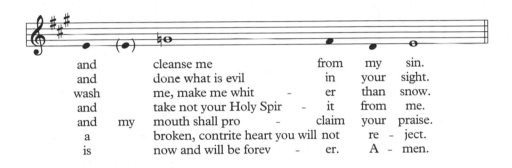

and cleanse me from my sin.
and done what is evil in your sight.
wash me, make me whit - er than snow.
and take not your Holy Spir - it from me.
and my mouth shall pro - claim your praise.
a broken, contrite heart you will not re - ject.
is now and will be forev - er. A - men.

Psalm Prayer (Ps. 51) 277

Our hearts long for your cleansing touch,
    Merciful One.
In your grace, wipe away our guilt,
    and renew our spirits,
        that we may serve you with joy all our days. **Amen.**

Ps. 51; adapt. by Elise S. Eslinger
Adapt. © 2006 Upper Room Books

Psalm 62
(God Is My Rock/*El Señor es mi fuerza*)

Refrain

Dm · Gm · Dm

God is my rock and my sal - va - tion, the
El Señ - or es mi fuer - za, mi

Am7 · **1** Dm · **2** Dm · Dm · Dm *Fine*

strength of my life. life. _____
ro - ca y sal - va - ción. ción. _____

F · Bb · Bb

1. You still call us to walk the paths of
2. In the midst of our fears and dark - ening
3. We en - trust you, the God of our sal -
4. Lord Al - might - y, the great strength of your

Bb/C · Bb/C · F

jus - tice, you help us see the way.
sha - dows you bring us hope and light.
va - tion, with all the fu - ture holds.
peo - ple, our strong De - li - ver - er.

F · Bb · Bb

As you give us the cour - age for life's
In your pres - ence we go through death's dark
Guide, pro - tect, and de - fend the poor and
Lib - er - a - tor, se - cure us in your

WORDS: Juan Antonio Espinosa (Ps. 62)
MUSIC: Juan Antonio Espinosa

© 1983 Discipleship Resources

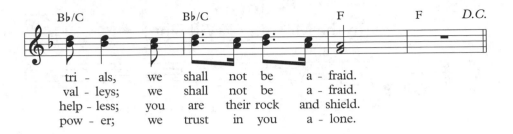

tri - als,   we   shall   not be   a - fraid.
val - leys;   we   shall   not be   a - fraid.
help - less;   you   are   their rock and shield.
pow - er;   we   trust   in you   a - lone.

1. Tú me guías por sendas de justicia,
   me enseñas la verdad.
   Tú me das el valor para la lucha,
   sin miedo avanzaré.

2. Iluminas las sombras de mi vida,
   al mundo das la luz;
   aunque pase por valles de tinieblas
   yo nunca temeré.

3. Yo confío el destino de mi vida
   al Dios de mi salud;
   a los pobres enseñas el camino,
   su escudo eres Tú.

4. El Señor es la fuerza de su pueblo,
   su gran libertador;
   Tú le haces vivir en la confianza,
   seguro en tu poder.

Psalm 63
(In the Morning I Will Sing)

Refrain

In the morn-ing I will sing glad songs of praise to you.

1. You are my God, I long for you from ear _ ly in the

morn - ing. My whole be - ing de - sires you like a

To Refrain

dry, worn, wa - ter - less land. My soul thirsts for you.

2. In the sanc - tu - ar - y let me see how might-y

are your works. Your con - stant love is

To Refrain

bet-ter than life it - self, and so I will praise you.

3. I will give you thanks as long as I shall live; I

WORDS: From *Good News Bible;* adapt. by David Goodrich (Ps. 63:1-8)
MUSIC: David Goodrich

raise my hands in prayer, and my soul will feast and be

To Refrain

filled, and I will sing and praise you.

4. As I lie in bed I re-mem-ber you, O Lord;

I think of you all night long, for you are my con - stant

help. In the sha - dow of your wings, I sing for

To Refrain

joy. I cling to you, your hand keeps me safe.

Psalm 63

280

(Your Love Is Finer Than Life)

Refrain

O God, I seek you, my soul thirsts for

you, your love is fin - er than life. _____

Use with psalm text of choice, chanted or read.

WORDS: Marty Haugen (Ps. 63)
MUSIC: Marty Haugen

281

Psalm 63
(Longing for God in the Shadow of the Cross)

Refrain 1

In the shad-ow of your wings I sing for joy.

or

Refrain 2

In the morn-ing I will sing glad songs of praise to you.

Cantor verses in Upper Room Worshipbook Accompaniment and Worship Leader *edition*

WORDS: Ref. 2 Michael Joncas (Ps. 63:1-8)
MUSIC: Michael Joncas

282

Psalm 63
(My Soul Is Thirsting)

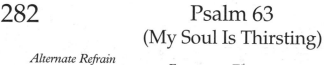

Alternate Refrain

In the morn - ing I will sing, will

Accompaniment in Upper Room Worshipbook Accompaniment and Worship Leader *edition; use with cantor verses, 280 or 281.*

WORDS: Ps. 63
MUSIC: David Clark Isele

sing glad songs of praise to you.

Psalm 63

283

(As Morning Breaks)

Refrain

As morn-ing breaks I look to you; I look to

you, O Lord, to be my strength this day, as morn-ing

breaks, as morn-ing breaks.

Read or chanted

1. O God, you are my God, for you I long; for you my soul is thirsting.
   My body pines for you, like a dry, weary land without water.
   So I gaze on you in your holy place to see your strength and your glory.
   Refrain

2. For your love is better than life, my lips will speak your praise.
   So I will bless you all my life, in your name I will lift up my hands.
   My soul shall be filled as with a banquet, my mouth shall praise you with joy.
   Refrain

3. On my bed I remember you. On you I muse through the night,
   for you have been my help; in the shadow of your wings I rejoice.
   My soul clings to you; your right hand holds me fast.
   Refrain

WORDS: The Grail (Ps. 63:2-3, 4-6, 7-9); ref. trans. ICEL
MUSIC: Michael Joncas

Words © 1963 The Grail, England; GIA Publications, Inc.; refrain trans. © 1974 ICEL; music © 1985 OCP Publications

Psalm 63
(O God, You Are My God Alone)

1. O God, you are my God alone, whom eagerly I seek,
   though longing fills my soul with thirst and leaves my body weak.
   Just like a dry and barren land awaits a fresh'ning show'r,
   I long within your house to see your glory and your pow'r.

2. Your faithful love surpasses life, evoking all my praise.
   Through ev'ry day, to bless your name, my hands in joy I'll raise.
   My deepest needs you satisfy as with a sumptuous feast.
   So, on my lips and in my heart, your praise has never ceased.

3. Throughout the night I lie in bed and call you, Lord, to mind;
   in darkest hours I meditate how God, my strength, is kind.
   Beneath the shadow of your wing, I live and feel secure;
   and daily, as I follow close, your right hand keeps me sure.

Sing to RESIGNATION, No. 244

The Iona Community

© 1993 Wild Goose Resource Group, Iona Community, Scotland; GIA Publications, Inc., exclusive North American agent

285

Psalm Prayer (Ps. 63)

We praise you with joy, loving God,
   for your grace is better than life itself.
You have sustained us through the darkness,
   and you bless us with life in this new day.
In the shadow of your wings we sing for joy
   and bless your holy name. **Amen.**

Ps. 63; adapt. by Richard Eslinger
Adapt. © 2006 Upper Room Books

Psalm 91
(Whoever Lives Beside the Lord)

1. Who - ev - er lives be - side the Lord, shel - tering in the Al - might - y's shade, shall say, "My God, in you I trust, my safe - ty, my de - fend - er."
2. From un - seen dan - ger and dis - ease God will keep you safe and sure; be - neath his wings a place you'll find, a ref - uge from all dan - ger.
3. You will not dread what dark - ness brings— hid - den dan - ger, dead - ly plague; nor will you fear, in day - light hours, the e - vil that sur - rounds you.
4. A thou - sand may die at your side, thou - sands more fall close at hand; but with God's truth for strength and shield, no threat will ev - er touch you.
5. God says, "I'll save from ev - ery harm those who know and love my name. In trou - ble I will hon - or them and show them my sal - va - tion."

WORDS: John L. Bell (Ps. 91)
MUSIC: Trad. Scottish, arr. by John L. Bell

287

Psalm 91
(In the Shadow of Your Wings)

Refrain

In the shad-ow of your wings, Lord, I cling to you.

Refrain

I.* You live in God's secret place;
  the Most High shades your sleep.
You say to the Lord, "My strong refuge,
  my God, in whom I trust."

II. God saves you from the fowler's snares,
  and from deadly disease.
The Lord's pinions are over you;
  you hide beneath God's wings.

I. Do not fear the terror of night,
  or the arrow that flies by day,
the pestilence stalking in darkness,
  the plague laying waste at noon.

II. A thousand may fall at your side,
  ten thousand at your right hand;
but you will not be stricken —
  the faithful God is your shield and tower. *Refrain*

I. Only look with your eyes,
  and see the oppressors punished.
As for you, the Lord is your refuge;
  you have made the Most High your shelter.

II. Evil will not befall you,
  nor harm approach your tent.
On your behalf, God commanded the angels
  to guard you in all your ways.

I and II may be read or chanted alternately by two leaders, leader and congregation, men and women, etc.

WORDS: Ps. 91, trans. by Gary Chamberlain
MUSIC: Elise S. Eslinger

I. Their hands will lift you high,
　　lest you catch your foot on a stone.
　You shall step on lion and snake,
　　tread down young lion and serpent.

II. "I will save those who cling to me,
　　and protect those who know my name.
　They call and I answer them;
　　I am with them in their distress.

I., II. "I will rescue them and reward them;
　　I satisfy them with long life,
　　and show them my saving power." *Refrain*

Psalm Prayer (Ps. 91)　　288

O God, you are our refuge and deliverer.
When we are wounded or ill you send angels—
　human and divine—to minister to us.
Through Christ we are bound to you in love
　our whole life through.
And we dwell secure in the shadow of the Most High.
Thanks be to God. **Amen.**

Ps. 91; adapt. by Ginger Howl
Adapt. © 2006 Upper Room Books

Psalm Prayer (Ps. 91)　　289

O Most High God, we are covered with your wings,
　guarded by your love, sheltered by your grace.
Your faithfulness is our hope and shield. **Amen.**

Ps. 91; adapt. by Larry Peacock
Adapt. © 2006 Upper Room Books

Psalm Prayer (Ps. 91)　　290

Sheltering God, you have made a nest among us.
Under the canopy of your wings
　we make our homes and find our sanctuary.
Our trust is in you!
Bear us on your wings of love
　that we might be wings of your hope to the world. **Amen.**

Ps. 91; adapt. by Kay Barckley
Adapt. © 2006 Upper Room Books

291

Psalm 95
(Come, Let Us Sing)

Refrain

Come, let us sing to the Lord, and

shout with joy to the Rock who saves us.

Refrain

1.★ Come, let us sing to the Lord;
   let us shout to our saving rock!
   Enter God's presence with praise,
   with music and shouts of joy.

2. For the Lord is a mighty God,
   the great ruler of all the gods.
   God's hands hold the depths of the world,
   and rule the peaks of the mountains.

3. It is God who made and rules the seas,
   whose hand created dry ground.
   Come, let us kneel and worship the Lord;
   let us bow before God our maker. *Refrain*

★May be read by one or more leaders or sung by cantor (psalm tones in Upper Room Worshipbook
Accompaniment and Worship Leader *edition).*

WORDS: Ps. 95, trans. by Gary Chamberlain; ref. words ICEL
MUSIC: St. Meinrad Archabbey

Refrain words © 1974 ICEL; verse trans. © 1984 The Upper Room; music © 1977 St. Meinrad Archabbey

292

Psalm 95
(Come, Sing with Joy to God)

1. Come, sing with joy to God, our Rock and Sav-ior
2. The heights and depths of earth are cra-dled in God's
3. Our God and Lord a-lone, through all the years the
4. Lord, we would hear your word, and not the test re-

WORDS: Ps. 95, para. by Arlo Duba
MUSIC: John Darwall
Paraphrase © 1986 Arlo Duba

DARWALL'S 148th
66.66.88

praise; come, en - ter in with shouts of joy, your
hand; the same al - might - y power made moun - tains,
same, you feed us, take us by the hand, call
peat of Mas - sah with its man - na and the

voic - es raise. O might - y God, you
sea, and land. Come wor - ship God, come
each by name. You are the shep - herd,
wa - ters sweet. We ask for sight, your

are the Lord, the God of gods by all a - dored.
kneel and bow be - fore the Lord our Mak - er now.
we the sheep; Lord, shel - ter us, our foot - steps keep.
rest re - store, and we shall praise you ev - er - more.

293

Psalm-Hymn
(We Sing to You, O God)

1. We sing to you, O God, the Rock who gave us birth,
   let our rejoicing sing your name in all the earth.
   To you, O God, let songs be raised,
   in joyful hymns, our feast of praise.

2. We wandered far from home out in a desert land,
   you shielded with your love our fearful pilgrim band.
   You kept us safe within your arms
   and sheltered us against the storm.

3. You bear us through the world, an eagle to its young,
   who rises on her wings and bears us toward the sun.
   We ride the vaults of light and air
   and trust in your unfailing care.

4. O God, eternal God, we hide within your wings,
   the everlasting arms to whom our praises ring.
   Your word is true, your way is just,
   you are the God in whom we trust.

Sing to DARWALL'S 148th, No. 292

Gracia Grindal (Deut. 32:11, 18; 33:27; Ps. 57:1; 66:2; 96:1-2)
Words © 1993 Selah Publishing Co., Inc.

294

Psalm Prayer (Ps. 95)

We come before you with singing and shouts of joy!
You are our Creator God and the Rock of our salvation.
We praise you! We adore you!
May your love reign in our hearts this day! **Amen.**

Ps. 95; adapt. by Judy Holloway
Adapt. © 2006 Upper Room Books

295

Psalm Prayer (Ps. 95)

Our shouts of praise greet you, Shepherd God.
We have been led by your loving hand,
   and we proclaim with joy that you are our salvation.
Reign in our hearts this day. **Amen.**

Ps. 95; adapt. by Elise S. Eslinger
Adapt. © 2006 Upper Room Books

Psalm 98
(Sing a New Song)

Refrain

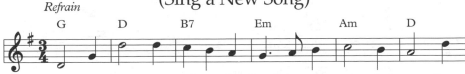

Sing a new song un-to the Lord; let your song be sung from

moun-tains high. Sing a new song un-to the Lord, sing-ing

al - le - lu - ia. _____
                              1. Yah-weh's peo - ple dance for
2. Rise, O chil - dren, from your
3. Glad, my soul, for I have

joy. O come be - fore the Lord.___ And play for him on
sleep; your Sav - ior now has come.___ ___ He has turned your
seen the glo - ry of the Lord.___ The trum - pet sounds; the

To Refrain

glad tam - bour-ines, and let your trum - pet sound.___
sor - row to joy and filled your soul with song.___
dead shall be raised. I know my Sav - ior lives.___

WORDS: Dan Schutte (Ps. 98), alt.
MUSIC: Dan Schutte
© 1972 Dan Schutte, admin. by OCP Publications

Psalm Prayer (Ps. 98)

Our souls rise up to meet you, living Lord, in a dance of joy!
With all creation we sing your praise in heart songs,
fresh, new, and ever thankful. Alleluia! **Amen.**

Ps. 98; adapt. by Elise S. Eslinger
Adapt. © 2006 Upper Room Books

298

Psalm 100
(Enter God's Gates)

Refrain

En - ter God's gates with thanks and praise.

Verse

1. Shout to the Lord, all the land; _ serve the Lord with joy;

come be-fore God with laugh-ter. Know that the Lord is God; _

_ we be - long to the Lord, our Mak - er, to

God, who tends us like sheep. Come to God's gates with

To Refrain

thanks; come to God's courts with praise; _

Verse

2. Praise and bless the Lord's name. _ Tru-ly the Lord is good.

To Refrain

God is al - ways gra-cious, and faith-ful age af-ter age. _

WORDS: Ps. 100, trans. by Gary Chamberlain
MUSIC: J. Jefferson Cleveland

Psalm 100
(O Many People of All Lands)

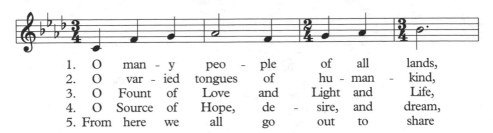

1. O   man - y   peo - ple   of   all   lands,
2. O   var - ied   tongues   of   hu - man - kind,
3. O   Fount   of   Love   and   Light   and   Life,
4. O   Source   of   Hope,   de - sire,   and   dream,
5. From   here   we   all   go   out   to   share

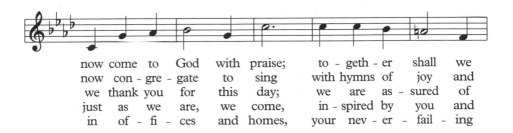

now come to God   with praise;   to - geth - er   shall   we
now con - gre - gate   to   sing   with hymns of   joy   and
we thank you   for   this   day;   we   are   as - sured   of
just   as   we   are,   we   come,   in - spired by   you   and
in   of - fi - ces   and homes,   your nev - er - fail - ing

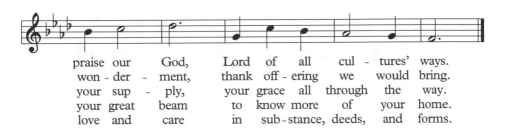

praise our   God,   Lord   of   all   cul - tures' ways.
won - der - ment,   thank off - ering   we   would   bring.
your sup - ply,   your grace   all   through   the   way.
your great   beam   to   know more   of   your   home.
love and   care   in   sub - stance, deeds,   and   forms.

WORDS: Natty G. Barranda (Ps. 100)
MUSIC: Lois F. Bello

Used by permission of Christian Conference of Asia

300

Psalm 100
(Rejoice in God)

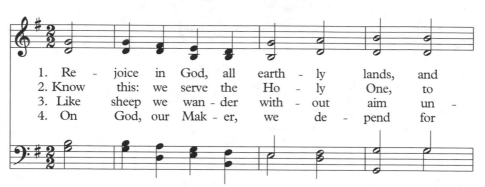

1. Re - joice in God, all earth - ly lands, and
2. Know this: we serve the Ho - ly One, to
3. Like sheep we wan - der with - out aim un -
4. On God, our Mak - er, we de - pend for

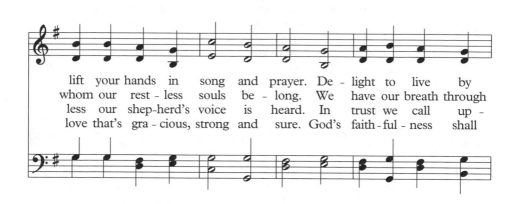

lift your hands in song and prayer. De - light to live by
whom our rest - less souls be - long. We have our breath through
less our shep - herd's voice is heard. In trust we call up -
love that's gra - cious, strong and sure. God's faith - ful - ness shall

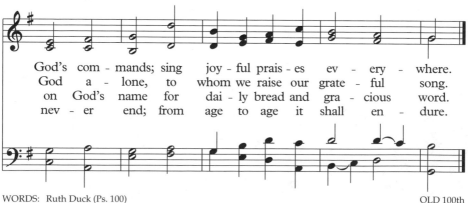

God's com - mands; sing joy - ful prais - es ev - ery - where.
God a - lone, to whom we raise our grate - ful song.
on God's name for dai - ly bread and gra - cious word.
nev - er end; from age to age it shall en - dure.

WORDS: Ruth Duck (Ps. 100)
MUSIC: Attr. to Louis Bourgeois

OLD 100th
LM

Wesley's Grace
301

Be present at our table, Lord;
be here and everywhere adored;
thy creatures bless, and grant that we
may feast in paradise with thee.

Sing to OLD 100th, No. 300

John Wesley

Doxology (Traditional)
302

Praise God from whom all blessings flow;
praise God, all creatures here below;
praise God above, ye heav'nly hosts,
praise Father, Son, and Holy Ghost.

Sing to OLD 100th, No. 300

Thomas Ken, alt.

Psalm Prayer (Ps. 100)
303

Holy God, with people of all lands we joyfully serve you
and sing praises in your presence.
Your mercy and faithfulness are our guiding lights.
Praise be to you, O God. **Amen.**

Ps. 100; adapt. by Ginger Howl
Adapt. © 2006 Upper Room Books

Psalm Prayer (Ps. 100)
304

Shepherding God, we join with all creation
in bringing you joyful thanks and glad songs of praise,
for your love endures and your faithfulness lasts forever. **Amen.**

Ps. 100; adapt. by Larry Peacock
Adapt. © 2006 Upper Room Books

Psalm Prayer (Ps. 100)
305

O Everlasting Love, what joy to be in your presence.
How wonderful to know that you created us.
How we marvel that you have made us your own.
Keep us mindful of your faithfulness.
Enfold us in your enduring love forever. **Amen.**

Ps. 100; adapt. by Jo Hoover
Adapt. © 2006 Upper Room Books

Psalm 103
(O Bless the Lord)

Refrain (in canon)

O bless the Lord, my soul, and all that is in me,

O bless the Lord, my soul, and

bless God's ho - ly name! _____

all that is in me, bless God's ho - ly name!

May be accompanied by hand clapping, tambourine, or other percussive instrument.

Verses (read or chanted)

Refrain

I. Bless the Lord, my inmost self!
    Everything in me, bless God's holy name.

II. Bless the Lord, my inmost self,
    do not forget what God has done —

I. pardoning all your sin,
    healing your every disease,

II. redeeming your life from the grave,
    crowning your head with constant compassion.

I., II. Your vital needs are satisfied;
    like the phoenix, your youth is renewed. *Refrain*

WORDS: Refrain, Ps. 103:1; verses, Ps. 103:1-13 trans. by Gary Chamberlain
MUSIC: Elise S. Eslinger

Refrain © 1985 The Upper Room; trans. © 1984 The Upper Room; music © 1985 The Upper Room

I. The Lord accomplishes justice—
   vindication for all the oppressed!

II. God's ways were made known to Moses,
    God's acts to Israel's offspring.

I. Compassion and grace—that is the Lord,
   slow to be angry, determined to love us!

II. God will not always oppose us,
    nor hold a grudge forever.

I., II. God does not act in accord with our sins,
        nor as our guilt deserves. *Refrain*

I. As high as the sky is above the world,
   so great is the grace given those who fear God.

II. As far as the east is from the west,
    God removes our offenses from us.

I., II. Like a father's love for his child
        is the love shown to those who fear God. *Refrain*

Psalm 103
(Bless the Lord, O My Soul)

307

Bless the Lord, O my soul and all that is with-in me praise and bless the Lord, O my soul. Bless God's ho-ly name.

Verses for cantor in Upper Room Worshipbook Accompaniment and Worship Leader *edition or read text on previous page. See also "Bless the Lord" (Ps. 103) in Taizé section, No. 377.*

WORDS: Timothy E. Kimbrough (Ps. 103)
MUSIC: Timothy E. Kimbrough

308

Psalm Prayer (Ps. 103)

You are compassion and grace, almighty God.
You have redeemed us. You have crowned us.
We join your creatures everywhere
    in blessing your name, now and always. **Amen.**

Ps. 103; adapt. by Elise S. Eslinger

Adapt. © 2006 Upper Room Books

309

Psalm 113
(Praise to the Lord)

1. Praise to the Lord, all of
2. There is none like our God in the

you, God's ser - vants. Bless - ed
heavens or on earth, who lifts the

be the name of our God now and
poor from the dust, seat - ing them with the

WORDS: Ron Klusmeier (Ps. 113)
MUSIC: Ron Klusmeier
© 1972 Ron Klusmeier

ev - er._____ From the ris - ing up of the
might - y, _____ who stoops to raise the

Refrain

sun _____ may the Lord be praised.
weak and low:

Praise to the name of the Lord. _____

Psalm Prayer (Ps. 113)   310

From the rising of the sun till its setting, there is none like you.
We praise you, knowing that you lift the poor from the dust.
May we, your servants, participate in your justice and mercy
 for all peoples. **Amen.**

Ps. 113; adapt. by Elise S. Eslinger

Psalm 116
(I Love You, Lord)

*Refrain**

1. I love you, Lord; _____ you hear my cry _____ and pit - y
2. I love you, Lord; _____ you hear my cry _____ and chase my

ev - ery groan. _____ Long as I live _____ and trou - bles
grief a - way. _____ O let my heart _____ no more des-

rise, _____ I'll has-ten to _____ your throne.
pair _____ while I have breath _____ to pray.

May be used with Psalm text read by Leader.

WORDS: Isaac Watts, alt. (Ps. 116:1-2)
MUSIC: African American spiritual; harm. by Richard Smallwood

Harm. © 1975 Century Oak Publishing Group/Richwood Music, admin. by Copyright Management Services, Inc.

Psalm 118
(This Is the Day/*Éste es el día*)

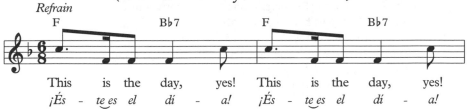

Refrain

This is the day, yes! This is the day, yes!
¡És - te es el dí - a! ¡És - te es el dí - a!

This is the day＿＿ that God has made! ＿＿
¡És - te es el dí - a que hi-zo el Se - ñor! ＿＿

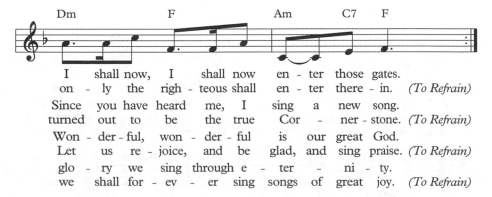

1. O - pen the doors of true jus - tice and mer - cy.
   This is the door that our God is pro - claim - ing,
2. I shall sing prais - es to you, our Re - deem - er.
   Know that the Rock that once had been re - ject - ed
3. God has en - tered, God our Cre - a - tor.
   This is the day that our Mak - er has of - fered.
4. To the Fa - ther, Son, and Spir - it,
   In the be - gin - ning, and now, and for - ev - er,

I shall now, I shall now en - ter those gates.
on - ly the right - teous shall en - ter there - in. *(To Refrain)*
Since you have heard me, I sing a new song.
turned out to be the true Cor - ner - stone. *(To Refrain)*
Won - der - ful, won - der - ful is our great God.
Let us re - joice, and be glad, and sing praise. *(To Refrain)*
glo - ry we sing through e - ter - ni - ty.
we shall for - ev - er sing songs of great joy. *(To Refrain)*

WORDS: Pablo Sosa (Ps. 118:19-24)
MUSIC: Pablo Sosa, arr. by Esther Frances

313   Psalm Prayer (Ps. 118)

The stone that the builders rejected has become our cornerstone.
With all who have been raised with Christ in baptism,
    we proclaim the resurrection of our Lord.
You reveal the way of the righteous, of justice and mercy.
This very day, you have acted!
You are our Rock and our Redeemer. **Amen.**

Ps. 118; adapt. by Richard Eslinger
Adapt. © 2006 Upper Room Books

314   Psalm 121
(Lifting My Eyes Up to the Hills)

1. Lift - ing my eyes up to the hills,
2. The Lord who guards you nev - er sleeps,
3. God is your guar - dian, God your shade,
4. The Lord shall shield you from all harm

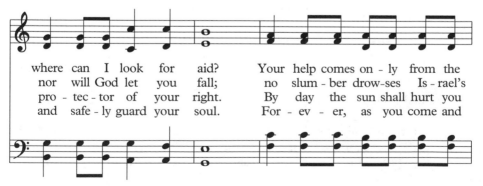

where can I look for aid? Your help comes on - ly from the
nor will God let you fall; no slum - ber drow-ses Is - rael's
pro - tec - tor of your right. By day the sun shall hurt you
and safe - ly guard your soul. For - ev - er, as you come and

WORDS: John L. Bell (Ps. 121)
MUSIC: John L. Bell

© 1993 Wild Goose Resource Group, Iona Community, Scotland; GIA Publications, Inc., exclusive North American agent

Lord who earth and heav - en made.
God; guar - dian of each and all.
none, nor shall the moon by night.
go, God's love shall keep you whole.

Psalm 121   315
(Our Help Comes from the Lord)

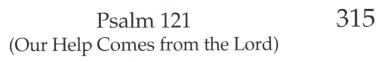

Our help comes from the Lord, the mak-er of heav-en and earth.

Cantor verses in Upper Room Worshipbook Accompaniment and Worship Leader *edition*

WORDS: Ps. 121:2
MUSIC: Verses The Grail; refrain by Michael Joncas

Psalm Prayer (Ps. 121)   316

Not from the hills but from you, O God,
my help, my shield, my shelter.
Keep us from evil and guard all our journeys. **Amen.**

Ps. 121; adapt. by Larry Peacock

317 Psalm Prayer (Ps. 121)

You have been our help forever and ever,
  guarding, watching, and protecting.
Through the day and all during the night, Loving Creator,
  you are with us. **Amen.**

Ps. 121; adapt. by Larry Peacock
Adapt. © 2006 Upper Room Books

318 Psalm Prayer (Ps. 121)

O God, ever wakeful, ever vigilant,
  your protection and loving care are always with us.
Even in times when evil seems rampant,
  in times of natural disaster,
  in times of anxiety or grief,
  you guard our going out and our coming in.
Through Jesus Christ we know your grace is sufficient. **Amen.**

Ps. 121; adapt. by Ginger Howl
Adapt. © 2006 Upper Room Books

319 Psalm Prayer (Ps. 121)

O Protector God, ever close and attentive:
  you know each step we take and each word we utter.
We rest our souls in you and have nothing to fear.
Thank you for this unmerited blessing. **Amen.**

Ps. 121; adapt. by Jerry Oakland
Adapt. © 2006 Upper Room Books

320 Psalm Prayer (Ps. 121)

Today, O God, I rest in the hope of your love and protection,
  for my help comes from you.
You will not let my foot slip. You watch over me day and night.
You keep me in the safety of your eternal love
  now and forevermore. **Amen.**

Ps. 121; adapt. by Sheri Daylong
Adapt. © 2006 Upper Room Books

Psalm 122
(I Rejoiced When I Heard Them Say)

1. I re-joiced when I heard them say: "Let us
2. Like a tem-ple of u-ni-ty is the
3. It is faith-ful to Is-rael's law, there to
4. For the peace of all na-tions, pray: for God's
5. For the love of my friends and kin I will

go to the house of God." And now our feet arc
cit-y, Je-ru-sa-lem. It is there all tribes will
praise the name of God. All the judg-ment seats of
peace with-in your homes. May God's last-ing peace sur-
bless you with signs of peace. For the love of God's own

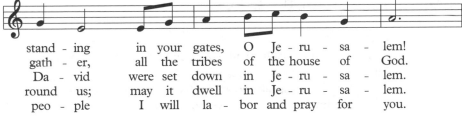

stand-ing in your gates, O Je-ru-sa-lem!
gath-er, all the tribes of the house of God.
Da-vid were set down in Je-ru-sa-lem.
round us; may it dwell in Je-ru-sa-lem.
peo-ple I will la-bor and pray for you.

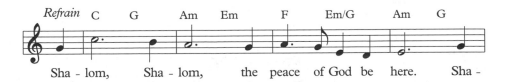

Refrain

Sha-lom, Sha-lom, the peace of God be here. Sha-

lom, sha-lom, God's jus-tice be ev-er near.

Gestures of greeting and peace may be offered during the refrain.

WORDS: Bernadette Farrell
MUSIC: Bernadette Farrell

322

Psalm Prayer (Ps. 122)

O God of the holy places, of the sacred and the profane,
    guide our steps to you and hear our prayers for your people.
May your goodness bring the blessing of peace
    throughout the earth, in every land. **Amen.**

Ps. 122; adapt. by Jerry Oakland
Adapt. © 2006 Upper Room Books

323

Psalm Prayer (Ps. 122)

Holy God, we pray with your people throughout the ages—
    Let there be peace in Jerusalem.
And not only Jerusalem, but may peace come to every great city,
    every hamlet, every home in the universe
    that you created and called "very good." **Amen.**

Ps. 122; adapt. by Ginger Howl
Adapt. © 2006 Upper Room Books

324

Psalm Prayer (Ps. 122)

O God of Peace,
    it is a delight to gather with your people in your holy presence.
Fill us with your desire for peace
    so that we may speak and act for harmony in our homes,
    our communities, and your world. **Amen.**

Ps. 122; adapt. by Jo Hoover
Adapt. © 2006 Upper Room Books

325

Psalm 126
(When God First Brought Us Back from Exile)

1. When God first brought us back from
2. Once more, O Lord, re - store your

WORDS: Carl P. Daw, Jr. (Ps. 126)
MUSIC: USA folk melody
Words © 1996 Hope Publishing Co.

WAYFARING STRANGER
Irregular

326

Psalm 126
(God Has Done Great Things for Us)

God has done great things for us, filled us with laugh-ter and mu - sic; ___ God has done great things for us, filled us with laugh-ter and mu - sic. ___

*Cantor verses in Upper Room Worshipbook Accompaniment and Worship Leader edition

WORDS: Marty Haugen (Ps. 126:1-6)
MUSIC: Marty Haugen
© 1988 GIA Publications, Inc.

327

Psalm Prayer (Ps. 126)

Wondrous God,
    bring us back to you,
        dry our tears, put a song in our hearts,
        raise up a harvest of joy.
You are still doing great things for us. **Amen.**

Ps. 126; adapt. by Larry Peacock
Adapt. © 2006 Upper Room Books

Psalm 130
(Out of the Direst Depths)

1. Out of the dir - est depths I make my deep - est plea. O gra - cious - ly bow down your ear and lis - ten, Lord, for me.
2. If you kept note of sins, be - fore you who could stand? But since for - give - ness is your right, our rev - erence you com - mand.
3. My soul longs for the Lord, and hopes to hear God's word. More keen - ly than some watch for dawn, I wait and watch for God.
4. Yes, with the Lord is grace and power to free and save. Re - demp - tion from their ev - ery sin God's peo - ple yet shall have.

Community silence may be observed between verses 3 and 4 as a vital sign of vigilant prayer.

WORDS: John L. Bell (Ps. 130)
MUSIC: John L. Bell

© 1993 Wild Goose Resource Group, Iona Community, Scotland; GIA Publications, Inc., exclusive North American agent

Psalm Prayer (Ps. 130)

Waiting for you, O God …
you will come, as surely as the morning,
bringing hope, forgiveness,
and redemption. **Amen.**

Ps. 130; adapt. by Larry Peacock
Adapt. © 2006 Upper Room Books

Psalm 131
(O Lord, My Heart Is Not Proud)

O Lord, my heart is not proud, nor haugh-ty my eyes.

I have not gone af-ter things too great, nor mar-vels be-

yond me. Tru-ly I have set my soul in

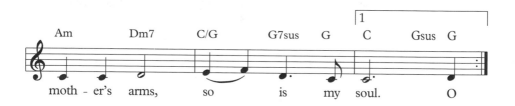

si - lence and peace; at rest, as a child in its

1

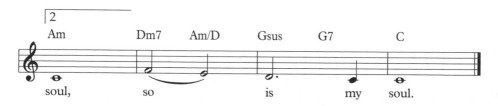

moth-er's arms, so is my soul. O

2

soul, so is my soul.

WORDS: Ps. 131:1-2, trans. The Grail, alt.
MUSIC: Margaret Rizza

Psalm Prayer (Ps. 131)

Loving God, we rest, still and quiet in your embrace.
With childlike trust and simple confidence,
we find peace in your arms. **Amen.**

Ps. 131; adapt. by Larry Peacock
Adapt. © 2006 Upper Room Books

Psalm Prayer (Ps. 131)

Calmed and quiet, resting in you,
abiding in your love,
carried like a child,
confident in hope.
My God. **Amen.**

Ps. 131; adapt. by Larry Peacock
Adapt. © 2006 Upper Room Books

Psalm Prayer (Ps. 131)

God of gentleness and compassion,
of tenderness and steadfast love:
we come into your embrace and are comforted.
Thanks and praise be unto you. **Amen.**

Ps. 131; adapt. by Jerry Oakland
Adapt. © 2006 Upper Room Books

Psalm Prayer (Ps. 131)

O God, so mighty and so gentle,
I bow before you in humble adoration.
With a calm and quiet spirit I climb into your lap,
there to rest.
In my resting fill me with hope
so that I may trust you forever. **Amen.**

Ps. 131; adapt. by Jo Hoover
Adapt. © 2006 Upper Room Books

335

Psalm 133
(How Good It Is)

1. How good it is, what pleasure comes,
   when people live as one.
   When peace and justice light the way,
   the will of God is done, the will of God is done.

2. True friendship then like fragrant oil
   surrounds us with delight;
   and blessings shine like morning dew
   upon the mountain height, upon the mountain height.

3. How good it is when walls of fear
   come tumbling to the ground.
   When arms are changed to farming tools,
   the fruits of life abound, the fruits of life abound.

4. What quiet joy can bloom and grow
   when people work for peace,
   when hands and voices join as one
   that hate and war may cease, that hate and war may cease.

Sing to DOVE OF PEACE, No. 120

Ruth Duck (Ps. 133)
© 1992 GIA Publications, Inc.

336

Psalm Prayer (Ps. 133)

O God, who created your people to dwell in families and communities,
  forgive us our acts of isolation and our attitudes of fear.
Bind us together in harmony and love,
  that we may receive your blessing. **Amen.**

Ps. 133; adapt. by Jerry Oakland
Adapt. © 2006 Upper Room Books

337

Psalm Prayer (Ps. 133)

O Loving God,
  we thank you for the blessing of unity
  which so frequently we reject.
Help us to see the wonder of the oneness you desire for us.
Fill us with love for you and for each other. **Amen.**

Ps. 133; adapt. by Jo Hoover
Adapt. © 2006 Upper Room Books

Psalm 134
(Come, Bless the Lord)

338

Come, bless the Lord, all you ser-vants of the Lord, who

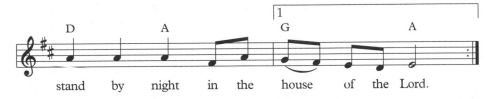

stand by night in the house of the Lord.

house of the Lord. Lift up your hands, lift up your hands, lift up your

hands to the ho-ly place and bless the Lord, and bless the

Lord, lift up your hands and bless the Lord!

(Spoken verse, then repeat from the beginning.)

Spoken verse: "May the Lord who made heaven and earth bless you from Zion."

WORDS: Steven B. Eulberg (Ps. 134)
MUSIC: Steven B. Eulberg
© 1996 Steven B. Eulberg

Psalm Prayer (Ps. 134)

339

How blessed we are, God of holy times and holy places.
We lift our hearts, hands, and voices in thanks and praise.
We bless your holy name, now and forever. **Amen.**

Ps. 134; adapt. by Elise S. Eslinger
Adapt. © 2006 Upper Room Books

340

Psalm 136
(Everlasting Grace Is Yours)

Cantor

1. Filled with thanks we sing to God:
2. Stretch - ing the earth a - round the wa - ter,
3. Strik - ing down the ty - rants of E - gypt,
4. Lead - ing us through rag - ing tor - rents:

All   *Cantor*

Ev - er - last - ing grace is yours!

God who is the
Burn - ing bright with
Free - ing us from the
Toss - ing the ar - mies

All

an - swer to our dreams,
shin - ing ra - diance,
ter - ror of pris - on,
deep in - to the sea,

Ev - er - last - ing grace is yours!

Cantor

God a - lone is won - der - ful and might - y,
Rul - ing the day with bril - liant splen - dor,
Op - ening wide the Red Sea wa - ters,
Strik - ing down the pow - er of the might - y,

All   *Cantor*

Ev - er - last - ing grace is yours!

Heav - en and earth cre -
Guard - ing the night with
Bring us through to
Sav - ing us from

WORDS: David Haas (Ps. 136)
MUSIC: David Haas
© 1995 GIA Publications, Inc.

at - ed in wis - dom,
moon and star - light,
life and free - dom,
all op - pres - sion,
Ev - er - last - ing grace is yours!

Refrain

Al - le - lu - ia! Al - le - lu - ia!

Ev - er - last - ing grace is yours! Al - le - lu - ia! Al -

le - lu - ia! Ev - er - last - ing grace is yours! ___

Psalm Prayer (Ps. 136)   341

We thank you, O God, for the remarkable story of your Presence
   in making us the people you would have us be.
You created us from nothing,
      saved us from sin,
      and liberated us for loving.
How can we refrain from thanksgiving?
For your steadfast love endures forever. **Amen.**

Ps. 136; adapt. by Stephen D. Bryant

342

Refrain

① *May be sung in unison before the reading begins, and as a canon at the end.*

By the wa - ters, the wa - ters of Ba - by - lon,

②

we sat down and wept, and wept for Zi - on.

③

We re-mem-ber, we re-mem-ber, we re-mem-ber Zi - on.

(Hum as verses are read by one or more readers.)

By the rivers of Babylon,
    there we sat down and wept,
    when we remembered Zion.
On the willows there
    we hung up our lyres.
For there our captors
    required of us songs,
    and our tormentors, mirth, saying,
    "Sing us one of the songs of Zion."
How shall we sing the Lord's song
    in a foreign land? *Refrain*
If I forget you, O Jerusalem,
    let my right hand wither!
Let my tongue stick to the roof of my mouth,
    if I do not remember you,
if I do not set Jerusalem
    above my highest joy!
O Lord, remember against the Edomites,
    the day of Jerusalem,
how they said, "Raze it, raze it!
    Down to its foundations!"
O daughter of Babylon, you devastator!
    Happy shall they be who repay you
    with what you have done to us!
Happy shall they be who take your little ones
    and smash them against a rock! *Refrain*

WORDS: Ps. 137; trans. by John Holbert, S T Kimbrough, Jr., and Carlton R. Young
MUSIC: Trad. Israeli melody

Psalm 137

(Beside the Streams of Babylon)

1. Be - side the streams of Bab - y - lon, we
2. On wil - low trees we hung our harps while,
3. How shall we ev - er sing God's song in
4. And let my tongue stick in my mouth if

sat our - selves and wept, re - mem - ber - ing the
add - ing to their wrongs, our cap - tors smirked a
such a for - eign land? If I my birth - place
ev - er I for - get Je - ru - sa - lem, which

land we loved and all the hope it kept.
cruel re - quest, "Sing one of Zi - on's songs."
dared for - get, let strength de - sert my hand.
far a - bove all oth - er joys I set.

WORDS: John L. Bell (Ps. 137)
MUSIC: Trad. Scottish, alt.

Psalm Prayer (Ps. 137)

We weep, O God, when we are held captive
　　to things that are not of you.
Let us remember in the midst of our captivity
　　to sing your song of hope
　　　　as we recall your promises to us.
Let us weep with hope,
　　and let us rejoice in your presence,
　　　　even when we do not see you or feel your presence.
For our trust is in you. **Amen.**

Ps. 137; adapt. by Sheri Daylong

345   Psalm Prayer (Ps. 137)

O God of all times and places, of all peoples and all nations,
     though our lives are filled with moments of misery,
          days of despair,
          periods of pain,
          times of trial,
          years of yearning,
     we pray for your comfort and strength on each day of life's journey
          as we walk in the light of your enduring grace. **Amen.**

Ps. 137; adapt. by Jerry Oakland
Adapt. © 2006 Upper Room Books

346   Psalm Prayer (Ps. 137)

O God, we sit beside waters of sorrow and despair.
We hear voices that hold us captive
     and realize that apart from you our hearts do not sing.
We turn to you for deliverance.
Guide us to the promised shore, the place of justice and mercy,
     that returning to you we may sing a new song. **Amen.**

Ps. 137; adapt. by Judy Holloway
Adapt. © 2006 Upper Room Books

347   Psalm Prayer (Ps. 137)

O God of judgment,
     when we have been wounded by the enemy,
     or by those who are supposed to love us;
     when we feel held captive by another's hand,
     or by our own thoughts and emotions,
     help us remember that vengeance is yours.
You hear our cry, and you take upon yourself our burden.
We give you thanks that we are human, and you are God. **Amen.**

Ps. 137; adapt. by Ginger Howl
Adapt. © 2006 Upper Room Books

Psalm Prayer (Ps. 139)

It is not you who shape God,
   it is God who shapes you.
If, then, you are the work of God,
   await the hand of the artist who does all things in due season.
Offer the Potter your heart,
   soft and tractable,
   and keep the form in which the Artist has fashioned you.
Let your clay be moist,
   lest you grow hard and lose the imprint of the Potter's fingers.

Ps. 139; adapt. by Irenaeus (2nd century)

349

Psalm 139

Refrain 1

Search me, O God, and know my

heart. Lead me in ways that en-dure.

or

Refrain 2

O God, you have searched me and known me.

or

Refrain 3

① *(Sing as a canon.)*

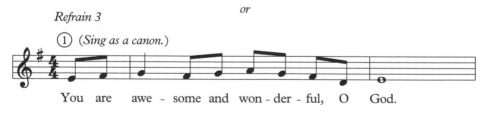

You are awe-some and won-der-ful, O God.

②

Won-der-ful are your works.

WORDS: Ps. 139; refrain 1 by Jane Marshall; refrain 2 by Beth A. Richardson (Ps. 139); refrain 3 by Fred Erwin (Ps. 139)
MUSIC: Refrain 1, Jane Marshall; refrain 2, Beth A. Richardson; refrain 3, Fred Erwin
Refrain 1 © 1984 The Upper Room; refrain 2 © 2001 Beth A. Richardson; refrain 3 © 2002 Fred Erwin

Choose a refrain to respond to this text, read by four groups or four readers located in four parts of the room.
Interpretive dance or body postures can provide heightened expression of the text.

Refrain

I.   O God, you have searched me and known me.
You know when I sit down and rise up, you discern my thoughts from afar.
You discern my path and the places I rest;
you are familiar with all my ways.
Before a word is on my tongue, you know it, O God, completely.
You guard me from behind and before,
and lay your hand upon me.
It is beyond my knowledge; it is a mystery; I cannot fathom it. *Refrain*

II.   Where can I escape from your spirit? Where can I flee from your presence?
If I ascend to heaven, you are there;
if I lie down in the grave, you are even there.
If I take wing with the dawn and alight at the sea's farthest limits,
there also your hand will be guiding me,
your powerful hand holding me fast.
If I say, "Let the darkness cover me and my day be turned to night,"
even darkness is not dark to you: the night is as bright as the day,
for darkness is as light to you. *Refrain*

III. It was you who formed my inward parts;
you fashioned me in my mother's womb.
I praise you, for I am fearfully, wonderfully made.
Wondrous are your works; that I know very well.
My frame was not hidden from you when I was being fashioned in secret,
intricately woven in the mystery of clay.
Your eyes saw my substance taking shape;
in your book my every day was recorded;
all my days were fashioned, even before they came to be. *Refrain*

IV. How deep your designs are to me, O God! How great their number!
I try to count them but they are more than the sand.
I come to the end—I am still with you.
[O that you would kill the wicked, O God,
and that the bloodthirsty would depart from me—
those who speak of you maliciously,
and lift themselves up against you for evil!
Do I not hate those who hate you, O Lord?
And do I not loathe those who rise up against you?
I hate them with perfect hatred;
I count them my enemies.]*
Search me, O God, and know my heart;
test me and know my thoughts.
Watch closely, lest I follow a path of error
and guide me in the everlasting way. *Refrain*

**Omit if desired.*

350

Psalm Prayer (Ps. 139)

Loving and tender Creator,
 you knit us into being. You truly know us.
 You forever love us.
Praise to you at morning's light.
Praise from heavenly heights,
 praise all our days.
Wonderful is your love. **Amen.**

Ps. 139; adapt. by Larry Peacock
Adapt. © 2006 Upper Room Books

351

Psalm Prayer (Ps. 139)

O Creator God,
 we thank you that though we may run, we cannot hide from you.
 There is nowhere we can go that you are not with us.
We praise you for the power of your presence
 every moment of the day and of the night.
We place our lives into your safekeeping.
 In the name of Christ we pray. **Amen.**

Ps. 139; adapt. by Jo Hoover
Adapt. © 2006 Upper Room Books

352

Psalm 141
(My Prayers Rise Like Incense)

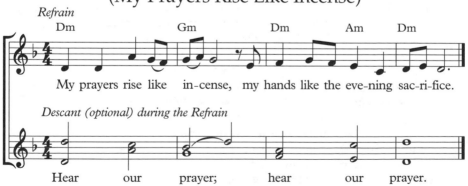

Refrain

My prayers rise like in-cense, my hands like the eve-ning sac-ri-fice.

Descant (optional) during the Refrain

Hear our prayer; hear our prayer.

*Accompaniment in Upper Room Worshipbook Accompaniment and Worship Leader *edition*

WORDS: Arlo D. Duba (Ps. 141)
MUSIC: Arlo D. Duba; descant by Elise Eslinger
Refrain © 1980 Arlo D. Duba; descant © 1985 The Upper Room

Leader, chanting freely

Dm   C   Dm

1.   I   call   to   you,   O   Lord,   come   to   me   quickly;
2.   Keep   guard   over   my   mouth; O Lord, watch the door of my lips;
3.   Should   the   righteous   re - buke   me,   let   me   accept   it   as   grace; but keep the
4.   But my   eyes are turned toward you,   O   Lord   my   God,   in

Gm   Dm   A7

hear   my   voice   when   I   cry   to   you.   Let   my
keep   my   heart   from   slipping   into   evil.
oil of the unrighteous ever from touching   my   head.   I   con -
you   I   take   refuge,   de - prive   me   not   of   life.

D   D7   Gm

prayer   rise   be - fore   you   like   incense,   and   my
Let   me   not   be   busy   with   evil - doers;   let   me
tinually   pray   a - gainst   their   wicked   deeds; when they   are
Keep   me   from   the   snare   the   evil   ones   set   for   me;   Let

Dm   Gm   A   *To Refrain*

hands   like   the   evening   sacrifice.
not   be   taken   in   by   their   sensuous   foods.
judged they will know the   truth   of   your   Word.
them   be   ensnared,   but   Lord,   grant   me   re - lease.

353

Psalm 141
(Let My Prayer Rise As Incense)

Let my prayer rise as in - cense, as in - cense be -

fore you, in - cense be - fore you, O God.

Let my prayer rise as in - cense, as in - cense be -

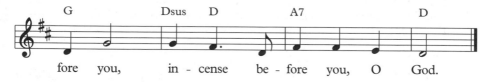

fore you, in - cense be - fore you, O God.

Sing as a response to the text of choice.

WORDS: Steven B. Eulberg (Ps. 141)
MUSIC: Steven B. Eulberg

© 1996 Steven B. Eulberg

354

Psalm Prayer (Ps. 141)

O God, we give you thanks that you sent us Jesus
    to show us how to live in a violent world as nonviolent people.
Replace our vengeful thoughts with prayers of adoration,
    rising before you like incense, that we may rest in peace. **Amen.**

Ps. 141; adapt. by Ginger Howl
Adapt. © 2006 Upper Room Books

Psalm 145

(I Will Exalt My God / *Te exaltaré*)

I will ex - alt my God, my King.
Te e - xal - ta - ré, mi Dios, mi Rey,

I will praise your name for - ev - er.
y ben - de - ci - ré tu nom - bre.

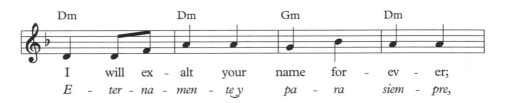

I will ex - alt your name for - ev - er;
E - ter - na - men - te y pa - ra siem - pre,

ev - ery day I'll praise your ho - ly name.
ca - da dí - a te ben - de - ci - ré.

Sing as response to text of choice, spoken or chanted.

WORDS: Casiodoro A. Cárdenas (Ps. 145)
MUSIC: Casiodoro A. Cárdenas

© Casiodoro A. Cárdenas

Psalm Prayer (Ps. 145)

356

We praise your name, O God.
The wonders of your creation give you glory.
All creatures and humans rejoice in your faithfulness,
the whole earth sings to you in joy. **Amen.**

Ps. 145; adapt. by Ginger Howl
Adapt. © 2006 Upper Room Books

Psalm 146
(Praise to the One)

Refrain (may be sung as a canon at the end of the psalm)

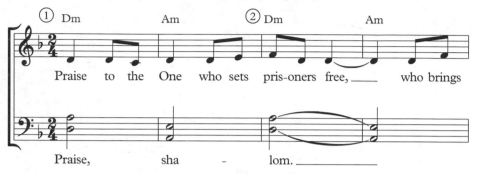

Praise to the One who sets pris-oners free, ___ who brings

Praise,   sha   -   lom. ___

sight to the blind, and gives food to the hun-gry, O

Praise,   sha   -   lom. ___

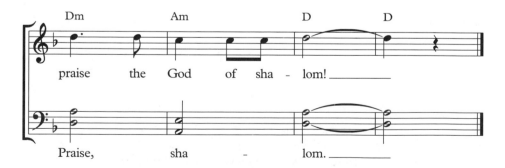

praise the God of sha - lom! ___

Praise,   sha   -   lom. ___

WORDS: Refrain Elise S. Eslinger (Ps. 146:7*b*, 8*a*); verses trans. by Gary Chamberlain, alt.
MUSIC: Elise S. Eslinger

Refrain

I.*   Praise the Lord!
> My inmost self, praise the Lord,
> praise the Lord as long as I live;
> I will constantly sing to my God.

II.   Do not depend on the noblest people,
> for no human power can save you.
> Their breath departs; they return to the ground;
> on that very day their plans will perish.

I.   Happy are those whose helper is Jacob's God,
> whose hope is in God, the Lord—
> the maker of earth and sky and sea,
> and all the things that are in them;

II.   who always does what is right,
> who brings justice to all the oppressed,
> who gives food to the famished,
> who sets the prisoner free;

I.   the Lord, who gives sight to the blind,

II.   who lifts up the humbled,

I.   who loves those who act justly,

II.   who protects the refugees,

I.   who comes to the aid of the orphan and widow,

II.   but subverts the plans of evil people.

I, II.   The Lord will always rule,
> your God, O Zion, forevermore.   (*Refrain may be sung as a canon.*)

*I and II may be read by Leader/All or by two groups within the assembly.

Psalm Prayer (Ps. 146)   358

God of our hope, you always do what is right:
> bringing justice to the oppressed, food to the famished,
> and sight to the blind.
You protect those who are weak and subvert the plans of evil people.
Praise wells up from our inmost selves,
> and we join the chorus of all whom you have redeemed.
We praise you, O God of *shalom*! **Amen.**

Ps. 146; adapt. by Richard Eslinger
Adapt. © 2006 Upper Room Books

359

Psalm 147
(Sing to God with Joy)

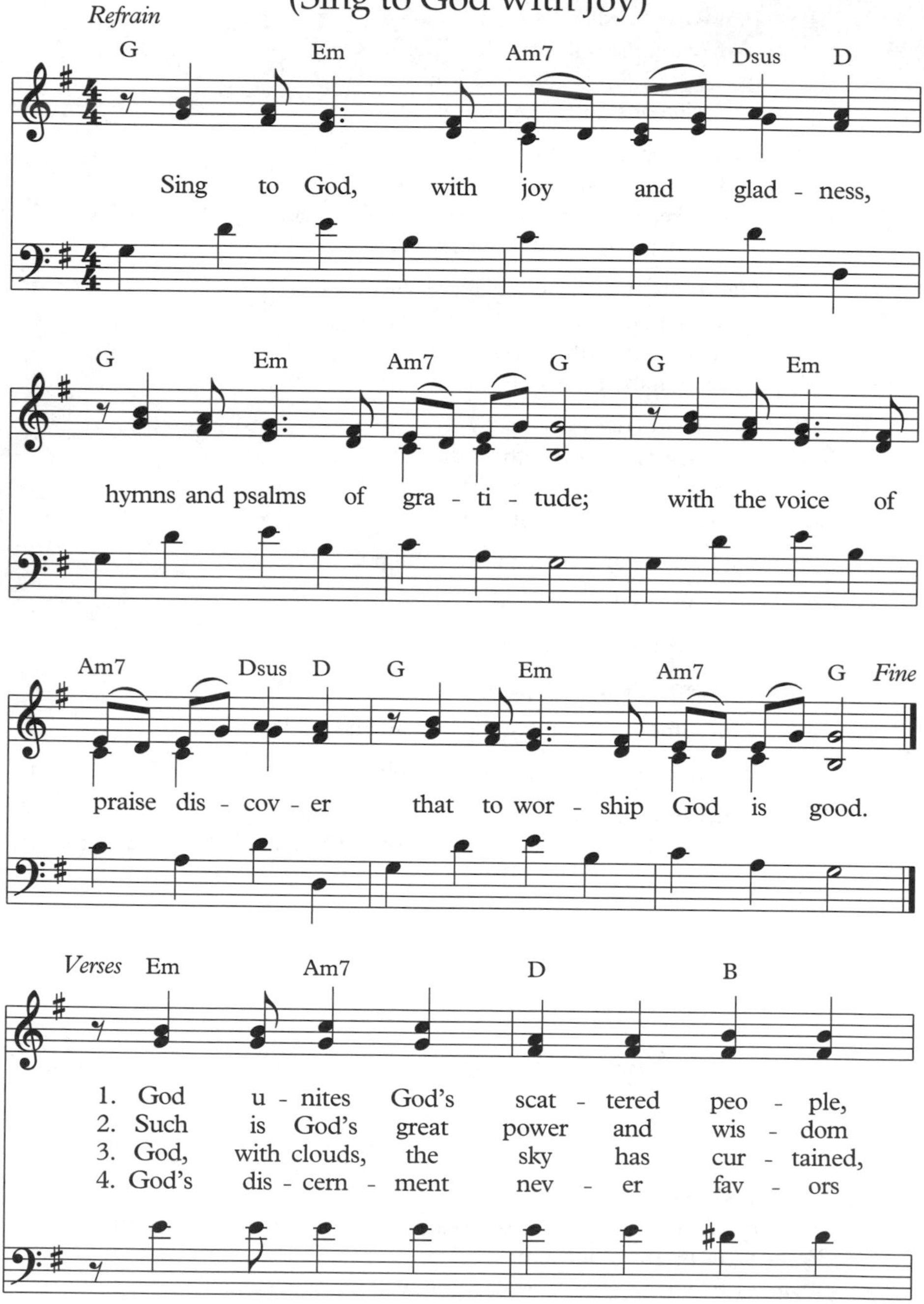

Refrain
G Em Am7 Dsus D
Sing to God, with joy and glad - ness,
G Em Am7 G G Em
hymns and psalms of gra - ti - tude; with the voice of
Am7 Dsus D G Em Am7 G Fine
praise dis - cov - er that to wor - ship God is good.
Verses Em Am7 D B
1. God u - nites God's scat - tered peo - ple,
2. Such is God's great power and wis - dom
3. God, with clouds, the sky has cur - tained,
4. God's dis - cern - ment nev - er fav - ors

WORDS: John L. Bell (Ps. 147)
MUSIC: John L. Bell

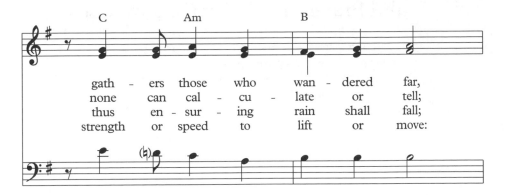

gath – ers those who wan – dered far,
none can cal – cu – late or tell;
thus en – sur – ing rain shall fall;
strength or speed to lift or move:

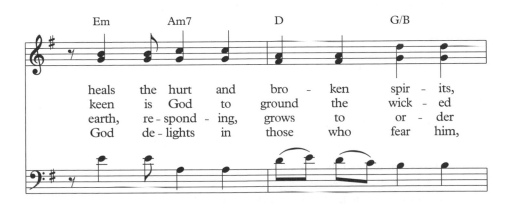

heals the hurt and bro – ken spir – its,
keen is God to ground the wick – ed
earth, re – spond – ing, grows to or – der
God de – lights in those who fear him,

tend – ing ev – ery wound and scar.
and with hum – ble folk to dwell.
food for crea – tures great and small.
trust – ing in his stead – fast love.

360 Psalm Prayer (Ps. 147 *or* General Use)

O God of generous love and abundant mercy,
   how good it is to sing your praises.
Your steadfast love has been known in all the generations;
   and we celebrate that love this day.
As we place our hope in you,
   may we be your faithful servants. **Amen.**

Ps. 147; adapt. by Jerry Oakland
Adapt. © 2006 Upper Room Books

361 Psalm Prayer (Ps. 147 *or* General Use)

We praise you, O great and glorious God.
We thank you that you take pleasure in your creation
   and that you are at work healing and restoring your people.
May our songs of love and praise be a faithful witness to you. **Amen.**

Ps. 147; adapt. by Judy Holloway
Adapt. © 2006 Upper Room Books

362 Psalm Prayer (Ps. 147 *or* General Use)

O God, you tend to the stars, the grass,
   the animals and birds with gentle care.
You provide food and drink for all your creatures.
In the same way, you lift the fallen,
   heal the sick and brokenhearted,
   establish peace where there is conflict.
We glorify your name and worship you with thanks and praise. **Amen.**

Ps. 147; adapt. by Ginger Howl
Adapt. © 2006 Upper Room Books

363 Psalm Prayer (Ps. 147 *or* General Use)

Our hands clap, our feet dance, and our voices shout:
   Amen! Hallelujah!
You are our sovereign, you are exalted!
Hallelujah! Amen!

Ps. 147; adapt. by Elise S. Eslinger
Adapt. © 2006 Upper Room Books

Psalms 148–150
(I Want to Praise Your Name)

1. Praise with the trum-pet, praise with the harp,
2. Moun-tains and val-leys, riv-ers and seas,
3. Moth-ers and fa-thers, daugh-ters and sons,

praise with the tim-brel, the dance and the lyre;
stars in the heav-ens and fish in the deep;
all of God's peo-ple, the old and the young;

let ev-ery-thing that has breath give praise to
let all cre-a-tion give praise to God on
let all who hun-ger to do God's will give

Refrain

God. _____
high. _____
praise. _____

I want to praise your

name. _____ I want to sing your good-

ness. Glo-ry, O God; glo-ry.

WORDS: Bob Hurd (Ps. 148; 149; 150)
MUSIC: Bob Hurd
© 1984 Bob Hurd, published by OCP Publications

365

Psalm 148
(Sing the Lord a New Song)

1. Sing the Lord a new song and praise God's whole cre -
2. Praise the Lord in heav - en, O sun and moon and
3. Praise the Lord, O heav - en of heav - ens, join God's
4. Kings and prin - ces, rul - ers in all the world and
5. All cre - a - tion, join in the praise of your Cre -

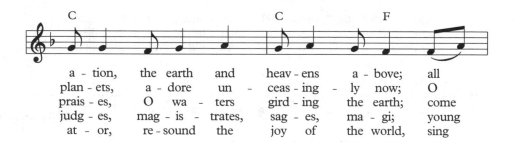

a - tion, the earth and heav - ens a - bove; all
plan - ets, a - dore un - ceas - ing - ly now; O
prais - es, O wa - ters gird - ing the earth; come
judg - es, mag - is - trates, sag - es, ma - gi; young
at - or, re - sound the joy of the world, sing

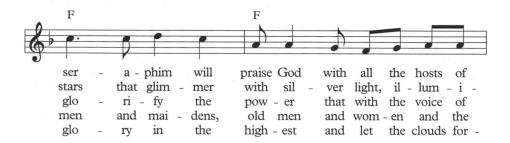

ser - a - phim will praise God with all the hosts of
stars that glim - mer with sil - ver light, il - lum - i -
glo - ri - fy the pow - er that with the voice of
men and mai - dens, old men and wom - en and the
glo - ry in the high - est and let the clouds for -

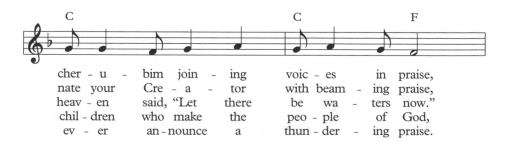

cher - u - bim join - ing voic - es in praise,
nate your Cre - a - tor with beam - ing praise,
heav - en said, "Let there be wa - ters now."
chil - dren who make the peo - ple of God,
ev - er an - nounce a thun - der - ing praise.

Performance notes in Upper Room Worshipbook Accompaniment and Worship Leader *edition*

WORDS: Tilly Lubis-Nainggolan (Ps. 148)
MUSIC: Trad. Batok melody (Toba, Indonesia)

great   is   God's name,   sing   praise and   re - joice;
great   is   your Mak - er,   re - joice in   God's name;
Great   is   your King,   glo - ry   be God's   do - main;
of - fer   God thanks,   you   are bless - ed   of   all;
Sing   al - le - lu - ia,   re - joice in   our   King!

great   is   God's name,   sing   praise and   re - joice.
great   is   your Mak - er,   re - joice in   God's name.
great   is   your King,   glo - ry   be God's   do - main.
of - fer   God thanks,   you   are bless - ed   of   all.
Sing   al - le - lu - ia,   re - joice in   our   King!

Psalm Prayer (Ps. 148)   366

Holy God,
    sometimes our only response to you must be an outburst of sheer joy!
All heaven and earth, and all human beings and animals,
    sing to you our hymn of praise. Alleluia! **Amen.**

Ps. 148; adapt. by Ginger Howl
Adapt. © 2006 Upper Room Books

Psalm Prayer (Ps. 148)   367

O God, creator of the universe and worlds beyond,
    we lift our praise to you.
You bless your creation with faithfulness,
    and you desire only the goodness of harmony and peace.
May we carry your praise into the world
    so that all creation is blessed by your goodness. **Amen.**

Ps. 148; adapt. by Judy Holloway
Adapt. © 2006 Upper Room Books

Psalm 149

Refrain I

Give praise to the Lord and sing a new

song, a - mid all the saints God's prais - es pro - long.

WORDS: *The Psalter, 1912*
MUSIC: Attr. to Johann M. Haydn

or

Refrain II

Come, let us sing to the Lord our song, to

joy - ful - ly thank God for our days.

WORDS: Jim Strathdee (Ps. 149)
MUSIC: Jim Strathdee
© 1977 Desert Flower Music

Refrain

Praise the Lord!

Sing to the Lord a new song,
God's praise in the assembly of the faithful.

Let Israel be glad in their maker,
let the children of Zion rejoice in their ruler.
Let them praise God's name with dancing,
making melody to the Lord with tambourine and lyre.

For the Lord takes pleasure in this people,
and adorns the humble with victory.   *Refrain*

Let the faithful exult in glory;
let them sing for joy on their couches.

Wild animals and all cattle,
creeping things and flying birds!

Rulers of the earth and all peoples,
leaders and all judges of the earth!
Young men and women alike,
old and young together!

Let them praise the name of the Lord,
whose name alone is exalted,
whose glory is above earth and heaven.   *Refrain*

The Lord has raised up a horn for the people,
praise for all the faithful,
for the people of Israel who are close to their God.

Praise the Lord!   *Refrain*

Psalm Prayer (Ps. 149)   369

Great and holy God,
we know that you alone hold power
to create and to destroy.
You alone exercise right judgments.
We know also that you delight in your creation—
that you rejoice in your children.
So we dance and sing,
we play instruments, and we shout for joy
that you are our God and we are your people. **Amen.**

Ps. 149; adapt. by Ginger Howl
Adapt. © 2006 Upper Room Books

Psalm 150
(Halle, Halle, Hallelujah)

Refrain

Hal-le, hal-le, hal-le-lu-jah! Hal-le, hal-le, hal-
hal-

hal-

le-lu-jah! Hal-le, hal-le, hal-le-lu-

le-lu, Hal-le-lu-jah!

le-lu-jah!

To Repeat or to Verses | *Last time*

Hal-le-lu-jah! _____ jah! _____

jah! Hal-le-lu-jah! Hal-le-lu, hal-le-lu-jah! jah! _____

Hal-le-lu-jah! _____ jah! _____

Refrain may be used as Gospel Alleluia in A Celebration of Word and Table.

WORDS: Refrain trad. Caribbean; vss. 1–2 by Hal H. Hopson
MUSIC: Refrain trad. Caribbean, arr. by John L. Bell; verse music by Hal H. Hopson

Psalm 150
(Tell God's Wonders)

Refrain 1

Tell God's won-ders, sing God's worth.   Hal - le - lu - jah!

or

Refrain 2

Praise the Lord with the sound of trum-pet, praise the Lord with the
Lou - ons Dieu a - vec la trom - pet - te, lou - ons Dieu a - vec

harp and lute,   praise the Lord; nev-er let your voice be   still.
harpe et luth,   chan-tons tous a-vec joie à l'É - ter - nal.

Refrain

Praise God in the sanctuary;
praise God in the mighty firmament!
Praise God for mighty deeds;
praise God according to surpassing greatness!
Praise God with trumpet sound;
praise God with lute and harp!
Praise God with tambourine and dance;
praise God with strings and pipe!
Praise God with clanging cymbals;
praise God with loud clashing cymbals!
Let everything that breathes praise our God!
Hallelujah! *Refrain*

Verses sung to Psalm Tones or read responsively, with either Refrain

WORDS: Refrain 1 by Henry Francis Lyle, alt.; refrain 2 by Natalie Sleeth; trans. by Andrew Donaldson;
       Psalm 150 NRSV, para.
MUSIC: Refrain 1 by Robert Williams; refrain 2 by Natalie Sleeth; psalm tones by Elise S. Eslinger

372

Psalm 150
(Praise Ye the Lord)

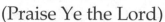

Praise ye the Lord, Hal - le - lu - jah!

Ev - ery-bod - y praise the Lord. _

1. Praise God with the sound of the trum - pet,
2. Praise God with ho - ly cym - bals,
3. Praise God in the ho - ly tem - ple,
4. Praise God on top of the moun - tains,

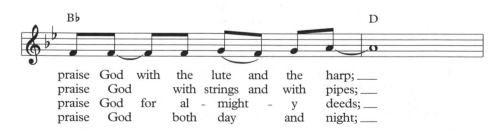

praise God with the lute and the harp; __
praise God with strings and with pipes; __
praise God for al - might - y deeds; __
praise God both day and night; __

WORDS: J. Jefferson Cleveland (Ps. 150)
MUSIC: J. Jefferson Cleveland
© 1981 J. Jefferson Cleveland

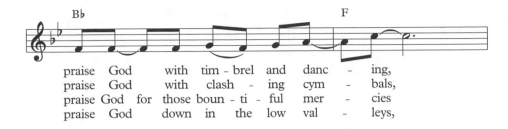

praise God with tim - brel and danc - ing,
praise God with clash - ing cym - bals,
praise God for those boun - ti - ful mer - cies
praise God down in the low val - leys,

praise God wher - ev - er you are. _____
praise God with all of your might. _____
for God ful - fills our needs. _____
praise God be - cause it's all right. _____

Psalm Prayer (Ps. 150) 373

When in our music God is glorified,
and adoration leaves no room for pride,
it is as though the whole creation cried
  "Alleluia!"

How often, making music, we have found
a new dimension in the world of sound,
as worship moved us to a more profound
  "Alleluia!"

So has the church in liturgy and song,
in faith and love, through centuries of wrong,
borne witness to the truth in every tongue,
  "Alleluia!"

And did not Jesus sing a psalm that night
when utmost evil strove against the light?
Then let us sing, for whom he won the fight:
  "Alleluia!"

Let every instrument be tuned for praise!
Let all rejoice who have a voice to raise!
And may God give us faith to sing always
  "Alleluia!"

May be sung to ENGELBERG, No. 131.

Fred Pratt Green

Global Songs and Responses

Simple Gifts

In memory of Brother Roger, founding leader of the Community of Taizé, assassinated in 2005 while leading prayers at the Church of Reconciliation, Taizé, France; and, in gratitude for the musical gifts embodied in diverse ways by courageous communities of Christians all over the earth.

Arising in recent decades among Christians the world round—in gracious contrast to fearsome global complexities and crises (and often in prophetic witness)—have been some amazing, simple gifts. These short songs serve as communal prayer and praise, are effectively learned by rote, and may be internalized more easily and quickly than lengthy texts or elaborate musical forms. Sung by Christian pilgrims and worshipers of all ages and stages of faith, these brief and accessible songs of community offer opportunity for reflection and contemplation as well as celebration. They are simple to sing but not simplistic in a biblical or theological sense. They may enhance hopeful and trusting address to God in the long tradition of sung liturgical prayer responses as well as in spontaneous praise. They may evoke the dance!

Singing such songs inevitably widens our vision of Christ's church, as these are offered in solidarity with those indigenous communities from which they arose—just as ancient psalms, canticles, and other liturgical songs bring us close to universal praise among the saints and in heaven. Such simple gifts punctuate our celebration, proclamation, table fellowship, commissioning, and blessing. They carry the flavor and *ethos* of unique, varied contexts from around the earth. Ordinary people in all times and places celebrate holy mysteries of faith and faithfulness.

Two particular communities have arisen that provide ongoing creation and expression of such sung prayer: the Taizé Community in France and the Community of Iona in Scotland.[1] These pages include major contributions from both of these European settings, as well as lively and moving music from Africa, South America, Eastern Europe, Asia, and Australia. The impact on the body of Christ of unique denominational projects, along with the richly reciprocal interchange of international composers and worship leaders in recent years, cannot be underestimated in importance. Never has it been truer that Christians are called urgently to "one faith, one Lord, one baptism," even as the love of Christ himself urges us constantly toward open, respectful exchange with those of faiths and cultures not our own. Hospitality of the heart and mind is the unique invitation conveyed yet again when we remember the One to whom we all belong.

Elise S. Eslinger
Editor and Compiler

---

1. Additional background, interpretation, and suggestions for use of these global songs and responses is provided in *Upper Room Worshipbook Accompaniment and Worship Leader Edition.*

376 **Adoramus Te, Domine**
(We Adore You, Lord Jesus Christ)

(hum) _____

A-do-ra-mus te, Do-mi-ne.
We a-dore you, Lord Je-sus Christ.

Cantor verses in Upper Room Worshipbook Accompaniment and Worship Leader *edition*

WORDS: Jacques Berthier
MUSIC: Jacques Berthier

ADORAMUS
Irregular

© 1991 Ateliers et Presses de Taizé, Taizé Community, France; GIA Publications, Inc., exclusive North American agent

377 **Bless the Lord**

Bless the Lord, my soul, and bless God's ho-ly name.

Bless the Lord, my soul, who leads me in-to life.

Cantor verses in Upper Room Worshipbook Accompaniment and Worship Leader *edition*

WORDS: Ps. 103:1
MUSIC: Jacques Berthier and the Taizé Community

BLESS THE LORD (TAIZÉ)
Irregular

© 1982, 1983, 1984 Ateliers et Presses de Taizé, Taizé Community, France; GIA Publications, Inc., exclusive North American agent

Come and Fill Our Hearts

Come and fill our hearts with your peace.

You a-lone, O Lord, are ho-ly.

Come and fill our hearts with your peace,

al-le-lu - ia!

WORDS: Jacques Berthier (Ps. 137)
MUSIC: Jacques Berthier

CONFITEMINI DOMINO
Irregular

379

Eat This Bread

1. Eat this bread, drink this cup,
2. Je - sus Christ, bread of life,

come to him and nev - er be hun - gry. Eat this bread,
those who come to you will not hun - ger. Je - sus Christ,

drink this cup, trust in him and you will not thirst.
ris - en Lord, those who trust in you will not thirst.

WORDS: John 6:35
MUSIC: Jacques Berthier

BREAD
Irregular

380

Gloria
(Glory to God)

Canon

Glo - ri - a, glo - ri - a, in ex - cel - sis De - o!
Glo-ry to God, glo-ry to God, glo-ry in the high - est!

WORDS: Luke 2:14
MUSIC: Jacques Berthier

GLORIA 3
Irregular

Glo - ri - a,   glo - ri - a,   al - le - lu - ia,   al - le - lu - ia,
Glo-ry to God,   *Glo-ry to God,*   *al - le - lu - ia,*   *al - le - lu - ia!*

In the Lord I'll Be Ever Thankful   381

In the Lord I'll be ev - er thank - ful, in the Lord I will re -

joice! Look to God, do not be a - fraid. Lift up your

voic - es, the Lord is near; lift up your voic - es, the Lord is near.

WORDS: Ps. 145:10, 18   ITLIBET
MUSIC: Jacques Berthier   Irregular

382 Jesus, Remember Me

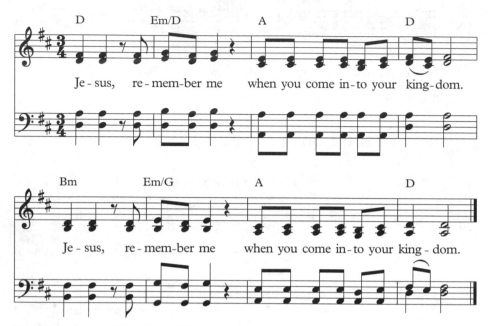

Je - sus, re - mem - ber me when you come in - to your king - dom.

Je - sus, re - mem - ber me when you come in - to your king - dom.

WORDS: Community of Taizé (Luke 23:42)
MUSIC: Jacques Berthier

REMEMBER ME
Irregular

© 1978, 1980, 1981 Ateliers et Presses de Taizé, Taizé Community, France; GIA Publications, Inc., exclusive North American agent

383 Jubilate, Servite
(Raise a Song of Gladness)

Ju - bi - la - te De - o om - nis ter - ra.
Raise a song of glad-ness peo-ples of the earth.

Ser - vi - te Do - mi - no in lae - ti - ti - a.
Christ has come, bring-ing peace, joy to ev-ery heart.

May be sung as a two-, three- or four-part canon.

WORDS: Ps. 100
MUSIC: Jacques Berthier

JUBILATE SERVITE
Irregular

© 1978, 1980, 1981 Ateliers et Presses de Taizé, Taizé Community, France; GIA Publications, Inc., exclusive North American agent

③
Al - le - lu - ia, al - le - lu - ia, in lae - ti - ti - a.
Al - le - lu - ia, al - le - lu - ia, joy to ev - ery heart.

④
Al - le - lu - ia, al - le - lu - ia, in lae - ti - ti - a.
Al - le - lu - ia, al - le - lu - ia, joy to ev - ery heart.

Laudate Dominum 384
(Sing Praise and Bless the Lord)

Lau - da - te   Do - mi - num,   lau - da - te   Do - mi - num,
Sing, praise and   bless the Lord.   Sing, praise and   bless the Lord.

om - nes   gen - tes,   al - le - lu - ia!   al - le - lu - ia!
Peo - ples!   Na - tions!   Al - le - lu - ia!   Al - le - lu - ia!

Verses in Upper Room Worshipbook Accompaniment and Worship Leader *edition*

WORDS: Pss. 117; 150:6; 47:1; 100:2-5
MUSIC: Jacques Berthier

LAUDATE
Irregular

385 Let Your Servant Now Go in Peace

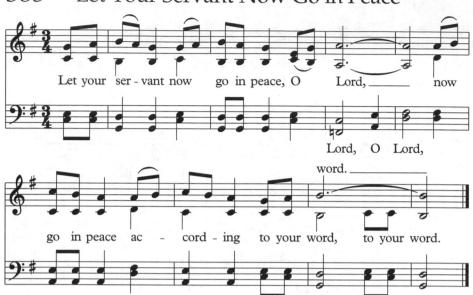

Let your ser-vant now go in peace, O Lord, _____ now

Lord, O Lord,

word. _____

go in peace ac-cord-ing to your word, to your word.

May be used as refrain for Canticle of Simeon in the Service of Night Prayer, p. 22.

WORDS: Jacques Berthier
MUSIC: Jacques Berthier

NUNC DIMITTIS
Irregular

© 1998 Ateliers et Presses de Taizé, Taizé Community, France; GIA Publications, Inc., exclusive North American agent

386 Lord Jesus Christ

Lord Je - sus Christ, your light shines with - in us.

Let not my doubts nor my dark-ness speak to me.

Cantor verses in Upper Room Worshipbook Accompaniment and Worship Leader *edition*

WORDS: Ps. 139
MUSIC: Jacques Berthier

LORD JESUS
Irregular

© 1998 Ateliers et Presses de Taizé, Taizé Community, France; GIA Publications, Inc., exclusive North American agent

Lord Je-sus Christ, your light shines with-in us.

Let my heart al-ways wel-come your love.

My Soul Is at Rest 387

My soul is at rest in God a-lone,

my sal-va-tion comes from God.

Cantor verses in Upper Room Worshipbook Accompaniment and Worship Leader *edition*

WORDS: Ps. 62:5-8
MUSIC: Jacques Berthier

REST
Irregular

388 Nada te turbe
(Nothing Can Trouble)

Na - da te tur - be, na - da te es-pan - te. Quien a Dios tie - ne
Noth-ing can trou - ble, noth-ing can fright-en. Those who seek God shall

na - da le fal - ta. So - lo Dios bas - ta.
nev - er go want - ing. God a - lone fills us.

Cantor verses in Upper Room Worshipbook Accompaniment and Worship Leader *edition*

WORDS: St. Teresa de Jesús; Taizé Community
MUSIC: Jacques Berthier

NADA TE TURBE
Irregular

© 1986, 1991 Ateliers et Presses de Taizé, Taizé Community, France; GIA Publications, Inc., exclusive North American agent

389 O Christe Domine Jesu
(Christ Jesus)

O Chri - ste Do - mi - ne Je - su! O
Christ Je - sus, Lord and Sav - ior! Christ

Cantor verses in Upper Room Worshipbook Accompaniment and Worship Leader *edition*

WORDS: Ps. 23
MUSIC: Jacques Berthier

O CHRISTE
Irregular

© 1982, 1983, 1984, 1991 Ateliers et Presses de Taizé, Taizé Community, France; GIA Publications, Inc., exclusive North American agent

O Lord, Hear My Prayer / The Lord Is My Song

390

Chri – ste Do – mi – ne Je – su!
Je – sus, Lord and Sav – ior!

O Lord, hear my prayer, O Lord, hear my prayer.
The Lord is my song, the Lord is my praise:

When I call an – swer me. O Lord, hear my prayer, O
All my hope comes from God. The Lord is my song, the

Lord, hear my prayer. Come and lis – ten to me.
Lord is my praise: God, the well-spring of life.

WORDS: Ps. 28:1-2; Isa. 12
MUSIC: Jacques Berthier

MY PRAYER
Irregular

391   Our Darkness

Our dark-ness is nev-er dark-ness in your sight: the deep-est night is clear as the day - light.

WORDS: Jacques Berthier
MUSIC: Jacques Berthier

OUR DARKNESS
Irregular

© 1991 Ateliers et Presses de Taizé, Taizé Community, France; GIA Publications, Inc., exclusive North American agent

392   Stay with Us

Stay with us, O Lord Je-sus Christ, night will soon fall. Then

WORDS: Jacques Berthier
MUSIC: Jacques Berthier

STAY WITH US
Irregular

© 1991 Ateliers et Presses de Taizé, Taizé Community, France; GIA Publications, Inc., exclusive North American agent

stay with us, O Lord Je-sus Christ, light in our dark - ness.

The Lord Is My Light 393

Theme I

The Lord is my light, my light and sal - va - tion: in

God I trust, in God I trust.

Theme II

The Lord is my light, my light and sal - va - tion: in

God I trust, in God I trust.

Each of the two themes can be sung alone, either in unison or as a canon for two voices entering at A1 and B1. The two themes can also be sung together, preferably with Theme I for female voices and Theme II for male voices.

WORDS: Ps. 27
MUSIC: Jacques Berthier

THE LORD IS MY LIGHT
Irregular

394

Ubi Caritas
(Live in Charity)

U – bi ca – ri – tas et a – mor,
Live in char – i – ty and stead – fast love,

u – bi ca – ri – tas De – us i – bi est.
live in char – i – ty; God will dwell with you.

Cantor verses in Upper Room Worshipbook Accompaniment and Worship Leader *edition*

WORDS: 9th cent. Latin (1 Cor. 13:2-8)   UBI CARITAS (TAIZÉ)
MUSIC: Jacques Berthier and the Community of Taizé   Irregular

395

Veni Sancte Spiritus
(Holy Spirit, Come to Us)

Ve – ni San – cte Spi – ri – tus.
Ho – ly Spir – it, come to us.

Cantor verses in Upper Room Worshipbook Accompaniment and Worship Leader *edition*

WORDS: Pentecost Sequence; adapt. by Jacques Berthier   VENI SANCTE SPIRITUS
MUSIC: Jacques Berthier   Irregular

Wait for the Lord

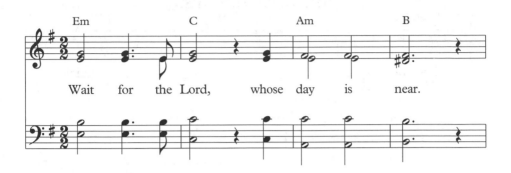

Wait for the Lord, whose day is near.

Wait for the Lord: keep watch, take heart!

WORDS: Ps. 130
MUSIC: Jacques Berthier

Creator and Healer of the World

Creator and Healer of the world,
    help us to see our part in your work
    of healing our world and its wounded people.
Show us what needs to be torn down
    and what needs to be built up,
    that all people may live in peace and safety,
    enjoying fullness of life. **Amen.**

Mary Lou Redding

398 Amen, We Praise Your Name
(Amen Siakudumisa)

WORDS: Trad. Xhosa (South Africa) attr. to S. C. Molefe as taught by Gobingca George Mxadana
MUSIC: Trad. Xhosa melody (South Africa) attr. to S. C. Molefe as taught by George Mxadana

MASITHI
Irregular

Praise, Praise, Praise the Lord

Melody in alto part

Praise, praise, praise the Lord! Praise God's ho-ly name. Al-le-lu-ia!

Praise, praise, praise the Lord! Praise God's ho-ly name. Al-le-lu-ia!

Praise God's ho-ly name. Al-le-lu-ia! Praise God's ho-ly name. Al-le-lu-ia!

Praise God's ho-ly name. Al-le-lu-ia! Praise God's ho-ly name. Al-le-lu-ia!

This song may be repeated, adding a vocal part on each repetition:
melody (alto) alone; melody plus tenor; melody plus lower parts; all voices.

WORDS: Trad. Cameroon; collected by Elaine Hanson
MUSIC: Trad. Cameroon; arr. by Ralph M. Johnson
Arr. © 1994 Earthsongs

AFRICAN PROCESSIONAL
Irregular

400 Hallelujah! We Sing Your Praises

Refrain

Hal - le - lu - jah! We sing your prais - es, all our hearts are filled with glad - ness. Hal - le - lu - jah! We sing your prais - es, all our hearts are filled with glad - ness.

1. Christ the Lord to us said: "I am
2. Now he sends us all out, strong in

Each refrain and stanza is sung twice in succession.

WORDS: Trad. South African
MUSIC: Trad. South African

HALELUYA! PELO TSO RONA
Irregular

| wine, | I am | bread, | I | am wine, | I | am |
| faith, | free of | doubt, | strong | in faith, | free | of |

| bread, | give | to | all | who thirst and hun | - ger." |
| doubt. | Tell | to | all | the joy - ful Gos | - pel. |

Come into God's Presence   401

1. Come in - to God's pres - ence sing - ing al - le - lu - ia,
2. Come in - to God's pres - ence sing - ing Je - sus is Lord,
3. Praise the Lord to - geth - er sing - ing wor - thy the Lamb,
4. Praise the Lord to - geth - er sing - ing glo - ry to God,

al	- le - lu	- ia,	al	- le - lu	- ia.
Je	- sus is	Lord,	Je	- sus is	Lord.
wor	- thy the	Lamb,	wor	- thy the	Lamb.
glo	- ry to	God,	glo	- ry to	God.

*May be sung as a canon.

WORDS: Anon.
MUSIC: Anon.

GOD'S PRESENCE
84.44

402 Alleluia

May be used as Gospel Alleluia in A Celebration of Word and Table, No. 34.

WORDS: Trad.
MUSIC: Norah Duncan IV
Music © 1987 GIA Publications, Inc.

DUNCAN
Irregular

403 Glory to God, Glory in the Highest

Additional suggestions in Upper Room Worshipbook Accompaniment and Worship Leader *edition*

WORDS: Trad. Peruvian
MUSIC: Trad. Peruvian

MACHU-PICHU
Irregular

Leader
To God be glo-ry for - ev - er!
¡A Dios la glo-ria por siem-pre!

All
To God be glo-ry for - ev - er!
¡A Dios la glo-ria por siem-pre!

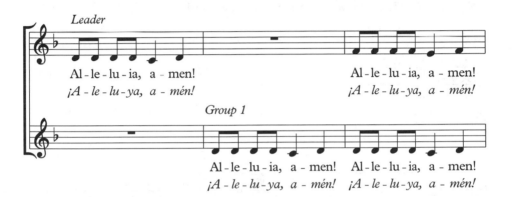

Leader
Al - le - lu - ia, a - men! Al - le - lu - ia, a - men!
¡A - le - lu - ya, a - mén! ¡A - le - lu - ya, a - mén!

Group 1
Al - le - lu - ia, a - men! Al - le - lu - ia, a - men!
¡A - le - lu - ya, a - mén! ¡A - le - lu - ya, a - mén!

Leader
Al - le - lu - ia, a - men!
¡A - le - lu - ya, a - mén!

Groups 1, 2   **Groups 1, 2, 3**
Al - le - lu - ia, a - men! Al - le - lu - ia, a - men! Al - le - lu - ia, a - men!
¡A - le - lu - ya, a - mén! ¡A - le - lu - ya, a - mén! ¡A - le - lu - ya, a - mén!

Al - le - lu - ia, a - men! Al - le - lu - ia, a - men! __
¡A - le - lu - ya, a - mén! ¡A - le - lu - ya, a - mén! __

404 Sing Alleluia to the Lord

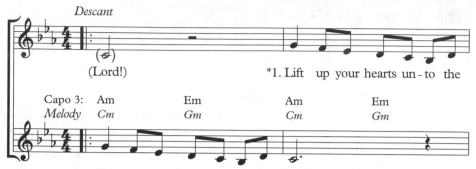

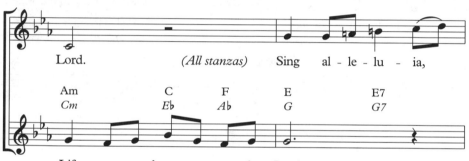

2. In Christ the world has been redeemed.
3. His resurrection sets us free.

4. Therefore we celebrate the feast.
5. Sing alleluia to the Lord.

Sing other stanzas in echo style.

WORDS: Early Christian liturgy; st. 5 Linda Stassen (1 Cor. 5:8)
MUSIC: Linda Stassen; harm. Dale Grotenhuis

SING ALLELUIA
Irregular

Final ending

lift up your hearts un-to the (Lord!)

Final ending

| Dm | Em | Am | Em | A |
| *Fm* | *Gm* | *Cm* | *Gm* | *C* |

lift up your hearts un-to the Lord.

Heleluyan

(Hallelujah)

405

He - le - lu - yan, he - le - lu - yan;
Hal - le - lu - jah, hal - le - lu - jah;

he - le, he - le - lu - yan; he - le - lu - yan,
hal - le, hal - le - lu - yah; hal - le - lu - jah,

he - le - lu - yan; he - le, he - le - lu - yan.
hal - le - lu - jah; hal - le, hal - le - lu - jah.

May be sung as a canon. Additional suggestions in Upper Room Worshipbok Accompaniment and Worship Leader *edition*

WORDS: Muscogee (Creek) Indian
MUSIC: Muscogee (Creek) Indian; transcribed by Charles H. Webb

HELELUYAN
Irregular

406

Holy God

Ho - ly, ho - ly, ho - ly God, ho - ly al - might-y God,

ho - ly, ho - ly, al-might-y God, have mer - cy up - on us.

WORDS: Trad. Orthodox liturgy
MUSIC: Trad. Orthodox liturgy; harm. Alfred V. Fedak
Harm. © 2000 Selah Publishing Co., Inc.

AGIOS, O THEOS
Irregular

407

Holy Darkness

Refrain

Ho - ly dark - ness, bless-ed night, ____ heav-en's

an - swer hid-den from our sight. As we a - wait you, O God of

si - lence we em - brace your ho - ly night. ____

WORDS: Daniel L. Schutte
MUSIC: Daniel L. Schutte
© 1988, 1993 Daniel L. Schutte, published by OCP Publications

HOLY DARKNESS
Refrain

On God Alone I Wait Silently 408

On God a - lone I wait si - lent - ly;

God my de - liv - er - er, God my strong tower.

May be used as psalm refrain (Ps. 62 or 46).

WORDS: John L. Bell (Ps. 62)
MUSIC: John L. Bell

STRONG TOWER
Irregular

© 1993 Wild Goose Resource Group, Iona Community, Scotland; GIA Publications, Inc., exclusive North American agent

Be Still and Know That I Am God 409

Be still and know that I am God.

Be still and know that I am God.

May be sung as a canon.
May be used as psalm refrain (Ps. 46).

WORDS: John L. Bell
MUSIC: John L. Bell

PSALM 46
Irregular

© 1989 Wild Goose Resource Group, Iona Community, Scotland; GIA Publications, Inc., exclusive North American agent

410

Kyrie Eleison #1
(Lord, Have Mercy)

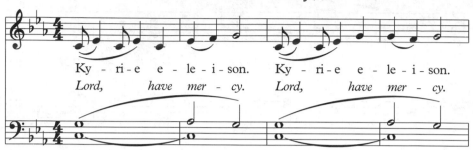

Ky - ri-e e - le - i - son. Ky - ri-e e - le - i - son.
Lord, have mer - cy. Lord, have mer - cy.

Lower voices may hum.

Ky - ri-e e - le - i - son. Ky - ri-e e - le - i - son.
Lord, have mer - cy. Lord, have mer - cy.

Additional verses: Christe eleison (Christ, have mercy); then repeat Kyrie Eleison #1.

WORDS: Early Greek
MUSIC: Dinah Reindorf; arr. from *Sing a New Creation*
Music © 1987 Dinah Reindorf; arr. © 2001 CRC Publications

REINDORF KYRIE
Irregular

411

Kyrie Eleison #2
(Lord, Have Mercy)

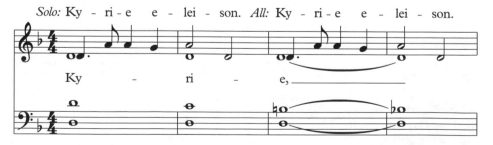

Solo: Ky - ri-e e - lei - son. *All:* Ky - ri-e e - lei - son.

Ky - ri - e,

WORDS: Early Greek
MUSIC: John L. Bell
Music © 1998 Wild Goose Resource Group, Iona Community, Scotland; GIA Publications, Inc., exclusive North American agent

BELL KYRIE
Irregular

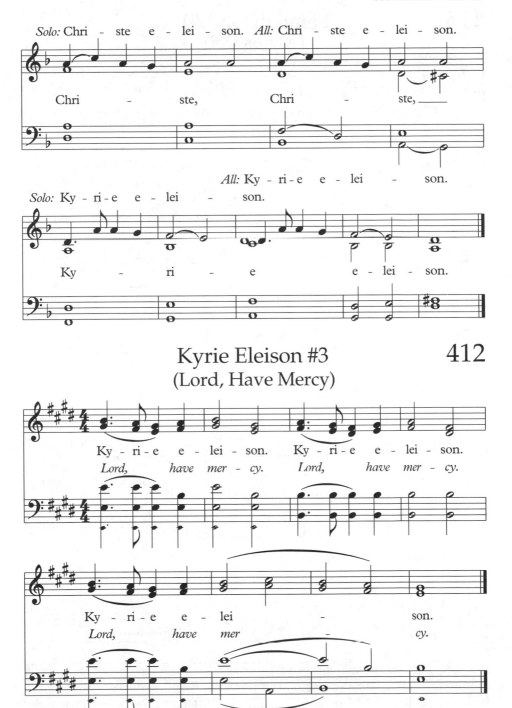

Kyrie Eleison #3
(Lord, Have Mercy)

412

Additional verses: Christe eleison (Christ, have mercy); then repeat Kyrie Eleison #3.

WORDS: Early Greek
MUSIC: Russian Orthodox liturgy

ORTHODOX KYRIE
Irregular

413

Lamb of God #1
(Agnus Dei)

WORDS: From the Mass
MUSIC: John L. Bell

BELL AGNUS
Irregular

Lamb of God #2
(Agnus Dei)

Cantor · *All*

Je - sus, Lamb of God, you take a - way the

sins of the world: have mer - cy, have mer - cy on

Cantor

us. _____ Bread of life and sav - ing cup,

All

you take a - way the sins of the world: have mer - cy, have

Cantor

mer - cy on us. _____ Je - sus, Lamb of

All

God, you take a - way the sins of the world: have

mer - cy, and grant us your peace. _____

WORDS: From the Mass
MUSIC: Michael Joncas (*The Psallite Mass*)
© 1988 GIA Publications, Inc.

JONCAS AGNUS
Irregular

415 Come Now, O Prince of Peace
(O-so-so)

1. Come now, O Prince of Peace, make us one bod-y,
2. Come now, O God of Love, make us one bod-y,

1. O - so - so o - so - so, pyong-hwa eui im-gum,
2. O - so - so o - so - so, sa - rang eui im-gum,

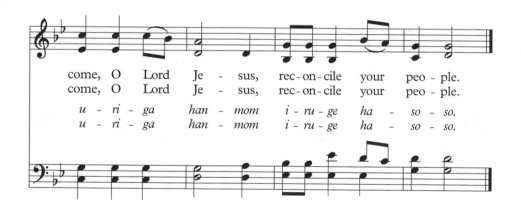

come, O Lord Je - sus, rec-on-cile your peo - ple.
come, O Lord Je - sus, rec-on-cile your peo - ple.

u – ri – ga han – mom i – ru – ge ha – so – so.
u – ri – ga han – mom i – ru – ge ha – so – so.

3. Come now and set us free,
   O God, our Savior,
   come, O Lord Jesus,
   reconcile all nations.

3. O-so-so o-so-so
   cha-yu eui im-gum,
   u-ri-ga han-mom
   i-ru-ge ha-so-so.

4. Come, Hope of unity,
   make us one body,
   come, O Lord Jesus,
   reconcile all nations.

4. O-so-so o-so-so
   tong-il eui im-gum,
   u-ri-ga han-mom
   u-ri-ge ha-so-so.

WORDS: Geonyong Lee; English paraphrase by Marion Pope (Isa. 9:6; John 17:22-23)
MUSIC: Geonyong Lee

GEONYONG
65.56

Listen

1. Lis - ten   to the song   of the wind.   Lis - ten   to the
2. Lis - ten   to the hope   of the poor.   Lis - ten   to the
3. Lis - ten   to the knock at the door.   Lis - ten   to the
4. Lis - ten   to the dreams in the night.   Lis - ten   to the
5. Lis - ten   to the cry   to be whole.   Lis - ten   to the
6. Lis - ten   to the sigh   of the soul.   Lis - ten   to the
7. Lis - ten,   si-lence speaks in the heart. Lis - ten,   si-lence

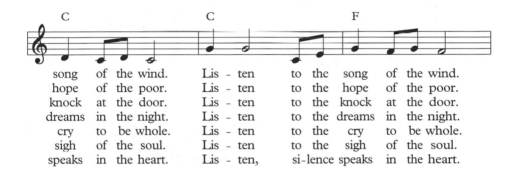

song   of the wind.   Lis - ten   to the song   of the wind.
hope   of the poor.   Lis - ten   to the hope   of the poor.
knock   at the door.   Lis - ten   to the knock at the door.
dreams in the night.   Lis - ten   to the dreams in the night.
cry   to be whole.   Lis - ten   to the cry   to be whole.
sigh   of the soul.   Lis - ten   to the sigh   of the soul.
speaks in the heart.   Lis - ten,   si-lence speaks in the heart.

Lis - ten,   God is sing - ing.   God is sing - ing.

WORDS: Thomas Turner
MUSIC: Thomas Turner

417 The Word Is in Your Heart

Refrain

The Word is near you, deep with - in you.

The Word is on your lips. _____

The Word who made you yet will save you.

The Word is in your heart. _____

May be used as sung "prayer for illumination."

WORDS: Bob Moore
MUSIC: Bob Moore
© 1993 GIA Publications, Inc.

THE WORD
Refrain

418 God Comes to Us

God comes to us on win-ter night, in ba-by's breath, by

fire - light, God comes to us _____

WORDS: Dirk Damonte
MUSIC: Dirk Damonte
© 1994 Excelsis Music

GOD COMES
887.887

on a star._____ God comes to us a-
midst our fears, un-spo-ken joys, un-end-ing tears, God
comes to us_____ where we are._____

Peace Is Flowing Like a River 419

1. Peace is flow - ing like a riv - er,
2. Joy is flow - ing like a riv - er,
3. Faith is flow - ing like a riv - er,
4. Hope is flow - ing like a riv - er,
5. Love is flow - ing like a riv - er,

flow - ing out through you and me; flow - ing out in-to the

des - ert, set - ting all the cap-tives free.

WORDS: Anon.
MUSIC: Anon.
© 1993 GIA Publications, Inc.

LIKE A RIVER
87.87

420 This Is the Body of Christ

This is the bod-y of Christ, _____ bro-ken that we may be whole; _____ this cup, as prom-ised by God, true to his word, cra - dles our Lord: _____ food for the good of the soul. _____

WORDS: John L. Bell
MUSIC: John L. Bell

CHRIST'S BODY
Irregular

© 1998 Wild Goose Resource Group, Iona Community, Scotland; GIA Publications, Inc., exclusive North American agent

Este es mi cuerpo
(This Is My Body)

Es - te es mi cuer - po, es - ta es mi san - gre,
This is my bod - y, this is my blood,

da - dos por ti, da - dos por ti.
giv - en for you, giv - en for you.

Gra - cias a Dios, gra - cias a Dios,
Thanks be to God, thanks be to God,

gra - cias a Dios, gra - cias a Dios. ___
thanks be to God, thanks be to God. ___

WORDS: Steven B. Eulberg
MUSIC: Steven B. Eulberg

MI CUERPO
Irregular

422   Water of Life

*Optional stanzas in Upper Room Worshipbook Accompaniment and Worship Leader *edition*
**Refrain 2 is an alternate text for Gathering.*

WORDS: Verses and Refrain 1, David Haas; refrain 2, Elise S. Eslinger
MUSIC: David Haas
© 1987 GIA Publications, Inc.

WATER OF LIFE
Irregular

Jesus, My God and My All

```
D                G              Bm           Bm
```

1. Je - sus,   my   on - ly de - sire. _____
2. Je - sus,   the   hope   of my   soul. _____
3. Je - sus,   the   mer - cy of   God. _____
4. Je - sus,   my   life - giv - ing Lord. _____
5. Je - sus,   the   wis - dom of   God. _____

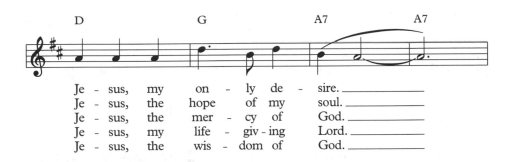

```
D                G              A7           A7
```

Je - sus,   my   on - ly de - sire. _____
Je - sus,   the   hope   of my   soul. _____
Je - sus,   the   mer - cy of   God. _____
Je - sus,   my   life - giv - ing Lord. _____
Je - sus,   the   wis - dom of   God. _____

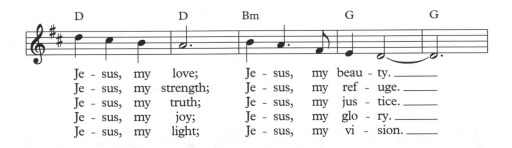

```
D          D        Bm         G          G
```

Je - sus,   my   love;   Je - sus,   my   beau - ty. _____
Je - sus,   my   strength; Je - sus,   my   ref - uge. _____
Je - sus,   my   truth;   Je - sus,   my   jus - tice. _____
Je - sus,   my   joy;   Je - sus,   my   glo - ry. _____
Je - sus,   my   light;   Je - sus,   my   vi - sion. _____

```
D                G              Dsus         D
```

Je - sus,   my   God   and my   all. _____

WORDS: Rufino Zaragoza, OFM
MUSIC: Rufino Zaragoza, OFM

JESUS, MY GOD
77.457

424 Come, Lord Jesus

1. Come, Lord Je - sus. Come, Lord Je - sus.
2. Come, O Prince of Peace. Come, O Prince of Peace.
3. Come, Im - man - u - el. Come, Im - man - u - el.

Come, Lord Je - sus;
Come, O Prince of Peace; } come and be born in our hearts.
Come, Im - man - u - el;

WORDS: Carey Landry
MUSIC: Carey Landry
© 1976 OCP Publications

COME, LORD JESUS
Irregular

425 Jesus Christ, Jesus Christ

Je - sus Christ, Je - sus Christ, Son of God a - mong us,

(Hum) _____

WORDS: John L. Bell
MUSIC: John L. Bell
© 1998 Wild Goose Resource Group, Iona Community, Scotland; GIA Publications, Inc., exclusive North American agent

JESUS CHRIST
Irregular

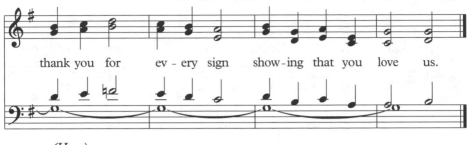

thank you for ev - ery sign show-ing that you love us.

(Hum) _____

Jesus, Come to Our Hearts   426

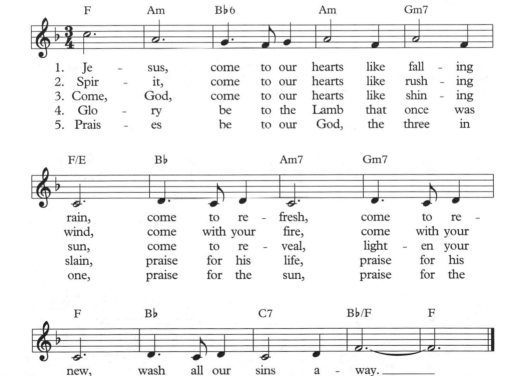

1.	Je -	sus,	come	to our	hearts	like	fall -	ing
2.	Spir -	it,	come	to our	hearts	like	rush -	ing
3.	Come,	God,	come	to our	hearts	like	shin -	ing
4.	Glo -	ry	be	to the	Lamb	that	once	was
5.	Prais -	es	be	to our	God,	the	three	in

rain,	come	to re -	fresh,	come	to re -
wind,	come	with your	fire,	come	with your
sun,	come	to re -	veal,	light -	en your
slain,	praise	for his	life,	praise	for his
one,	praise	for the	sun,	praise	for the

new,	wash	all our	sins	a -	way. _____
life,	blow	all our	doubts	a -	way. _____
Word,	drive	all our	gloom	a -	way. _____
death,	praise	that he	lives	a -	gain. _____
wind,	praise	for the	fall -	ing	rain. _____

WORDS: William Worley
MUSIC: William Worley

10.4.4.6

427 Lord Jesus Christ

Lord Je-sus Christ, lov-er of

Lord Je-sus Christ, Lord Je-sus, lov-er of

Lord Je-sus Christ, lov-er of

all, trail wide the

all, of all, trail wide the hem of your

all, all, trail wide the

gar - ment, bring heal-ing, bring peace.

bring peace.

WORDS: John L. Bell
MUSIC: John L. Bell

LORD JESUS
Irregular

In Love You Summon

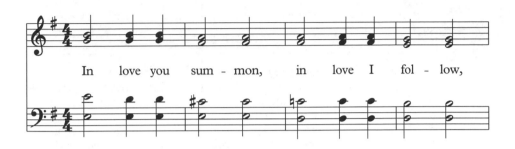

In love you sum-mon, in love I fol-low,

liv-ing to-day for your to-mor-row.

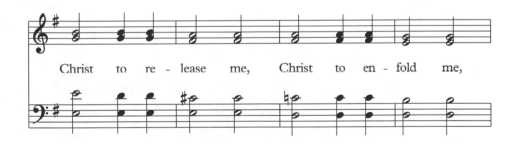

Christ to re-lease me, Christ to en-fold me,

Christ to re-strain me, Christ to up-hold me.

WORDS: John L. Bell
MUSIC: John L. Bell

LOVE SUMMON
Irregular

429 Drink Living Water

1. Come, you hun-gry, come, you thirst-y;
2. Come, you wea-ry, bring your bur-dens;
3. Come, you poor ones, come, you low-ly;
4. Come, re-ject-ed, come, a-ban-doned;
5. Come, you emp-ty, come, you bar-ren;
6. Come, you wound-ed, bring your suf-fer-ing;
7. Come, you a-ged, bring your or-phans;
8. Come to my arms, come to my heart;

Refrain

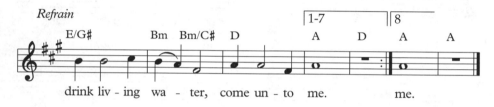

drink liv-ing wa-ter, come un-to me. me.

Additional suggestions in Upper Room Worshipbook Accompaniment and Worship Leader *edition*

WORDS: Colleen Fulmer
MUSIC: Rufino Zaragoza

LIVING WATER
Irregular

© 1990 Colleen Fulmer and Rufino Zaragoza, published by OCP Publications

430 Akekho Ofana No Jesu
(There's No One Like Jesus)

1. A-ke-kho o-fa-na no Je-su. A-
1. There's no one, there's no one like Je-sus. There's

WORDS: Trad. Zulu
MUSIC: Trad. Zulu, arr. by Dean McIntyre

Arr. © 2005 The General Board of Discipleship of The United Methodist Church

ke - kho o - fa - na na - ye. A - ke - kho o - fa - na no
no one, there's no one like him. *There's no one, there's no one like*

Je - su. A - ke - kho o - fa - na na - ye.
Je - sus. There's no one, there's no one like him.

2. Sahamba, sahamba akekho.
   Sahamba, sahamb' akekho.
   Sahamba, sahamba akekho.
   Sahamba, sahamb' akekho.

3. Sajika, sajika lutho.
   Sajika, sajika lutho.
   Sajika, sajika lutho.
   Sajika, sajika lutho.

4. Safuna, safuna lutho.
   Safuna, safuna lutho.
   Safuna, safuna lutho.
   Safuna, safuna lutho.

5. Akekho ofana no Jesu.
   Akekho ofana naye.
   Akekho ofana no Jesu.
   Akekho ofana naye.

2. *We walked and we walked, there is no one.*
   We walked and we walked, there's no one.
   We walked and we walked, there is no one.
   We walked and we walked, there's no one.

3. *We turned and we turned, there is nothing.*
   We turned and we turned, there's nothing.
   We turned and we turned, there is nothing.
   We turned and we turned, there's nothing.

4. *We searched and we searched, there is nothing.*
   We searched and we searched, there's nothing.
   We searched and we searched, there is nothing.
   We searched and we searched, there's nothing.

5. *There's no one, there's no one like Jesus.*
   There's no one, there's no one like him.
   There's no one, there's no one like Jesus.
   There's no one, there's no one like him.

431 He Became Poor

He be-came poor that we may be rich

lov - ing the world and leav - ing his throne;

King of all kings and Lord of all lords,

Flesh of our flesh and bone of our bone.

WORDS: John L. Bell
MUSIC: John L. Bell

Radiant Light Divine

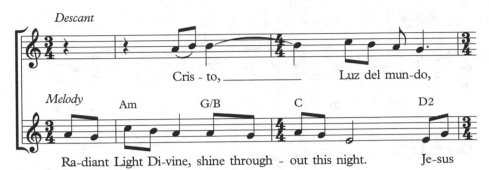

Descant

Cris - to, _____ Luz del mun-do,

Melody

Ra-diant Light Di-vine, shine through - out this night. Je-sus

Luz y A - mor.

Ho - ly One, praise to you, our Light, as the

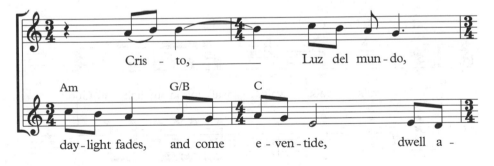

Cris - to, _____ Luz del mun - do,

day-light fades, and come e - ven - tide, dwell a -

Luz y A - mor.

mong us, Ho - ly Fire.

WORDS: Based on *Phos Hileron*
MUSIC: Rufino Zaragoza

RADIANT LIGHT
Irregular

433 Walking in the Light of God

WORDS: Trad. Zulu
MUSIC: Trad. Zulu, arr. by Dean McIntyre

2. 'Ham-ba, 'ham-ba, 'ham-ba, 'ham-ba, walk-ing in the light of God.

To Refrain

'Ham-ba, 'ham-ba, 'ham-ba, 'ham-ba, walk-ing in the light of God.

3. 'Ham - ba koo kah nigh nee, 'ham - ba koo kah nigh nee,

To Refrain

'ham - ba, koo kah nigh nee, walk-ing in the light of God.

434 I Am the World's True Light
(Yo soy la luz del mundo)

I am the world's true light.
Yo soy la luz del mun - do.

If you will fol - low me, your light will re-flect my
El que me si - ga ten - drá la luz que le da la

bright - ness and you'll nev - er walk in the night. I
vi - da. Y nun - ca an-da-rá en la os-cu - ri - dad. Yo

A - le - lu - ya, a - le - lu - ya,

a - le - lu - ya, a - le - lu! La, la, la, la, la, la.

God is our light, God is our peace,
Dios es la luz, Dios es la paz,

May be sung by any combination of voices. Additional suggestions in Upper Room Worshipbook
Accompaniment *and* Worship Leader *edition*

WORDS: Rudolfo Ascencio, trans. by Michael Hawn (John 8:12) TRUE LIGHT
MUSIC: Rudolfo Ascencio Irregular

God is our love. God is our light,
Dios es a - mor. *Dios es la luz,*

God is our peace, God is our love.
Dios es la paz, *Dios es a - mor.*

Those Who Wait on the Lord 435

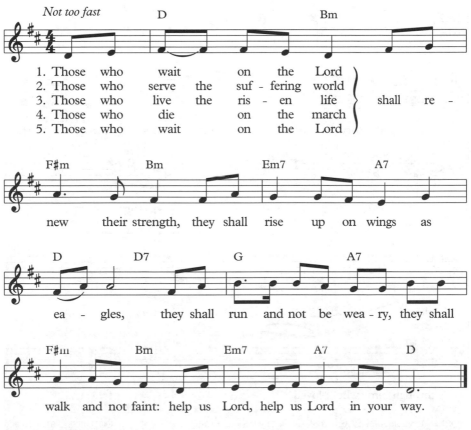

Not too fast

1. Those who wait on the Lord
2. Those who serve the suf - fering world
3. Those who live the ris - en life
4. Those who die on the march
5. Those who wait on the Lord
   } shall re -

new their strength, they shall rise up on wings as

ea - gles, they shall run and not be wea - ry, they shall

walk and not faint: help us Lord, help us Lord in your way.

WORDS: Trad. American
MUSIC: Trad. American, arr. by John Bell

THOSE WHO WAIT
Irregular

436 Goodness Is Stronger Than Evil

Sing deliberately

Good-ness is strong-er than e - vil; love is strong-er than hate; light is strong-er than dark - ness; life is strong-er than death. Vic-tory is ours, vic-tory is ours through him who

Oh, vic-tory is ours, vic-tory is ours

loved us. Vic - tory is us.

through him who loved us. Oh, us.

WORDS: From *An African Prayer Book*, selected by Desmond Tutu
MUSIC: John L. Bell

GOODNESS IS STRONGER
Irregular

Words © 1995 Desmond Tutu, admin. by Doubleday (a division of Random House); music © 1996 Wild Goose Resource Group, Iona Community, Scotland; GIA Publications, Inc., exclusive North American agent

If You Believe and I Believe

Slowly

If you be-lieve and I be-lieve and we to-geth-er pray, the

Ho-ly Spir-it shall come down and set God's peo-ple free, and

set God's peo-ple free, and set God's peo-ple free, the

Ho-ly Spir-it shall come down and set God's peo-ple free.

WORDS: Trad. Zimbabwean (Matt. 18:19)
MUSIC: Zimbabwean variant of an English folk melody, arr. John Bell

BELIEVE
Irregular

438   We Will Take What You Offer

WORDS: John L. Bell
MUSIC: John L. Bell

OFFER
Irregular

Somlandela
(We Will Follow)

WORDS: Trad. Zulu
MUSIC: Trad. Zulu, arr. by Dean McIntyre
Arr. © 2005 The General Board of Discipleship of The United Methodist Church

440

Mayenziwe
(Your Will Be Done)

WORDS: Trad. South African (Xhosa)
MUSIC: Trad. South African

MAYENZIWE
Irregular

Take, O Take Me As I Am

Take, O take me as I am. Sum-mon out what I shall be; set your seal up-on my heart and live in me.

WORDS: John L. Bell
MUSIC: John L. Bell

O TAKE ME
Irregular

© 1995 Wild Goose Resource Group, Iona Community, Scotland; GIA Publications, Inc., exclusive North American agent

Marked and Sealed

442

We are marked as Christ's own,
sealed by your constant love.
Live your yearning in us, O God,
for love is strong as death.

Nancy Bryan Crouch, OSL
© 2006 Upper Room Books

443 Dona Nobis Pacem
(Song of Blessing)

Additional suggestions in Upper Room Worshipbook Accompaniment and Worship Leader *edition*

WORDS: Trad.
MUSIC: Trad.

DONA NOBIS PACEM
Irregular

Go in Peace, Walk in Love

1. Go in peace, walk in love, gen - tle Shep - herd,
2. Go in peace, walk in love, Spir - it wings en -
3. Go in peace, walk in love. May your path be

Optional canon

3. Go in peace, walk in love.

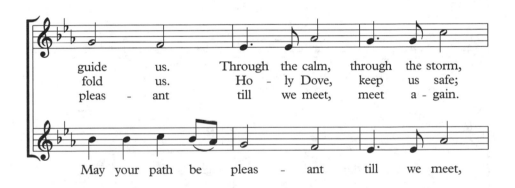

guide us. Through the calm, through the storm,
fold us. Ho - ly Dove, keep us safe;
pleas - ant till we meet, meet a - gain.

May your path be pleas - ant till we meet,

|1, 2| |3|

Shep - herd, walk be - side us.
strength - en and up - hold us.
God is ev - er - pres - ent._____

|1, 2| |3|

meet a-gain. God is ev - er - pres - ent.

WORDS: Trilby Jordan
MUSIC: Albert Zabel
© 1990 Trilby Jordan and Albert Zabel

WALK IN LOVE
Irregular

445 May the Lord, Mighty God

Opt. Descant for stanza 2

2. Lift up and see God's face,

Melody

1. May the Lord, might - y God,
2. Lift up your eyes and see God's face

God's grace for - ev - er;
bless and keep you for - ev - er;
and God's grace for - ev - er;

may the Lord, might - y God,

grant you peace, per - fect peace,
may the Lord, might - y God,

bless and keep you for - ev - er.

cou - rage in ev - ery en - deav - our.
bless and keep you for - ev - er.

WORDS: From the Liturgy
MUSIC: Trad. Chinese, adapt. by I-to Loh

WEN TI
Irregular

Adapt. © 1983 Abingdon Press, admin. by The Copyright Co.

The Peace of the Earth

The peace of the earth be with you, the peace of the heav-ens too; the
peace of the riv - ers be with you, the peace of the o-ceans too.

Deep peace fall-ing o - ver you;
Deep peace, deep peace

God's peace grow - ing in you.
God's peace, God's peace

WORDS: Trad. Guatemalan, trans. by Christine Carson
MUSIC: Trad. Guatemalan, arr. John L. Bell

GOD'S PEACE
Irregular

447

God to Enfold You

God to en-fold you, Christ to up-hold you,

Spir-it to keep you in heav-en's sight;

so may God grace you, heal and em-brace you,

lead you through dark-ness in-to the light.

WORDS: John L. Bell
MUSIC: John L. Bell

GOD ENFOLDING
Irregular

God's Eye Be within Me

God's eye be with-in me, God's foot be be-fore me,

God's Spir-it be 'round me to shield and re-store me.

God's free-dom to choose me, God's jus-tice to fuse me,

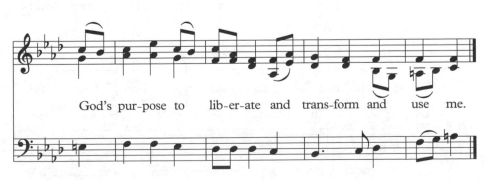

God's pur-pose to lib-er-ate and trans-form and use me.

WORDS: John L. Bell
MUSIC: Trad. Irish, arr. John L. Bell

COLUMCILLE
Irregular

Words and arr. © 1998 Wild Goose Resource Group, Iona Community, Scotland; GIA Publications, Inc., exclusive
North American agent

449

You Shall Go Out with Joy
(The Trees of the Field)

WORDS: Steffi Geiser Rubin (Isa. 55:12)
MUSIC: Stuart Dauermann

© 1975 Lillenas Publishing Co., admin. by The Copyright Co.

THE TREES OF THE FIELD
Irregular

For You Shall Go Out with Joy
(Go in Joy)

For you shall go out with joy

and be led forth in peace:

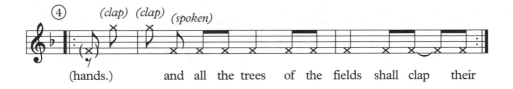

The moun-tains and the hills shall break forth in - to sing-ing.

(hands.) and all the trees of the fields shall clap their

Optional Ending

For you shall go out in joy!

May be performed by four groups, each singing and repeating a single line.

WORDS: Don E. Saliers (Isa. 55:12)
MUSIC: Don E. Saliers
© 1977 Don E. Saliers

BUCKHANNON
Irregular

451 May You Run and Not Be Weary

WORDS: Handt Hanson
MUSIC: Handt Hanson, arr. by Henry Wiens

PRINCE OF PEACE
Irregular

Prayer of Jesus

Praying with Christ:
Our Path to the Heart of God

A long time ago some students asked a teacher how to pray. The disciples sensed that prayer opened a path that led to the heart of God, and they wanted Jesus to show the way. All of us are like those disciples, always beginning, forever seeking, daily wanting to be close to God, to know the intimacy that Jesus spoke of and lived in.

Jesus responds with an invitation: Pray. Pray these words. Pray this pattern. Keep praying; keep turning toward God who is love, who is holy, who is near.

For nearly two thousand years, people around the world have prayed the Lord's Prayer. A thousand voices in chorus or an individual in silence, strangers meeting together for the first time or longtime friends, hand in hand in a circle or kneeling before a cross, in so many ways and in so many places, people have joined the ongoing stream of prayer, crying for justice, for bread, for forgiveness, for deliverance.

In many languages, in King James English, common hymn tunes or New Zealand poetry, people give voice to their deepest yearnings. The prayer of Jesus gives shape to our human longings, a hunger for God and community. It gives voice to our desire for a touch of heaven to be enfleshed here on earth, our earnest petition for food to feed body and soul for all, our deep plea for forgiveness for the wrongs we commit and the hurts we absorb, our persistent and urgent request for guidance and deliverance. We ask God, who is bigger and more gracious than any of the names or words we use to describe God, to infuse our lives and the world with holy purpose and will. In these common words, our longings are turned into prayer.

Here you will find several translations, languages, and musical settings of the Lord's Prayer. Some may be unfamiliar to you and open a new way of understanding and praying an ancient text. Let the Spirit guide and teach you. Try using only one petition of the prayer as a breath prayer or prayer focus for a day or a week. Try the Lord's Prayer as an evening examination of conscience. This prayer practice invites you to reflect on your day, asking where God's purpose unfolded, how you broke bread and with whom, how you practiced forgiveness. Adapt the parts of the prayer as a lens to look at your day or week.

The Lord's Prayer is more than a Sunday recitation. It leads us to the heart of God and guides our living.

Larry J. Peacock, Director
Rolling Ridge Retreat Center
North Andover, Massachusetts

453 The Lord's Prayer

Guitar chords provided in Upper Room Worshipbook Accompaniment and Worship Leader *edition*

WORDS: Matt. 6:9-13
MUSIC: Anon.; arr. by Al Oppenheimer

LORD'S PRAYER (OPPENHEIMER)
Irregular

454

The Lord's Prayer

Chanted freely

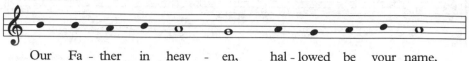

Our Fa - ther in heav - en, hal - lowed be your name,

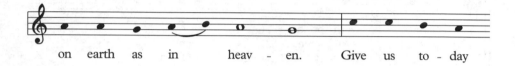

your king - dom come, your will be done,

on earth as in heav - en. Give us to - day

our dai - ly bread. For - give us our sins

as we for - give those who sin a - gainst us.

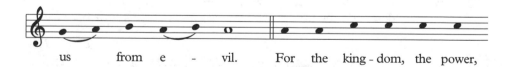

Save us from the time of trial and de - liv - er

us from e - vil. For the king - dom, the power,

and the glo - ry are yours now and for - ev - er.

WORDS: Matt. 6:9-13
MUSIC: Plainsong

Text from *Prayers We Have in Common*, 2nd revised ed., © 1975 ICET

The Prayer of Jesus

Ho - ly One, our on - ly home, hal - lowed be your name. May your day dawn, your will be done, here as in heav - en. Feed us to - day, and for - give us as we for-give each oth - er. Do not for-sake us at the test, but de - liv - er us from e - vil. For the glo - ry, the pow-er, and the mer - cy are yours, now and for - ev - er. A - men; A - men; A - men.

WORDS: Mother Thunder Mission (Matt. 6:9-13)
MUSIC: Native American melody, arr. Elise S. Eslinger
Arr. © 2005 The Upper Room

456

Padre nuestro

Pa-dre nues - tro _____ que es-tás en el

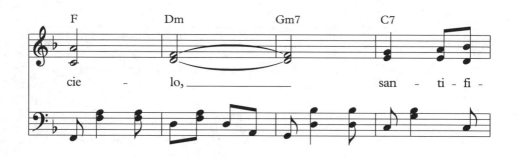

cie - lo, _____ san - ti - fi -

ca - do, san - ti - fi - ca - do se - a tu

nom - bre.

WORDS: Carlos Rosas
MUSIC: Carlos Rosas; arr. by Raquel Mora Martínez
© 1976 Mexican-American Cultural Center

PADRE NUESTRO
Irreg.

457   Life-Giver, Lover of Us All

1. Life-giver, Lover of us all,
   upon your holy name we call;
   your new day come, your will be done,
   on earth as in all realms beyond.

2. We pray this day for bread to live,
   forgive our sins as we forgive,
   and give us strength in time of test.
   Grant us release from evil's death.

3. For all the cosmos is your own,
   your pow'r of love which we have known,
   the splendor, radiant, without end.
   To God be praise! Amen. Amen.

Sing to TALLIS' CANON, No. 209

Laurie Y. J. Aleona
© 1988 Laurie Y. J. Aleona

458   Prayer at Night's Approaching

Life-giver, Pain-bearer, Love-maker,
Source of all that is and that shall be,
Father and Mother of us all,
Loving God, in whom is heaven:

The hallowing of your name echo through the universe!
The way of your justice be followed by the peoples of the world!
Your heavenly will be done by all created beings!
Your commonwealth of peace and freedom
    sustain our hope and come on earth.

With the bread we need for today, feed us.
In the hurts we absorb from one another, forgive us.
In times of temptation and test, strengthen us.
From trials too great to endure, spare us.
From the grip of all that is evil, free us.

For you reign in the glory of the power that is love,
    now and for ever. Amen.

Jim Cotter
© 2001 Cairns Publications

Acknowledgments

Abingdon Press
(c/o The Copyright Company)

American Bible Society
1965 Broadway
New York, NY 10023
(212) 408-1200

Appleseed Music, Inc.
250 West 57th Street; Suite 1218
New York, NY 10107
(212) 586-6553
All material used with all
rights reserved and used with
permission.

Augsburg Fortress Publishers
P.O. Box 1209
Minneapolis, MN 55440-1209
(800) 328-4648

Kay Barckley
kbarckley@utemple.org

Albert F. Bayly
(c/o Oxford University Press)

Laurie Aleona
500 N. Emerson Avenue, #301
Wenatchee, WA 98801

Brummhart Publishing
The Rev. Ms. Kathleen Hart Brumm
708 Blooming Grove Drive
Rensselaer, NY 12144-9420
khbising2@aol.com

AnnaMae Meyer Bush
860 Byerly, SE
Ada, MI 49301

Cairns Publications
Dwylan, Stryd Fawr
Harlech, Gwynedd LL46 2YA

Pastor Casiodoro A. Cardenas
c/o Christian Assembly Church
P.O. Box 71816
Durham, NC 27722

Christine Carson and WGRG
(c/o GIA Publications, Inc.)

Celebration
P.O. Box 309
Aliquippa, PA 15001

Century Oak Publishing Group
(c/o MCS America)

Chalice Press
Christian Board of Publication
1221 Locust Street, Suite 670
St. Louis, MO 63166-0719

Changing Church Forum
c/o Handt Hanson
13901 Fairview Drive
Burnsville, MN 55337

Choristers Guild
2834 W. Kingsley Rd.
Garland, TX 75041-2498
(972) 271-1521
customerservice@mailcg.org

Christian Conference of Asia
96 Pak Tin Village Area 2
Mei Tin Road, Shatin NT
Hong Kong SAR, CHINA
cca@cca.org.hk

Church Publishing, Inc.
Attn: Permissions
445 Fifth Avenue
New York, NY 10016
(212) 779-3392 - fax

The Estate of
J. Jefferson Cleveland
c/o Dr. William B. McClain
Wesley Theological Seminary
4500 Massachusetts Ave., NW
Washington, DC 20016

Jaroslav Vajda
(c/o Concordia Publishing House)

Concionero Abierto
Eparlaco 634
1406 Buenos Aires, Argentina
sosasilva@infovia.com.ar

Concordia Publishing House
3558 South Jefferson Ave.
St. Louis, MO 63118-3968
(314) 268-1000
All material used with all
rights reserved and used with
permission.

Jamie Cortez
(c/o OCP Publications)

CRC Publications
2850 Kalamazoo Ave., SE
Grand Rapids, MI 49560

David Higham Associates
Limited
5-8 Lower John Street
Golden Square
London W1F 9HA
dha@davidhigham.co.uk

Lucien Deiss
Suite 400
Franklin Park, IL 60131

Desert Flower Music
P.O. Box 1476
Carmichael, CA 95609

Discipleship Resources
General Board of Discipleship
1908 Grand Avenue
Nashville, TN 37212
(615) 340-7000

Dr. Arlo Duba
University of Dubuque
Theological Seminary
2000 University Avenue
Dubuque, IA 52001

Ruth Duck
1616 Sheridan, Unit 6F
Wilmette, IL 60091

Delores Dufner
(c/o OCP Publications)

Earthsongs
220 NW 29th Street
Corallis, OR 97330
email@earthsongsmus.com

Ekklesia Music, Inc.
Attn: Dan Feiten
2127 South Fillmore Street
Denver, CO 80210

Elise Eslinger
1843 Ruskin Road
Dayton, OH 45406

Dr. Richard Eslinger
1843 Ruskin Road
Dayton, OH 45406
RLEslEagle@aol.com

ELLC (English Language
Liturgical Consultation)
David Holeton, EELC
Secretariat
Korunni 69
CZ-13000
Prague 3
hippolytus@volny.cz

Steven B. Eulberg
Owl Mountain Music
1281 East Magnolia, Unit D
Fort Collins, CO 80524

Excelsis Music
c/o Rev. Dirk Damonte
Los Altos United Methodist
Church
655 Magdalena Avenue
Los Altos, CA 94024

Bernadette Farrell
(c/o OCP Publications)

John B. Foley, SJ
(c/o OCP Publications)

Fred Bock Music Co., Inc.
PO Box 570567
Tarzana, CA 91356
(818) 996-2043
All items used with all
rights reserved and used by
permission.

Colleen Fulmer
(c/o OCP Publications)

Kathy Galloway
c/o Sandra Kramer
4th Floor, Savoy House
140 Sauchiehall Street
Glasgow, UK G2 3DH

Gamut Music Productions
704 Saddle Trail Court
Nashville, TN 37076

Rev. Steve Garnaas-Holmes
271 South Street
Concord, NH 03301

GBGMusik
General Board of Global
Ministries
475 Riverside Drive
New York, NY 10015

General Board of Discipleship
1908 Grand Avenue
Nashville, TN 37212
(615) 340-7000

GIA Publications, Inc.
7404 S. Mason Avenue
Chicago, IL 60638
(708) 496-3800 x 62
www.giamusic.com

Bishop William Boyd Grove
900 Washington Street, East
Charleston, WV 25301

HarperCollins Publishers
10 East 53rd Street
New York, NY 10022-5299
(212) 207-7000
All items reprinted by
permission of HarperCollins
Publishers.

Ruth Watson Henderson
Kingsway-Lambton United Church
85 The Kingsway
Toronto, Ontario M8X 2T6

Hinshaw Music, Inc.
P.O. Box 470
Chapel Hill, NC 27514-0470
(919) 933-1691
All items used with permission.

Hope Publishing Company
380 South Main Place
Carol Stream, IL 60188
(800) 323-1049

Juliana Howard
2713 15th Street, North
St. Cloud, MN 56303

Jane Park Huber
(c/o Westminster John Knox
Press)

Bob Hurd
(c/o OCP Publications)

ICET
(c/o ELLC)

ICEL
(c/o ELLC)

Integrity Music
Integrity Media, Inc.
1000 Cody Road
Mobile, AL 36695-3425
(251) 633-9000
Scripture in Song is a member
of ASCAP.

Willard F. Jabusch
(c/o OCP Publications)

Trilby Jordan
1224 150th SE
Bellevue, WA 98007

Kevin Mayhew Publishers
Buixhall
Stowmarket
Suffolk IP14 3BW
United Kingdom

Ron Klusmeier
345 Pym Street
Parksville, BC V9P 1C8

Geonyong Lee
School of Music, KNUA
1753 Seocho-dong, Seocho-ku
Seoul, Korea
leegy@knua.ac.kr

Les Presses de Taizé
(c/o GIA Publications, Inc.)

Lillenas Publishing
(c/o The Coypright Company)

Lubis-Nainggolan and the CCA
(c/o Christian Conference of Asia)

Maranatha Praise, Inc.
(c/o Music Services, Inc.)

MCS America
1625 Broadway
Nashville, TN 37203-3138

Medical Mission Sisters
8400 Pine Road
Philadelphia, PA 19111

Mexican-American Cultural
Center
3019 West French Place
San Antonio, TX 78228

Music Services, Inc.
1526 Otter Creek Road
Nashville, TN 37215
(615) 371-1320

New Song Creations
R.R. 1, Box 454
Erin, TN 37061

North American Liturgy
Resources
(c/o OCP Publications)

OCP Publications
Attn: Leanna Nudo
P.O. Box 18030
Portland, OR 97218-0030

Herbert O'Driscoll
1000 Jasmine Avenue
Vitoria, BC V8Z 2P4

Oxford University Press
198 Madison Avenue
New York, NY 10016-4314
(212) 726-6000

Panel on Worship
Church of Scotland
121 George Street
Edinburgh, Scotland EH2 4YN

Larry J. Peacock
Rolling Ridge Retreat Center
660 Great Pond Rd
North Andover, MA 01845

Marjean Postlethwaite
4116 York Avenue, South
Minneapolis, MN 55410-1152

Presbyterian Publishing
Corporation
100 Witherspoon Street
Room 2047
Louisville, KY 40202-1396
(502) 569-5021
randres@presbypub.com

James Quinn SJ
(c/o Selah Publishing Company)

Random House, Inc.
Permissions Department
1745 Broadway
New York. NY 10019
All items used by permission
of Doubleday, a division of
Random House, Inc.

The Estate of John S. Rice
c/o Cathlin D. Rice
P. O. Box 458
Indian Hills, CO 80454
cathlinrice@yahoo.com

Rev. Rodney Romney
6180 Gleneagles Drive
Idaho Falls, ID 83401

St. Benedict's Monastery
104 Chapel Lane
St. Joseph, MN 56374-0220

St. Dominic Priory
2601 Lindell Boulevard
St. Louis, MO 63108

St. Meinrad Archabbey
200 Hill Drive
St. Meinrad, IN 47577

Rev. Don E. Saliers
Cannon Chapel
Emory University
Atlanta, GA 30322

Daniel L. (Dan) Schutte
(c/o OCP Publications)

Scripture in Song
(c/o Integrity Music)

Selah Publishing Co., Inc.
4143 Brownsville Road,
Suite 2
Pittsburgh, PA 15227
(412) 886-1020
www.selahpub.com

Stainer & Bell Ltd.
(c/o Hope Publishing Company)

The Anglican Church in
Aotearoa, New Zealand and
Polynesia
204 N Warren Street
PO Box 885
Hastings, New Zealand
GenSec@hb.ang.org.nz

The Church Pension Fund
445 Fifth Avenue
New York, NY 10016

The Copyright Company
1025 16th Avenue, South
Nashville, TN 37212
(615) 321-1096

The Grail
(c/o GIA Publications, Inc.)

The Hymn Society
(c/o Hope Publishing
Company)

The Iona Community
(c/o GIA Publications, Inc.)

The Lorenz Corporation
501 East Third Street
Dayton, OH 45402-2118
(937) 228-6118
info@Lorenz.com
All items used with all rights
reserved and international
copyright secured.

The Pilgrim Press
700 Prospect Avenue, East
Cleveland, OH 44115
www.thepilgrimpress.com

The United Methodist
Publishing House
(c/o The Copyright Company)

The Upper Room
(c/o Upper Room Books)

Desmond Tutu
(c/o Random House, Inc.)

Upper Room Books
1908 Grand Avenue
Nashville, TN 37212
(615) 340-7000

Westminster John Knox Press
(c/o Presbyterian Publishing
Corporation)

WGRG
(c/o GIA Publications, Inc.)

Rev. Jay Wilkey
Director of Music
Newport Presbyterian Church
P.O. Box 53385
Bellevue, WA 98015-3385

Charles Wolff
3453 East Rockledge Road
Phoenix, AZ 85044

World Library Publications
(c/o GIA Publications, Inc.)

Albert Zabel
2928 Thomas Avenue
Huntington, WV 25705

Rufino Zaragoza
(c/o OCP Publications)

462 Index of Titles and First Lines

Index of Scripture